ISBN 978-0-332-27420-1
PIBN 10588296

THE EXPOSITION

OF THAT FAMOUS DIVINE

THOMAS GOODWIN, D.D.

ON THE

BOOK OF REVELATION.

CONDENSED FROM THE ORIGINAL

BY A CLERICAL MEMBER OF THE CONVOCATION AT OXFORD.

LONDON:

PUBLISHED BY SIMPKIN, MARSHALL, AND CO.

SOLD ALSO BY BENNETT, IVY LANE;

AND ALL OTHER BOOKSELLERS IN TOWN AND COUNTRY.

MDCCCXLII.

PLYMOUTH:
JENKIN THOMAS, PRINTER, CORNWALL-STREET.

PREMONITION

TO THE READER,

(AS IN THE OCTAVO EDITION OF GOODWIN'S EXPOSITIONS.)

In laying before the Church of Christ, (to whom I hereby dedicate this volume,) an octavo edition of the Expositions of that peerless divine and star of the first magnitude, that shone through two-thirds of the seventeenth century, Dr. Thomas Goodwin; the only apology I have to make is for the labor of reducing more than a thousand folio pages to the present cheap form and portable size, by condensing the same without sacrificing scarce an idea of the original. The diminution of the type, margin, and paragraphs, might account for the work being of an equal number of pages: and it has been further compressed by relieving the Exposition on the Ephesians of a multitude of repetitions, chiefly used at the commencement of the sixty sermons into which the original divides it; the more convenient form of a division by verses, and the more perspicuous mode of sub-dividing verses under prominent heads, (an index for which is found at the top of each page,) being substituted: I have also used in general a less circuitous phraseology; preserving withal so carefully every important expression, and the force of every phrase, that in some pages I have not ventured to omit, or add, or alter, a word of several sentences together; whilst I trust I have succeeded, without affecting the originality of the style, not only in condensing, but in removing from several passages that obscurity which still surrounds some others. Although the truth of most of the statements is set forth in an irresistible light, there are a few in which no one reader will perhaps fully concur: still as an editor, I owe it to the Church as well as to him, "who being dead yet speaketh," to give a faithful transcript of all the author's ideas, from the animalcula to the hugest behomoth, from the hedge-star to the brightest luminary in the heavens: and while the babe will find here its milk, the robust its strong meat, and every one his portion; there are some astounding notions, with which only minds of peculiar dimensions can grapple, but which once grasped afford a reward indeed. In studying such a divine class-book with the bible before him, the strongest intellect will find exercise enough, and the weakest understanding, (enlightened by the Spirit of God,) may wade easily through this river of life and pleasure.

Of the works of this gigantic theologist, the Comment on the Epistle to the Ephesians takes up eight hundred pages of the first of five very scarce and expensive folio volumes; and though it was never prosecuted beyond the commencement of the second chapter, it contains a complete body of divinity, and is remarkable for its undesigned testimony against the spirit of Popery, and all those "damnable heresies," which have so alarmingly threatened the vitality of the Protestant Church; while his Exposition of the Book of Revelation, (taken from two hundred pages of the second folio,) most fully anatomizing and detecting

Antichrist and the mystery of iniquity, peculiary interests these our days; and as it contains withal the same rich vein of ideas and practical observations as that of the Ephesians, I scruple not to say, " Blessed is he that readeth and they that hear the words of this volume, *and keep these things which are written therein." The life of the Author is prefixed to the fifth folio, and it is hoped the perusal of his experience, as well as of the present portion of his writings, will be acknowledged by the Holy Ghost, in comforting and strengthening the hearts of God's " own elect," in these perilous times : for as he lived to see the beginning, and as we are now in the last of " the latter days," he wrote under the same impressions with which we still read ; so that he seems, as if by a prophetic spirit, to have " written for our admonition, upon whom the ends of the world are come :" and I feel assured, that except our pulpits are made to ring again with the trumpet-sound of the glorious scriptural doctrines here set forth, no other barrier can be efficient against the universal domination of the Papacy.*

An objection may arise among some members of our Church, tending to invalidate the testimony of this pre-eminent minister of *Christ, and to reflect on his present editor ;* " but *he was a seceder," (as the glory of Naaman was marred by a single syllable ;* " but *he was a leper :") This* but *I would* re-but, *by observing, That Dr. Goodwin lived in communion with our Church upwards of thirty years, and for some time was under the patronage of Charles I. during which period several of his works were written ; and as they all contain the same spirit and doctrine, who could discern, from what is before him, whether it was under Charles or James, or in the days of Cromwell, that he was vice-chancellor of Oxford? it is only evident, that in whatsoever firmament he appeared, " he was a burning and a shining light." Let any bishop, or priest, or lay-divine, dying in our own communion, be pointed out as having written so deeply, so fully, so convincingly, so blessedly, on* the whole of all *the mysteries of grace, and I will confess my error in re-editing such an author, as another such I do not believe has been given to the world since the age of apostles : and should the Church of Christ require it, I shall, by God's grace and strength, prepare another corresponding volume, containing some* of *his treatises and discourses, which are the most perfect master-pieces of theology on the most important subjects I ever perused.*

The reader should be admonished, that I have chosen to express the Greek words in Roman, and the Hebrew in Italic capitals, the Latin being in small Italics with capital initials : and as I was now tempted to write my manuscript with one hand, and correct the press with the other, I hope I shall not again have to deplore so many errata *of all sorts as the reader will discover ; of whom I thus take leave, praying the Holy Ghost to be with him in the patient perusal of those pages, that therein he may see " the glory of God in the face of Jesus Christ."*

THE EDITOR.

Plymouth, July, 1842.

THE LIFE OF

DR. THOMAS GOODWIN,

AS COMPOSED OUT OF HIS OWN PAPERS AND MEMOIRS.

THOMAS, the eldest son of Richard and Catharine Goodwin, of the family of Collingwood, was born Oct. 5th, A.D. 1600, at Rolseby, a little village in Norfolk. His parents devoting him to the ministry, gave him a learned as well as a religious education, and placed him in Christ's College, Cambridge, A.D. 1613; where he continued about six years; and from this College, which flourished in learning, (the number of its students also being then about two hundred,) he removed to Catharine Hall; of which he was chosen a fellow, and a lecturer, A.D. 1620. Though so young, his unwearied industry and improvement of talents gained him great esteem in the University: yet all this time he "walked in the vanity of his mind," under the entire influence of ambitious hopes and designs, aiming at applause and reputation, so as to rise, and in any manner to advance himself, by preferment. But God had destined him to higher ends, and was graciously pleased to turn the thoughts of his heart and the course of his life to his own service and glory. Being "born out of due time," he was naturally of a weak constitution; and though not likely to live, he was preserved, "when he yet hung upon his mother's breasts," as one in whom God meant to manifest his grace in the miraculous conversion of his soul to himself. Sparks of conscience kept his childish years from gross sins, and set him upon the performance of common duties. He had some workings of the Spirit of God at six years of age, weeping for his sins, when he set himself to think of them, and having flashes of joy at the thoughts of divine things; he was also affected with good motions of love to God and Christ for their love to man, and with grief for sin as displeasing them: but all this goodness of assisted nature reached not to true sanctifying grace; yet he concluded it was grace; for he reasoned with himself, That it was not of nature. At fourteen years of age he received the sacrament, preparing himself as he was able, by examining whether he had grace; all the signs of which, according to Ursin's catechism, he thought he found in himself: the love of God to such a sinner, and Christ dying for him, affected him greatly; and he had much inward joy and comfort at this his first sacrament, while the usual Ps. ciii. was sung during the administration: his heart was wonderfully cheered, thinking himself sure of heaven, and judging all these workings as infallible tokens of God's love to him, and of his grace in him; not considering it as mere stronger fits of nature's working. But hereby God made way for the greater advancement of the power of his grace in him, by shewing him how far he may go, yet deceive himself; grace being a thing surpassing the power of nature; and therefore God suffered him to fall away, not from these good motions, which he could raise at pleasure, but from the practice of them; till his heart began to suspect them as counterfeit. For the next sacrament at Whitsuntide he made great preparations, attending Dr. Sibb's lectures at Trinity Church, and reading Calvin's Institutes; some parts of which were very sweet to him, and the solid delivery of truth therein very pleasing: He now was greatly affected at the thoughts of his going to heaven with the holy men in Christ's College, looking with special joy on Mr. Bentley, (a dear child of God, and fellow of the College,) as one with whom he should live for ever: When ready to receive the sacrament, (being then and for several years after the least in stature of the whole University,) his tutor, Mr. Power, obliged him to desist, and to go out before the whole College; which damped him much, and made him greatly pity himself, that his soul was disappointed of its expectations of being so confirmed, from that sacrament, as never to fall away again: Hereupon he left off praying, not knowing how to go to God, through discouragement; he also left off going to hear Dr. Sibbs; and no longer studied sound divinity, but gave himself up to such studies as should enable him to preach after the flattering manner of Dr. Senhouse.

It now fell out that Arminianism was set on foot in Holland, and the rest of those provinces; and it continued hottest at the very time our author was wrought upon as above. Being inquisitive, he perceived that their doctrine acknowledged a work of the Spirit, moving and stirring at first; but the freedom of the will, assisted by such aids and helps, was to carry it: This they called *grace*, sufficient at first in exciting the will to turn to God, and helping it with power to turn when a man would thus set himself to work; affirming withal, that such converts by the freedom of the same will may, and often do, either fall away totally, or repent again: he observed, however, that several holy youths in his College, (who had made known to him the workings of God on them in humiliation, faith, and change of heart,) continued their profession stedfast without falling off again. Now though the Arminian doctrines suited his own experience, in those natural workings of conscience off and on in religion, yet the example of these godly youths in their constant perseverance, made so strong an impression on him, that in his very heart and judgment he thought those doctrines untrue; and he was fixed under a conviction that his state was neither right nor sound; but yet he could not imagine wherein it failed and was defective. Notwithstanding his thus falling away, he still set himself upon every sacrament, to examine himself anew, to repent, and to turn to God; after that, returning to neglect of prayer, and to his former ways of unregenerate principles and practices, and living in hardness of heart and profaneness. Thus given over to the strength of his lusts, and further than ever from all goodness; despairing of God's grace to convert him, he resolved to follow the world, and its glory and honor, by all possible means. In his way to a merriment at his former College, on hearing a funeral-bell, one of his companions pressed him to go to the sermon; and though he loathed that kind of preaching that good men used, yet seeing many scholars go in, he thought it was some eminent man, or he would come out again; but his loathing was diminished on finding the preacher to be Dr. Bambridge, a witty man, the first words of whose sermon on Luke xix. 41, 42, (which he had heard once before,) pleased him so well, as to make him very attentive all the while: The danger of deferring repentance, That every man had his day of grace offered to him, called by our Lord "this thy day," which being neglected God justly hides from a man's eyes the bestowing of his peace, (as every man may be made for ever in this world by minding his opportunity,) That the neglect of this time of salvation was followed by impenitency, blindness, obduracy, from which we should ever pray to be kept—all this was vehemently urged, without deferring longer to turn immediately to God, lest that day's opportunity should be let slip, and lest the day of grace and salvation should be past, and the door of mercy shut for ever. To his companion who pressed him to turn in to hear that sermon, he expressed his hope to be the better for it as long as he lived, and refused to go with the rest to the place of engagement, (being on monday, Oct. 2nd, A.D. 1620,) for he was at once struck down by a mighty power: his grosser sins came in upon him; which he then wondered at, as being unseasonable; and so the working began, and was prosecuted still more and more, higher and higher: in his endeavouring not to think the least thought of his sins, he was passively held under the remembrance of them, and affected; so as he was rather passive all the while in it, than active; his thoughts being held under, while this work went on.

About two years after, preaching at Ely minster for Dr. Hill, a prebendary, master of his College; he told the auditory, (meaning himself in the person of another,) "That for a man to be converted, who is ordinarily ignorant of what conversion should be, and of what particular passages it consists; and yet to be guided through all its dark corners and windings, would be a wonder to think of; as if one were to go to the top of that lanthorn, to bring him into all the passages of the minster, in-doors and out, without knowing a jot of the way, and in danger every step of treading awry and falling down :" So it was with him : he knew no more of the work of conversion, than these two general heads; that a man is first troubled for sin, and then comforted by the manifestation of God's favor to him. Thus the reviewal of his having been so strangely guided in the dark, became an evidence of the truth of the work of grace upon him. In this and every following intercourse, he was acted by the Spirit of God upon him, and his thoughts passively held fixed, until each head and sort of thoughts were finished; and then a new thought begun and continued; so that he looked at these as so many conferences God had with him, by way of reproof and conviction. His thoughts were kept fixed and intent on the consideration of the next immediate causes of those past gross acts of sinning; and abundant discovery was made to him of his inward lusts, and how all sorts of concupiscences had wrought in him; so that he was amazed to see how greedily he had sought the gratification of every lust. Natural conscience is ready to discover gross acts of sin against knowledge; (as in the dark we more readily see the furniture in a room, than flies and motes,) but the new sort of illumination now vouchsafed him, discovered his heart in all his sinnings, and carried him down to see his inwards, as by the searching of candles, bringing to light the violent eagerness and insatiableness of his lusts. He found, under the dispensation of this new light, the apparent difference of his former experience, wherein he had indeed enlightenings, and great strivings of the Holy Ghost, both unto and in the performance of holy duties, prayers, hearings, &c. without discovering the sinful inordinacy of his lusts, as the root and ground of all his other sinnings: and those devotions differed also from the present sight of his inward corruption; for this secret thought ran along with them, That God could not but accept such real services as he thought he performed; so that the opinion of merit prevailed over the commonly received doctrine which taught him otherwise; but the clear sight of his heart-lusts made that notion vanish, for his former thoughts of which he now detested himself: the sinfulness of these lusts he perceived to be chiefly in *ungodliness*, as their spring; and that having been "a lover of pleasure more than a lover of God," (according to Jer. ii. 13, "My people have committed two evils; they have forsaken me the fountain of living waters, and hewed them out cisterns, broken cisterns, that can hold no water,") he had acted them in things that were most lawful, but wherein even "the plowing of the wicked is sin," Prov. xxi. 4. Thus the sinfulness of his sins was exceedingly enlarged, through the light accompanying every action which he could cast his remembrance on, or go over in his view; and thus a new horrid vein and course of sin, lying at the bottom of his heart, in the rising and working of all his lusts, was also revealed to him; so that his heart was kept in a continual course of ungodliness, wholly obstructed from acting towards God in any way, or from having any holy or good movings at all. God, "with whom (only and immediately) he had to do," and not with his own bare single thoughts, having proceeded thus far in "humbling him under his mighty hand," continued orderly to possess his thoughts with a further progress herein, holding him intent to consider and pierce into the first causes of so much actual sinfulness, and presenting to him, as in answer, (for this was transacted as a conference by God with him,) the original corruption of his nature, and the inward evil constitution and depravation of all his faculties, and the inclinations and dispositions of his heart unto all evil, and his averseness from all spiritual good and acceptableness to God: he was convinced that in these respects he was *flesh;* as if this was the definition of *man,* "that which is born of the flesh is flesh:" And here he stood astonished at the sight and workings of his heart, as if in the heat of summer, by a clear light and piercing eye, he had discerned millions of crawling things in a sink of liquid corruption. When holy Mr. Price heard Mr. Chatterton preach, it was as the shining of the sun of righteousness on a dunghill; but our authors apprehensions of his own heart were, That it was utterly without Christ. He was deeply impressed that all the sins that were ever committed, proceeded from the same root of the corruption of men's nature; and that if tempted thereto he should himself have committed the same. But what affected him yet more, was a sight and sense that his heart was empty of all good; as the apostle saith, "*I* know that in me, that is, in my flesh, there dwelleth *no* good thing," whereas in the righteous, "there is *some* good thing towards the Lord God of Israel:" Thus all his boasted ingenuity and goodness was naught before the goodness of God. He was next led to inquire into, and consider, the original cause at the bottom of all this said sinfulness of heart and life; and from Rom. v. 12, ("By one man sin entered into the world, and death by sin; and so death passed upon all men, in that all have sinned,") he debated thus with himself: That it was in Adam all sinned; for infants sin not "after the similitude of Adam's transgression," (which is cautiously added to shew that they are simply involved in his act of sinning, without actually sinning themselves;) whence we become guilty "by the disobedience of one, whereby we are all made sinners;" for disobedience notes an act of sinning, not a sinful nature or habit. Thus was his spirit so strongly convicted of this great truth, *That the guilt or demerit of one man's disobedience had corrupted our nature,* that once at midnight he rose, and fell on his knees before God, formally assuming and taking on him, the guilt of Adam's sin, as truly as any of his own actual sins.

While thus engaged in heart-conclusions about his own sinfulness and the utter corruption of all his actions, and that he was nothing but flesh, as born of flesh; it came in full upon his mind that he should wrong himself to end in such a conclusion, for he thought he had abundance of experience of the workings of true grace, enlightenings, and ravishments of spirit, and of faith in Christ, especially on sacramental occasions. He recollected the course of his spirit until he was thirteen years of age; and how when he was seven years old, a servant of his grandfather, (with whom he lived,) reproved him very vehemently for some sin as leading him to hell-torments; from which time he began to be affected with thoughts of God and religion, though in a childish way; for he began to weep and mourn on fresh convictions of fresh sins; but though for a while abstaining from them, he found himself weak and overcome again: still as he could weep for his sins in secret, when he could weep for nothing else, he concluded it was not hypocrisy; for God noticed Hezekiah's turning to the wall with tears: and having known the Scriptures from a child, like Timothy, he waxed confident, from the promise of obtaining whatever he asked of the Father in Christ's name; which he would be sure to do for all he would have of God. Thus renewing his repentance for relapses into sins, he "thought as a child," That whatever was more than *nature* must be *grace;* and that his religious fits and affections, of which he was once destitute, must be the work of God, (who came to him, only as a way-faring man tarries for a night and departs:) but as the Holy Ghost moved on the waters, and sustained the chaos that was created, so he excites good motions in carnal hearts; as in a frost, the ice-drops and snow melt, and the earth becomes slabby, only where the sun shines; yet there is no general thaw: so these lighter impressions, and slighter workings, made him so presumptuous as to think he had more grace, though but a school-boy, than his relations or any of the town-folks he knew. Having been admitted a junior-sophister of his College a year before the usual time of standing, he obtruded himself among the rest of his form, as a communicant, being ashamed to go out of the chapel alone: he had exercised himself on this occasion in self-examinations, and meditations on the sufferings of Christ, which he presumed to apply to himself with much thankfulnes to God. His devotions were the more kindled by the residence of six fellows, who were chief tutors of his College, and called Puritans, because of their strict godliness; (and besides, Cambridge was still full of talk of the power of Mr. Perkin's ministry; and also, Dr. Ames, professor of divinity at Franeker, who wrote "Puritanismus Anglicanus," had by the urgency of the master, not long before our author's time, been driven from his fellowship of Christ's Church and from the University itself; but the worth and holiness of that man was sufficiently known by what he afterwards did in the Low Countries:) These fellows had several godly pupils, whose ways he observed; and he took the opportunity of acquainting himself with Ursin's renowned summary of the orthodox religion, which was explained to them at their saturday-night's chamber-prayers. The powerful and steady examples of these, and especially of one of their tutors, Mr. Bentley, (whose innocent, meek, and humble spirit, was proved amidst dangerous fits of apoplexy to which he was subject,) had decided him in respect to the Arminian controversy: still the stirring affections he felt at the prayers, and the ravishing elevations of his animal spirits, were but as the morning dew; and at the end of a week he left off private prayer, and all his other godly exercises; till the return of another sacrament, when he fell to loving the godly tutors and pupils again, so as to continue more constant in duties for a longer time together. The University church of St. Mary vied in all the florid sermons and strains of wit, from which he was withdrawn for eight weeks, accompanying the godly of his College to hear the plain and wholesome preaching of Dr. Sibbs, keeping to private prayer, and getting more acquainted with those holy students; so that he longed for the next sacrament to confirm him by the body and blood of Christ in his new way, and to keep him from falling again in love with scholastic divinity: But on occasion of his tutor's restraining him from the Lord's table, (as before mentioned,) he suddenly left off his begun courses, and again constantly attended at St. Mary's, and returned to his lusts and pleasures, (though kept from gross sins,) and to the ambition of vain-glory and applause; and with a lower kind of enmity against good men and things, he resolved to preach against those at Lynn Regis and their ways, (where the eminent Mr. Price was afterwards minister,) and to take part with the whole town against them, which his wicked spirit, through the studies he had pursued, was too eager and fitted to do: till it came to this, That if God would give him the pleasure he desired, and the preferment he sought, and not damn him at last, he might keep heaven to himself; and as for the powerful preaching of Mr. Rogers, of Dedham, and such others, he defied their troubling his conscience.

When God by a true work of grace effectually converted him to himself, the vanity of his former religion, and the deficiency of the root of all his devotions, was abundantly manifested; and as he reflected on certain passages of scripture, God vouchsafed him a new and further light into the bottom of his heart, to discern, That self-love and self-flattery, acted to the utmost by wordly motives, were but the roots of all these gaudy tulips he counted for grace: thus the flowers of all his former devotions withered to nothing, as in the parable of the stony ground, where the heart wanted moisture to nourish it. He was surrounded by the prospect he lay under of all these heads of sinning, and so shut up as to see no way of escape; and together with the sight of this sinfulness, hell opened its mouth upon him, threatening to destroy and devour him for ever and ever. Though subjugated and bound over to these apprehensions, he was kept however from the soreness of God's wrath piercing him through and through; and though he had a solid and strong and just conviction of sin abiding on him, as in his unbelief, yet he suffered not the terrors of the Almighty, bound as he was hand and foot, and subacted under the pressure of the guilt of wrath and subjection to the just judgment of the Lord. It was not many hours before God, faithful to his word of promise in not suffering the regenerate to be tempted above what they are able, in his pity made a way for him to escape, that he might be able to bear it; and loving him with the same love as his own dear elect children, suffered not a destroying apprehension to continue long upon him previous to his believing. In Ezek. xvi. the election of grace are compared to a still-born child, covered over with the blood of its birth, its navel uncut, itself unwashed, but cast out as a carcase in the open field, till the compassion of God bid it, with earnest vehemence, "Live, yea live:" So God in an instant was pleased to alter the whole course of his former dispensation towards him, after all that heap amassed from the continual ebullitions of original sin: no eye pitied him or could help him; till he who created the world and the matter of all things by a word, put a new life and spirit into his soul by the whisper of his promise. As is the still yet certain sound of a distant voice; or as the gospel, whispered out of Zion, sounded over the whole earth; so this speaking of God to his soul, though so gentle a sound, made a noise over his whole heart, and filled and possessed all his soul, while God took him aside, and as it were privately said to him, "Do you turn to me, and I will pardon all your sins, though never so many, as I forgave and pardoned my servant Paul; and I will convert you unto myself, as I did Mr. Price," (a notable convert in Cambridge, and a most striking example of a singular conversion, and the holiest man without exception, and then preacher at King's Lynn, whither our author's parents had removed from Rolseby:) These secret whispers and speeches of God to him he related a year-and-half after to Mr. Price, and since then frequently to others, in declaring this his conversion; for they ever stuck in his mind: examples set before us by God, being written and propounded to us for our hope, (Rom. xv. 4,) and alleged not only to illustrate and explain rules, but to prove and confirm them: That God pardoned such a man in such a condition, is often brought home as implying a secret promise to another man in the same condition. Preaching at Ely two years after, he urged Paul's instance as an example to win others, (in allusion to his own experience,) and that such examples were flags of mercy to win a company of rebels: that of Paul was full and pertinent to the purpose for which God held it out to him; he considering with himself the amplitude of his pardon, that it involved all sorts of sins of the highest nature, in which Paul had so walked, that he was even upon the narrow brink of sinning against the Holy Ghost: and God had suggested to him, that he would pardon him for all his sins, though never so great, (for boldness, hardness of heart, and heinousness of sinning,) as he had done Paul, and would change his heart, as he had Mr. Price's. The confirmations whereby he judged the said instructions and suggestions to come immediately from God, were, *First,* The posture and condition of his spirit when they took him, his heart being at the time immoveably fixed in the contrary persuasions of his being in a damned state, without hope of a remedy for the guilt of those sins in which he had continued: and it was when God had set a guard upon him as the prisoner of hell, that the contrary apprehensions and impressions came in so instaneously, and so deeply rooted in his heart, that he remembered them ever since. *Secondly,* It was a word in season, (which Christ himself was taught to speak to distressed souls, Isa. l. 4,) like that to Abraham the father of the faithful, which became a Jewish proverb, " In the mount the Lord will (provide or) be seen;" which "*Jehovah-jireh*" the Jews apply to the immediate remedy God out of pity affords a man in such distress and straits as none but himself can remedy; and it is a word fitted and proper to such an occasion, and peculiar to the case in hand; a word quick and sudden, and interrupting all contrary expectations and fears, as when God spake in haste, calling, " Abraham, Abraham." *Thirdly,* What was suggested to him was not an ungrounded fancy, but the pure word of God, the ground of faith and hope; it was the promise and performance of God's forgiving Paul the most heinous sins that ever any committed who was saved; Paul confessing himself the chiefest of sinners; and his example being the most pertinent that could be found in the book of God. *Fourthly,* He was powerfully persuaded that the said suggestions were of God, from the fulfilment of God's words to him; for, 1st, He felt all the powers of his soul in an instant clean altered, and changed in the disposition of them; as the discourses of our English divines set forth the manner of conversion in the effects of it. 2ndly, He found the works of the devil dissolved in his heart, from that time, in an eminent manner; his understanding enlightened; his will melted and softened; the stone made flesh, disposed to receive and to turn to God: and, 3dly, He found his spirit cloathed with a new nature, inclining him to good instead of evil. It was not merely such good motions from the Spirit of God, as formerly incited him to flushings and streamings of transitory affections, exciting joy in his animal spirits, when he applied himself to a holy duty; but he found a new in-dwelling or habitual principle of opposition to in-dwelling sin, and a hatred of it; so that he concluded with himself, That this new workmanship wrought in him, was of the same kind, as to matter of holiness, with that image of God, expressed in Eph. iv. 24, and Col. iii. 10. Thus he was at first comforted in seeing and finding two contrary principles; the Spirit as truly lusting against the flesh, as the flesh against the Spirit; and he found apparent the difference of the opposition of conscience only against a lust, and that of the Spirit or new work of grace in the heart; (the Spirit not contradicting and checking, but making a real natural opposition as of fire to water;) and this difference he found not by reading or hearing it spoken of; but like Augustin, he perceived it of himself, and wondered at it: his was a combat proper and peculiar to the regenerate; not found in God or Christ who are fulness of holiness, or in devils who are all sin, or in angels who are entirely holy, or in sinners who have no grace in them to fight with their corruptions in such a manner. 4thly, The consequence of what took place in his heart was, an actual turning from all known sins, and an entertaining the truth of all the principles of godliness, as far as he received them from the word of God, and the best examples of godly men with whom he lived. Assisted by God's direction, he looked back on his sinful state, and took a summary survey of his chief sins and lusts; which he found to be, love of pleasure more than of God, corrupt ends, and especially such vain-glorious acàdemic praise as he sought with his whole soul: and God was pleased to direct him to take up, as his rule of turning to him, a sincere aim at his glory, as the scope of all his inward thoughts, words, actions, designs, and ends whatsoever; assisting him to consider severally all the sorts of actions he had gone through in his life, and to take them asunder, especially the most principal, in particulars, every one in order. And here in the first place he compared the aim and drift of his studies, (upon which he had spent his whole time,) with what served most to the glory of God in the work of the ministry: this overturned all the dearest hopes and projects and designs of his heart; for the interests of these were more than life to him. The University was addicted to a vain-glorious eloquence, wherein the wits strove to exceed one another; and that which he most of all affected in his foolish fancy, was to have preached like Dr. Senhouse, of St. John's, (afterwards made bishop,) a few of whose sermons were in print, being the greatest farrago of all sorts of flowers, similitudes, or elegancies of art, found in any of the fathers, poets, or historians: not that he expected to attain all the accomplishments wherein this man abounded, but he studied his collections so as to imitate him all he could, when he should come to preach. But this way of his soon received a fatal wound from Dr. Preston's opposition to it, as vain and unedifying; whose catechetical sermons in the chapel of that College he happened while unregenerate to hear, though unmoved thereby to alter his studies; nor could all the world, or angels, or men, have moved him; but on this turning to God, and setting up God's glory as the resolved end of all his actions and ways, he soon discovered the unprofitableness of such a design, and resolved to leave all, and to preach nothing but sound wholesome words; in which principle and practice he continued for three-score years, without once attempting to introduce any of his own withered flowers, that he had gathered, and had valued more than diamonds; nor did these even tempt him or offer themselves to his memory; but he preached what was most edifying, either for conversion of souls, or for bringing them up to eternal life. Thus his *master-lust* was mortified. There was nothing of constraint or force in this work of God on his soul, but he was carried on with the most willing and ready mind; and what he did was what he chose to do. He parted with his sins, (once so dear to him as the apple of his eye, yea as his life,) with the greatest freedom, resolving never to return to them any more, and deliberately counting the cost of so great a change. Though he considered the opinion the world had of the true convert, and sincere to God, who walked in such ways of purity and holiness, yet it hindered him not at all: he swam and broke through the weeds that entangled him in these waters, with as much ease as Samson did his withs; for he was made a vassal and perfect captive to another binding, (as when Paul went bound in the Spirit up to Jerusalem,) and he said within himself of all his old companions, "What do ye breaking my heart? for I am ready not to be bound only, but to give up my life, so as I may serve God with joy in those ways." He looked not back, (as Lot's wife,) but with his whole soul's desire to return no more to the enjoyment of any lust, all his childish imaginations of preferment were cast down, and fell like bubbles vanishing into air: every strong hold and high thing, (such as scholars generally make the card of their life to sail by,) was captivated to the obedience of Christ, 2 Cor. x. 5. He was brought to be content with the meanest condition all his days, so he might fulfil ever so mean a course of life with uprightness and sincerity towards God. He took his leave for ever of all ecclesiastical preferments; and though afterwards president of Magdalen College in Oxford, the motive of his heart was the fair opportunity of his ministry doing good in the University, and that he might bring in godly young men, fellows and students, to serve God in the ministry in after-times; and he accordingly inquired and sought after such jewels, and was grieved when he failed of his aim: and this principle he brought with him from his first sttiеon in Catharine Hall, Cambridge, (where he was instrumental in Dr. Sibb's election to the mastership of that College, and in Dr. Arrowsmith, Mr. Pen of Northamptonshire, &c. becoming fellows;) and he was confirmed therein, in that after seven years absence from Cambridge, on his return from Holland he received, almost monthly, for some years, serious and hearty acknowldgments from several young men, who had the light of their conversion by his ministry at Cambridge. This encouraged him to return again to a University; and his success at Oxford is left to Christ till the latter day. But the most eminent property of his said conversion was, That the glory of the great GOD was set up in his heart, as the square and rule of each and every particular practice both of faith and godliness; and of all signs of sincerity, there neither is nor can be any clearer than this witness, "He that seeketh his glory that sent him, the same is true, and no unrighteousness is in him," (John vii. 18;) Christ speaks this of himself, out of his own experience of what He did, who is the *truth* itself; as the *glory* of God is God Himself, who doth all things for Himself: and therefore he that thus acteth for God predominantly above all other ends, must necessarily be judged truly righteous. None can extract out of man's heart what is not in it; and there is not the least spark of regard for the glory of God, as the chief end, in the heart of the unregenerate: sparks will come from a flint struck against iron or steel; but not from a piece of ice, for there are none in it, nor the least disposition towards any. True conversion is, when upon the change of a man's last end, there is a change made upon the whole man and all the powers of his soul; if a man changes but to one particular end, the effect is answerably limited and partial; as when a prodigal thus becomes sparing and covetous, the only effect is, a care to keep his money and not spend it lavishly: but godliness, respecting the glory of God above all, hath a general and universal end, extending its influence upon all things. Hence our author's task was to survey, and go over, every particular kind of act, both as to what he must forbear, and for what end, and with what heart; as also to observe each particular practice of godliness, which he had for a long time wretchedly neglected: so that he fixed on this summary of his whole life, That he had made lusts and pleasures his only end, and done nothing with aims at God's glory; and therefore he would begin his turning to God by making God's glory the measure of all for the time to come.

The above account of the work of the Holy Ghost on our author's soul, in his own conversion to God, was designed to give, from his own experience, (as himself said,) a testimony of the difference between the common grace by some thought sufficient, and special saving grace, which is alone sufficient, and which always invincibly and effectually prevails, as it did in him, enduring through a long life and course of various temptations and trials unto the end. In the first enlightenings and workings of conscience, he experienced how far common grace might go, and yet fail at last so as utterly to wither and decay: in the other lasting work on his soul, which was victorious to eternity, he felt an extraordinary divine power changing it, and entirely subduing it to God. In reading the acts of the Synod of Dort, and reviewing the first workings of common grace in him, he found them consistent with the Arminian opinions; but on comparing his own experiences of efficacious grace with the doctrines of the orthodox protestant divines, he found the one perfectly to agree with the other. A man cannot be disputed out of such an inward sense of things as established him in the truths of the gospel and possessed him with a due tempered warmth and zeal to assert and vindicate them with such arguments and reasons, as the truth is never destitute of, to resist gainsayers. It was however many years before he came to have a clear knowledge of the gospel, and a full view of Christ by faith, with joy and peace in believing. "A blessed age this, said he in his latter years; now the time of faith is come; and faith is principally insisted on unto salvation: in my younger years we heard little more of Christ, than as merely mentioned in the ministry, and in printed books: I was diverted from Christ for several years, to search only into the signs of grace in me: it was almost seven years ere I was taken off to live by faith on Christ, and on God's free love, which are alike the objects of faith." For so long a time were his thoughts intent on the conviction God had wrought in him of the heinousness of sin, of his own sinful and miserable state by nature, of the difference between the workings of natural conscience though enlightened, and the motions of a holy soul changed and acted by the Spirit in an effectual work of peculiar saving grace: accordingly he kept a constant diary of observations of the case and posture of his mind and heart towards God, with suitable pious and pathetic meditations: His sermons being the result of these, had a great deal of spiritual heat in them, and were blessed by God to the conviction and conversion of many young scholars who flocked to his ministry. He maintained great intimacy of Christian friendship with Mr. Price, of Lynn, as the greatest man for experimental acquaintance with Christ he ever met with ; and as he poured into his bosom his spiritual complaints, so his conference with him, by letter and discourse, was blessed by God to lead him into the spirit of the gospel, to live by faith in Christ, deriving from him life and strength, for sanctification and all comfort and joy through believing. In answer to Mr. Price, (who had poured the balm of the gospel into his wounded soul, to its healing and comfort,) he thus wrote, " I am come to this pass now, that signs will do me no good alone ; I have trusted too much to habitual grace for assurauce of justification : I tell you Christ is worth all, to whom coming my weary soul finds that rest, which in all its unquiet motions it could not find elsewhere." And his own account of this work of faith is thus : " It fell out that soon after my being humbled for sin, the doctrine of justification through Christ by faith came into my thoughts ; but my spirit was turned off from it by this prejudice, That it had been the deceit of carnal men for continuing in their sins, and so I might be deceived in that way and course, remembering how I had been deceived in believing on Christ crucified with joy and ravishment in my carnal state : which from time to time was a hinderance to me from going to Christ : and I was pitched on this great principle, That if I found myself sanctified, (as I certainly did,) I then was justified ; the one being only the evidence of the other : and thus my mind was set on examining the inherent work wrought in me by the Spirit ; and I pursued after mortification of lusts, and inward holiness, thinking thus to have the comfort of my justification, yet being thus kept from going to Christ actually, though dealing with God and his mercy in Christ, as having done all on his part to be done in redeeming and reconciling us : so that I dealt immediately with God and his pure mercy and free grace. But it fell strongly into my mind, that there was a necessity of Christ's righteousness to justify me, as well as of his grace which had sanctified me ; and God took this course to convince me of it, and to set me a work about it : He used the very conviction I had of original sin from Adam, in its two branches, in the guilt of Adam's actual transgression imputed to me, and the corruption of my nature thence derived : I had had a mighty and large conviction and deep sense of these ; and that all lusts were sins ; which greatly helped me clearly to take in the absolute necessity of justification by Christ's righteousness, and to glory in it, discerning the perfect difference of it from sanctification : I began to reflect, That Christ was the head for salvation, as Adam had been for sin and condemnation ; and that therefore as there were two branches of sin and condemnation derived to me from Adam ; (the one an imputation of his fact to me, the other a violent and universal corruption of nature inherent in me ;) just so it must be in Christ's salvation of me : and hence I must have an imputation of his righteousness for justification, as well as a holy nature derived from him for sanctification ; the former being perfect, the latter not : The notion of this did mightily and experimentally enlighten me." This experience of the refreshing comforts of the knowledge of Christ and free justification by his righteousness alone, made him now zealous of preaching for the consolation of afflicted consciences, and not for conviction and terror as heretofore : so Dr. Sibbs once told him, That if ever he would do good, he must preach the gospel and the free grace of God in Christ Jesus. The only copy of his sermons on the glory of the gospel, called his *Primitiæ Evanglicæ*, or *Evangelical First-fruits*, was thus remarkably preserved : The portmanteau in which they were, was cut off from his horse by a thief in the evening, just against St. Andrew's church-yard in Holborn ; the clerk or sexton, coming on the Lord's day morning to ring the bell, found a bundle of papers tied up with a string, at the foot of a great tree, in which were some acquittances of a Cambridge bookseller, who accompanied him to London ; which led to the discovery.

He was chosen A. D. 1628, to preach the lecture to the town of Cambridge, at Trinity Church. Dr. Buckridge, Bishop of Ely, made some difficulty at first about admitting him to it, unless he would solemnly promise, in pursuance of the King's proclamation, not to preach about any controverted points in divinity : but as the most essential articles of the Christian faith were controverted by one or other, and as such a promise would scarce leave him any subject to preach on, he alleged, That it was not his Majesty's intention to inhibit him or any other from preaching against the gross errors of Popery. He continued lecturer till A. D. 1634, when dissatisfied in his conscience with the laws of conformity, he left the University and his preferments. As he acted herein with all sincerity, according to the light given him, and the full persuasion of his own mind, apart from all worldly motives which would have swayed him contrariwise ; so he expressed himself with great joy of faith and thankfulness and praise for the faithful love of Jesus Christ to him, in the performance of the promise in Luke xviii. 29, 30. Having cheerfully parted with all for Christ, he was abundantly compensated not only in the comforts and joy of his love, (which are incomparably above all other things,) but in that love and esteem of good men which God gave him, who alone also made his ministry acceptable and successful to the conversion and comfort of many souls. He married Elizabeth, daughter of alderman Prescott, A.D. 1638; of so sweet a temper, lively wit, and sincere piety, as endeared her to all who knew her: her two sisters were married, one to Sir William Leman, and the other to Sir Nicholas Crisp: He had by her an only daughter, Elizabeth, (married to Mr. John Mason, a citizen of London,) who was a living image of her parents, in natural endowment of mind, as well as in grace and piety; she lost her mother when about ten years of age, and died two years before her father. The persecution growing hot in England, our author resolved on removing into some foreign country, where he might exercise his ministry and enjoy Christ's ordinances, agreeably to his conscience. Accordingly he went over into Holland, A. D. 1639, and settling at last at Arnheim, was pastor of the English Church in that city: while there some differences arising in the English Church at Rotterdam, he and the elders of the Church of Arnheim went thither; and God was pleased by their brotherly advice and counsel to compose the difference, and to re-establish the disturbed peace of that Church. On returning to England and becoming pastor of a Church in London, he was appointed, by an ordinance of Parliament, A. D. 1643, a member of the venerable Assembly of divines at Westminster. He took a brief account of every day's debates about church-government and discipline which arose in that Synod; of which his son possessed about fourteen volumes of his manuscripts: his way of arguing was with such modesty and Christian meekness, as procured the esteem of them who differed from him and the other dissenting brethren in his judgment. He had an invitation, A. D. 1647, from the Rev. John Cotton, (in whom grace and learning were so happily conjoined,) and others in new England, to come over to them; to which he was so much inclined, that he had put a great part of his library on ship-board; but he was over-persuaded by some, to whose counsel and advice he paid a great deference. He was married again, A. D. 1649, to Mary, a descendant of the ancient family of the Hammonds, in Shropshire; whose ancestor was an officer in the army of William, Duke of Normandy, when he invaded England, A. D. 1066. Though not seventeen years of age, she had the gravity and prudence of a matron: her conjugal affection, her tender care, her wise administration of the affairs of her family, the goodness of her disposition, and above all her grace and piety, left an honorable remembrance of her. By her he had two sons, (Thomas, who compiled this memoir of his father; and Richard, who died in a voyage to the East Indies, where he was sent as one of the Company's factors a year after his father's death,) and also two daughters who died in their infancy. In the same year of his second marriage he was admitted President of Magdalen College in Oxford, where his zeal to promote piety and learning, his candour, his ingenuity, his catholic charity for all good men of every persuasion, won the hearts of those who were most averse to him. In disposing of any place of preferment, he was not biassed by party-affection but by goodness and merit. Messrs. Brown and Byfield, and Dr. Fairfax, who continued fellows many years after he left the College, retained an affection and esteem for him, ever speaking of him with most honourable mention. Several persons of piety and learning belonged to the church of which he was pastor; as Messrs. Thankful Owen, President of St. John's; Francis Hovel, Master of Jesus College; Theophilus Gale; Stephen Charnock; Blower, Barron, Terry, Lowman; and others. On the revolution, A. D. 1660, he resigned his Presidentship to Dr. Oliver, and removed to London, where he was pastor of the same church which he had gathered in Oxford, a great part of the members of it following him to that city. In the faithful discharge of this office and labour in the Lord Jesus Christ he continued till his death.

It was at this time he lived a retired life spent in prayer, reading, and meditation. He read much; and the authors he valued and studied, were Augustin, Calvin, Musculus, Zanchius, Parœus, Walœus, Gomarus, Attingius, and Amesius; among the school-men, Suarez and Esthius; but the scriptures were his chiefest study, (in which he was assisted by the best collection of commentators;) and as they are an inexhaustible treasury of divine knowledge, so by an eager search into and comparing of them, he discovered those truths which are not to be found in other authors. His mind soared with greatest delight, (not of merely speculative pleasure,) in the love and free-grace of God, and the excellencies and glories of Christ; which were the life and food of his soul; and as his heart was affected with them, he wrote them with a spiritual warmth better felt than expressed. Though he read much, yet he was more intense in thinking; whereby he made himself master of the subject of his discourse. In that deplorable calamity of the dreadful fire of London, A.D. 1666, reducing a considerable part of the city to ashes, he lost about half his library, to the value of five hundred pounds: that part of it however which was lodged very near where the fire began, which he accounted irrecoverably lost, was by the diligence of his friend, Mr. Moses Lowman, preserved from the flame with extreme hazard; while the other part, which he thought might have been timely secured, being lodged at a distance in Bread-street, was all burnt through the negligence of the persons sent to take care of them: God thus struck him in a very sensible part; for he loved his library too well: yet he blessed God that the rebuke of his affliction fell not on his divinity-books, but on those of human learning. As the exercise of faith, and of its fruits, relieved him; he hereupon meditated and wrote a discourse of "Patience and its perfect work," printed soon after. A fever seized him in Feb. 1679, putting an end to his life in a few days; in all the violence of which he discoursed with that strength of faith, that assurance of Christ's love, that holy admiration of free-grace, that joy in believing, and with such thanksgivings and praises, as extremely moved and affected all that heard him. Mr. Collins, (then pastor of the same church of which he had formerly been pastor, and with the reluctant consent of which he removed to Oxford, A.D. 1649,) praying earnestly for him, "That God would return into his bosom all those comforts which he had by his ministry of free-grace poured into so many distressed souls," he felt the prayer answered in the abundant comforts and joys with which he was filled. "I am going said he, to the Three Persons which whom I have had communion; they have taken me, I did not take them: I shall be changed in the twinkling of an eye: I shall be rid of all my lusts and corruptions, which I could not be here; these croaking toads will fall off in a moment." On mentioning those great examples of faith in Heb. xi. he said, "All these died in faith: I could not have imagined I should ever have had such a measure of faith in this hour; no, I could never have imagined it: My bow abides in strength: Is Christ divided? no: I have the whole of his righteousness; I am found in him, not in my own righteousness, which is of the law, but in the righteousness which is of God, which is by faith of Jesus Christ, who loved me and gave himself for me: Christ cannot love me more than he doth; I think I cannot love him more than I do: I am swallowed up in God." He thus exhorted his two sons to value the privilege of the Covenant: "It hath taken hold of me: my mother was a holy woman, she spake nothing diminishing of it: it is a privilege which cannot be valued enough, nor be purchased with a great sum of money, (Acts xxii. 28:) Be careful of provoking God to reject you: Now I shall be ever with the Lord." With such assurance of faith, and such fulnesss of joy, his soul left this world, and went to see and enjoy the reality of that blessed state of glory, which in a discourse on that subject he had so well demonstrated. He died in the eightieth year of his age.

The following is an abstract taken from the testimony of Messrs. Thankful Owen and James Barron, to this great person's eminent fitness for, and happy performance of such an undertaking as was his Exposition on the Epistle to the Ephesians, which he was chosen to interpret after his return to England: "The special light God so clearly gave him in the mysteries of corrupt nature and of the gospel, shone through all his works, and particulary this Comment; which could be best understood by one, who had the Apostle's sense, (that *Gustus Spiritualis Judicii,*) temptations, and experience; for our author was a man of inward conflicts and of outward sufferings. Cheery of the light he attained, he lived over the truths he knew, even to the hazard of what was most dear to him; and thus he abounded as he knew, according to John vii. 17, Matt. xiii. 12. His genius dived into the bottom, and waded through the depths of the points treated of; which he '*studied down,*' as he used to say; consulting all the weightiest authors on these subjects, and valuing every ray of light, in aid of the fresh lustre added thereto by his own experience; besides the advantages he had from the converse of most eminent Christians, those living and walking bibles: he thus became peculiarly qualified to treat also of cases of conscience, and practical points. Being a man mighty in prayer to that God, with whom he had high and intimate communion; and addicted to retirement and deep contemplation, he filled his head and heart with spiritual notions, as the sand of the sea. He delighted in searching into points neglected by others, and in opening difficult texts; and he discovered 'the depths of Satan,' by anatomizing 'the old man' in himself and others. He was much exercised in the controversies of his day; and having an insight into the covenant of grace, he was a witness to the Greek Fathers' ignorance of that grace, and the consequent rise of Pelagian and other errors in the church, as Jansenius observes: But before undertaking such a province, he had gone over the grand points of religion before intelligent auditories, who helped to draw out his gifts. Touching his Expositions, we know no man so happy in pitching on the true, genuine, and full scope of a text; and he delighted to exhibit the most comprehensive sense of the Holy Ghost, in the various references and aspects one passage had upon others. By 'comparing spiritual things with spiritual,' he was enabled to open dark scriptures by means of such as were less obscure; fetching light, as in optics, by various positions of the glass; bringing gospel-truths from types and prophecies, and reflecting back light again on these shadows from gospel-truths: thus small rays concentrated by him, emitted a glorious light, while he left no difficulty unassailed and unvanquished: He valued the least iota, and showed what momentous things depended on the least of God's words. His observations being clear, genuine, and natural, as well as scriptural, the highest controverted points and sublimest gospel mysteries, were brought down by him in a plain and familiar way, without the affectation of hard and scholastic terms; for what had first been stated in his own heart, he made easy to the sense and experience of others. While he brings not scripture to his learning, there is a variety of learning included under what he brings to bear upon scripture; and a vein of strong spiritual reason, carrying its own light and evidence with it, runs through all his discourses. In breaking open the mines of the glorious grace of God and the unsearchable riches of Christ, according to the divine decrees, (into which the further we search the greater treasures we find, *Plenius Responsura Fodienti,*) none could more clearly resolve the plot of salvation into pure grace. His discourses, being so evangelical, carry the soul on to a higher holiness from a higher and nobler spring of action than was found in man before the fall: and when he steps out of the beaten track, and beyond the elevation of writers in general, he doth it with regard to 'the analogy of faith,' and to a just veneration for the reformed religion; wondering greatly at the daring attempts of persons unskilful in the word of righteousness, against those great and momentous points of our religion, which are the glory of our reformation, and which will prove 'gold, silver, precious stones,' when their 'wood, hay, and stubble' will be burnt up. On the whole, we consider him as a person raised up by God for such eminent service in his age, as Augustin and others were in their times: and therefore we are not a little astonished at the unworthiness of some in this age, who use all their arts and interest to suppress the light of this and other great luminaries of the Church, and to eclipse stars of the first magnitude, for such little niceties and nothings as the best and purest times were unacquainted with. We need add no more, than that the writings of such an author cannot but carry with them his own signature, he having drawn to the life the picture of his own heart by his own hand."

AN

EXPOSITION

OF THE

BOOK OF REVELATION.

THE FIRST PART.

THE THREE FIRST CHAPTERS

CONTAIN seven epistles to seven particular churches; but from the fourth chapter to the close of the Revelation is laid down a more general prophecy, reaching from John's time to the end of the world. This former portion of the book concerns things past, present, and to come, (c. i. 19;) but the latter only "things which must be hereafter," c. iv. 1. In the vision of the general prophecy is the story of all times, acted and represented by angels, for whom the stage of Christ's church is erected; a scene is supposed where the things were done, and a chorus of spectators, (or church-members,) judging and approving, and giving their plaudit of glory to God by the mouth of the four beasts and the four and twenty elders; (see c. iv.): and as in such scenic exhibitions there is wont to be a prologue, so there is as artificial a one acted in c. v. as any in any poem; from whence, in c. vi. the representation of the story begins.

THE FOURTH CHAPTER.

VERSE I.—John is called up from the earth into the air, or "*heaven*," the place of his vision, where a door seemed to open; on entering which he sees as follows:

VERSE II.—"*And immediately I was in the Spirit;*" denoting such a repletion or filling with the Spirit as possessed all the powers of his soul to attend to the vision; (the phrase is as when we say a man is *in love* or *in liquor;* or as a mill is *in the wind:)* it filled all; it carried all in him to the thing in hand, and wholly acted his faculties by a supernatural motion of the Spirit on his understanding and sense; for it was to an extraordinary purpose, even to see and write these visions of the Holy Ghost: yet to us it should be ordinary so far as to our being,

2 O

and walking, *in the Spirit;* giving up ourselves, our powers and faculties to the Spirit's rule and guidance, to move all wheels in us. *N.B.* From this "*immediately*" we observe, That a believing soul may presently be in the Spirit, who soon and suddenly comes upon a man.

The following is a vision of the church, which is made the scene of all things prophesied of in this book; for all things are done either *for* or *concerning* it; the judgments on the world are recorded for the church's sake, as executed by God out from the church. Now this vision of the throne, beasts, and elders, is a representation of the church, wherein God hath his throne. I.—It is a *church*, for 1, There only is God worshipped, (v. 8—10,) and known and glorified, Ps. lxxvi. 1; xxix. 9. 2, The throne here is evidently God's seat in his temple, the church; as in c. xvi. 17. 3, The allusion here is to the tabernacle and to the temple, with their ornaments and utensils, as types of the New Testament church; where the mercy-seat in the Holy of Holies is "the throne," and the candlestick is "the seven golden lamps," and the sea of brass is "the sea of glass." II.—It is a church of *men*, not of angels; For, 1, The elders and beasts sing their redemption by Christ's blood; from whom, 2, The angels are distinguished as being "round about" them; see c. v. 9, 11. III.—It is a Church *on earth;* For, 1, It alludes to the marshalling of the Jews about the tabernacle. 2, Here are "seven spirits," or that variety of the gifts of the Holy Ghost which ceases in heaven. 3, Here is "a sea of glass" for the priests and worshippers to wash in, so that their feet at least still contract defilement, as in John xiii. 10. 4, The distinction of beasts and elders, (i. e. officers and brethren,) also ceaseth in heaven. IV.—It is a church *universal;* For, 1, Being in all *ages*, it is placed in the beginning here, and after introduced as spectators. 2, It is in all *places*, c. v. 9. V.—It is the true pattern of a church, according to the rules of the squaring-measure of the word, the mould into which all churches are cast; though in c. xi. 1, John is bid to measure the temple of that age, as having swerved from the original form in Antichrist's apostacy. So that here is the church, consisting of three states, (Christ the *head;* the four beasts its *officers;* and the twenty-four elders are the *brethren,)* with its appurtenances of lamps, laver, &c. or the Spirit and blood of Christ, &c. "*I saw a throne*" alludes to the mercy-seat, as in Isa. vi. 1; Ezek. xliii. 4, 5, 7, Jer. xvii. 12. *N.B.* To set up a church is to set up God and Christ a throne; the church being their only visible throne on earth, till the kingdoms of the world become theirs visibly. "*He who sitteth on the throne*" is God in Christ, in whom God is reconciled to his church, and by whom he rules it, c. iii. 21; xii. v; vii. 10: Isa. vi. 1; Ezek. i. 26.

VERSE III.—"*There was a rainbow round about the throne;*" as the memorial of the covenant of grace, being a sign of the covenant of nature, Isa. liv. 9; and it is "round about the throne," that in whatever way God goes forth in his dispensations towards his church, he may be still reminded of mercy; and that his church also, in all her intercourse with him, may remember to trust in the covenant of grace; her prayers passing to the throne through the same rainbow.

VERSE IV.—The situation of the church, whose elders and beasts are "*about the throne*," (see v. 5, 6,) is after the quartering of Israel about the tabernacle, Num. ii. where the Levites were next the tabernacle, and the tribes about the Levites; as here the officers' station is *between* the throne and those elders, which Beza interprets *in the midst*, so Gen. xxiii. 6. "The beasts," though their place is nearest the throne, are mentioned after the elders, as being but servants of the church and elders, in whom is the radical power. "The elders," 1st, Are so called because the New Testament church is *adult*, and no longer under age, (Gal. iv. 1, &c.) and as being *grave* in all her assemblies, proceedings, and administration. 2dly, They are "twenty-four," in allusion to the heads of those orders of Levites who were porters and singers, 1 Chron. xxiv. xxv.; and are double the heads of the twelve tribes, to shew the increase of the church. 3dly, They are "cloathed in white raiment" as priests; and 4thly, "On their heads were crowns of gold," to shew their rule in judicial matters concerning the church, as in 1 Cor. v. 12. 5thly, They are "round about the throne," (like the *round table*, in Cant. i. 12,) the meanest soul being as near and dear to God as the greatest, and all equal, where Christ is "the tree in the midst of the paradise of God," c. ii. 7.

VERSE V.—"*And out of the throne proceeded lightnings and thunderings and voices*," meaning God's judgments, (Ps. xviii. 13, 14; xxix. 3,) as he sits in his church, and as these are exercised for his church's sake, Ps. lxviii. 35: Amos i. 2. "*Voices*" also extends more generally to promises and answers to prayer. By "*The seven lamps which are the seven spirits of God*," the Holy Ghost, and his various gifts and operations and manifestations of himself in the church, is noted out, (c. i. 4; 1 Cor. xii. 11,) who gives both light and heat, as did the candlestick in the temple.

VERSE VI.—"*There was a sea of glass like unto crystal;*" in allusion to Solomon's sea, and purer than that of *brass*, in Ex. xxx. 17—20, typical of Christ's blood to wash in, for justification of person and sanctification of life, (Heb. x. 22: 1 Cor. xi. 11: Titus iii. 5;) especially that we may wash before we worship. "*And there were four beasts full of eyes before and behind;*" meaning church-officers, who being between the throne and the elders, are as leaders of the praise, being the mouth of the congregation, v. 9, 10. These are called ZOOA, or *living ones*, having in them life, and being means of quickening others: being *four* also, and the throne *four-square*, they are in the midst between each angle, as complete for number, and looking every way to all the necessities of the church, both for soul and body; and "*they are full of eyes*," as overseers; "*within*" to see to their own hearts, as well as "*without*" to see to others.

VERSE VII.—"*And the first beast was like a lion*," being the *ruling elder*, who needs courage to deal with men's spirits in case of sins calling for the church's notice and admonition. "*The second beast was like a calf*," or ox; being the laborious *pastor*, who takes pains in "treading out the corn," 1 Tim. v. 18. "*The third beast had a face like a man*;" or the *deacons*, whose *humane* hearts disposed and inclined them to mercifulness and pitifulness. "*And the fourth beast was like a flying eagle*:" or the *teacher*, whose eyes quickly spy out all errors, and who soars aloft into all mysteries.

VERSES VIII—XI. "*They had each of them six wings apiece*;" to shew the aptness and readiness of the four beasts to fly and act all manner of ways; and "*They rest not day nor night*, (but labour continually,) crying *Holy, Holy, Holy*," worshipping God in Trinity; (see Isa. vi. 2, 3,) and as the mouth of the congregation; for, "*When those beasts give glory and honour and thanks to him that sat on the throne, who liveth for ever and ever, the four and twenty elders fall down before him that sat on the throne, and worship him that liveth for ever and ever, and cast their crowns before the throne, saying, Thou art worthy, O Lord, to receive glory and honour and power; for thou hast created all things, and for thy pleasure they are, and were created*."

THE FIFTH CHAPTER.

The *stage* being built in the fourth chapter, and the *chorus* consisting of the church, being set; here begins the *prologue*, such as for elegance and stateliness was never heretofore invented: 1, Here is a *book sealed*, presented in his hand who sits on the throne, containing God's decrees to be executed until the day of judgment; and, 2, Here is a *proclamation*, made to all creatures, to find out one worthy to open it; but, 3, None such were found in heaven or earth; (v. 3:) Wherefore, 4, John weeps, thinking there would be an end of his visions, and that he must put up his pen, v. 4: In this strait, 5, Christ comes and undertakes to open this book, and to fulfil all its decrees: at this, 6, The chorus fall down and worship; v. 8.

VERSE I.—This "*book, written within and on the backside, and sealed with seven seals*" is not the scriptures generally, but a volume of the affairs of the world and church, and of God's decrees about them: for on opening each seal is seen a vision, containing the matter of the ensuing vi. vii. viii. and ix. chapters; and when the seals are all taken off, (c. x. 8,) John is bid to eat the book, that he might prophesy again the other part of this prophecy: It is therefore this *Revelation*, and the government of the world and of the church, therein set forth, which Christ by taking the book, undertakes to manage, perform, and execute; see c. i. 1. Whereupon,

VERSE II.—"*A strong angel proclaims, Who is worthy to loose the seals of this book,*" &c. The use of the seals is not here simply to shew, that the matter cannot be known, (as in Dan. xii. 4;) but to set out the glory of Him who only was "*able to take the book and loose the seals,*" &c. God causes a general *proclamation* to be made to all creatures, (as Saul did, promising rewards for some noble service, 1 Sam. xvii. 25—27,) by "*a strong angel,*" whose voice might reach to all; in order, 1st, To stir up strong desires in John and all who read this prophecy, to search into its meaning, to which there was an exhortation, and also an exciting promise, c. i. 3. 2ndly, To set out the weakness of the creature, that the honor of Christ might the more appear, in that he only can do this: God thus endears mercies to us, as he did a wife to Adam, by first bringing all creatures to him, that so he might see that there was not a *meet* help for him among them all: So in the work of salvation, God lets the soul try all means, duties, helps, &c. and then brings it to Christ, that his power may appear: he first lets the world try what their *wisdom* could do, and then sends the *foolishness* of preaching to save them that believe, 1 Cor. i. 21, 25. Now that no creature can satisfy for sin, is proved to the glory of Christ, in that none but he can even open this book, much less redeem us, v. 9. *N.B.* We must learn to renounce all kings, priests, and prophets, except CHRIST; and to say to all creatures "I will be saved by none of you:" Were the work of redemption yet to be done, and should God make this proclamation, "Call a council, and find me out a party able and suitable for the purpose of redemption;" how should we howl and weep as undone, none being found: and after trying what we could do for ourselves, suppose God should set out Christ at last, as able to save to the utmost? but he would not thus put us to the non-plus, and therefore took another course, commending his love the more by finding out Christ, and speaking to him to die for us, so doing the work of redemption to our hands. "*Who is worthy?*" it is not simply an act of *power*, but of *authority by worth*, to break open the seals: so it was the worth of Christ's *person* that put the value on his *satisfaction*. else in the act of "*opening the book,*" a mere creature might have had as much habitual grace, and performed as much duty; but personal worth carries it, as in Heb. vii. 26.

VERSE III.—"*None were found worthy*," (neither angel, man, devil, nor spirit, were able,) "*to open the book, neither to look thereon*," so as to *understand* it, for John *saw* it, v. 1. Now to loose the seals and to open the book, is not simply to know God's mind in his decrees, but to make the vision of them to John, and to execute and fulfil them in their times; (as men take a commission, not only to look on it, but to fulfil it:) which being sealed, the purport of the proclamation is, Who is able to be God's commissioner herein? so c. vi. 1: and still as the Lamb opens every seal, John is shewn what shall be done by him that hath *eyes* of providence, and *horns* of power; and who is a lion's whelp and an old lion, and a sceptre and a law-giver, (Gen. xlix. 9, 10,) to take God's laws from him, and to see them kept by an executive, and not merely a legislative power.

VERSE IV.—"*And I wept much;*" in despair of seeing the visions for which John was called up to heaven: this check was to set off the mercy, to try his heart, and to render his joy greater. *N.B.* The greatest mercies may have the greatest stops, even to hopelessness; as often in the first work of conversion, and in other great works.

VERSE V.—Here John is gradually comforted; first, by a bystander endeavouring to uphold his heart; and v. 6, by the sight of the Lamb; as Job, (xlii. 1,) first "heard of God by the hearing of the ear, and then his eye saw him." So God first lets fall something giving the soul hopes of Christ, (thus to draw it patiently to wait,) and then shews it Christ himself, who is here diversely expressed, *First*, As "*The root of David*," (Isa. xi. 10, 14, 30,) as well as "the *branch*," (Mal. iv. i,) being David's Son and Lord also, the root being the first-born, as Rom. viii. 29; Ps. lxxxix. 27; Col. i. 15; Eph. iii. 15. *Secondly*, As "*The lion of the tribe of Judah*," (Gen. xlix. 9,) so called because, 1st, out of Judah came all the worthies and lion-like men, (2 Sam. xvii, 10.) 2dly, Judah had the kingdom under the emblem of "the lion among beasts;" and therefore also he was both sceptre-bearer and legislator. 3dly, Judah took the prey, as Joshua, Caleb, &c. took the land, and then couched, (Num. xxiii. 24; 1 Kings iv. 20, 21;) so Christ having led captivity captive, sits down quietly in heaven, couching and lying in wait, till he sees opportunity to avenge the enemies of his church; when he shall appear as an old lion roused, suddenly leaping on his prey; especially in the latter days, "when the gathering of the people shall be to him:" Gen. xlix. 10: and so in Mich. v. 2, 8, the kingdom and conquest of Christ is set forth in the calling of the Jews, as also in Christ's birth. Now that kingdom is the scope of this book.

VERSE VI.—"*And in the midst of the elders stood a lamb as it had been slain*," &c. John had heard of Christ as a lion, but he sees him as a lamb: so many a poor soul is afraid of him, till it comes to see him and be acquainted with him: but in the end he will be found to be a lamb with seven eyes, to run to and fro through the earth for the good of his saints; and with seven horns, to defend them, and to butt his and their enemies. Well may we wonder at and praise this mixture in him of kingly courage and strength as a lion, and also of priestly meekness as a lamb slain, who stood "*in the midst of the throne*," nearer than the four beasts who stood between the throne and elders; he being mediator between the church and God. "*As it had been slain*;" as if but yesterday newly slain, his blood perpetually remaining fresh; yet only *as* slain, because not remaining dead but alive, as c. i. 18. "*Stood a lamb*," ready to help; as Stephen saw him ready to receive his spirit: it shews also his readiness to intercede: "*Having seven horns*" of power, to push therewith, (as in c. xvii. 12;) and thereby to open the seven seals, and also to fulfil the sound of the seven trumpets, and to empty the contents of the seven vials. Antichrist hath but two horns; and though his kings have ten, yet Christ is king of kings, and stronger than that roaring lion, whom they fear together. "*And seven eyes, which are the seven Spirits of God sent forth into all the earth*:" These are not the Holy Ghost's gifts of grace, but eyes of providence, (as in Zech. iv. 10,) and imply the perfection of Christ's knowledge to order all affairs on earth, and to discern and guide all for his church's good; as in 2 Chron. xvi. 9: his human nature is the instrument of all God's power; all must pass through his hands; all works of providence go through his view: he knows whatever is done in the whole world. Now Christ is specially in this chapter represented as a lion and a lamb; 1st, To keep up the Old Testament language; 2dly, In reference to the work of redemption by the price of his blood, and by the power of his conquest, v. 9; 3dly, As the opener of this book and the executor of it's contents; for 1, He must die for it, seeing each revelation to us cost him the same price as our salvation; for our sins else would have hindered the opening of God's counsels to us, which as a slain lamb he is worthy to reveal, v. 9. 2, As a lion he needed courage to encounter God's wrath, and by breaking through a consuming fire to approach his throne and take the book: "Who is this that engaged his heart to approach unto me?" (Jer. xxx. 21;) no angel durst presume to come so near to God. 3, As a lion he needed to overcome death, rising again to execute what is written in this book. A lion is said to sleep the first three days from his birth, after which being roused by the roaring of the old lion he sleeps the least of any creature: so Christ rose by the power of the Father, to sleep no more. 4thly, Being risen, this lion of the tribe of Judah, who is the law-giver, (Ps. lx. 7,) as God's commissioner to execute his decrees, is also a lamb with seven horns and eyes, to fulfil what he prophesies, and to open the seals, and to blow the trumpets, and to pour out the vials. God gave Christ the platform of occurrences to come, and power and wisdom to order their accomplishment. As both lion and lamb, he is both king and priest, and makes us so too; yet he governs with lamb-like quietness, as well as with lion-like force; and all by a promised succession from Judah and David, here therefore mentioned: In a word; "*The root of David*," shews his right and title to the kingdom he is to receive; and "*The lamb slain*," shews his purchase of it besides at the price of his own blood; and "*The lion of the tribe of Judah*," shews the power whereby he conquers, obtains, and possesses it.

VERSE VII.—This heavenly chorus or company here, when they once see Christ "*Come and take the book out of the hand of him that sat upon the throne*," so undertaking the accomplishment of this prophecy, (the conclusion of which is his instalment into his kingdom,) shout out beforehand, saying, "We shall reign on earth," (v. 10,) looking on all that was to precede his kingdom, and come between it and his vision, as already done; and having chiefly in their eye this kingdom to come.

VERSE VIII.—Hence to the end of the chapter is a doxology or praise for the Lamb's taking the book; which song consisteth of four parts, as sung by four companies: 1st, The *elders and beasts*, representing the church upon earth, begin to raise the song, v. 8. 2dly, The *angels* join their voices, v. 11. 3dly, The *creatures* come in also, v. 13. 4thly, The *beasts* close all, saying, "Amen," v. 14. *N.B.* 1, The sons of men are the most eminent praisers of God, being leaders in the choir and concluding the heavenly song; for redemption is the highest of God's works, and concerns men; though angels follow also and join in praising him for it too, and all creation besides: Therefore we should bless God for his mercy and goodness to others, as do angels for us, whose highest grace it is to praise God for that redemption in which they are not personally interested; how much more then should we bless God in a sense of our own intereset, to raise our hearts a degree higher still, as in v. 9, 10. The praisers are described as having *harps* and golden *vials*, in allusion to the Levitical service, where they had musical instruments and incense in bowls and vials, called "the bowls of the altar," Zech. ix. 15; xiv. 20: By these are signified prayers and praises, Ps. cxli. 2. and songs of spiritual melody in the heart, Eph. v. 19: Indeed the odour here is interpreted as "*the prayers of the saints*," whose hearts are "*the golden vials*," having faith more precious than gold, (1 Pet. i. 7,) which is the spring of all their prayers: and also their harps are their hearts, *Sursum Corda Sursum Chordæ:* Moreover "*every one*" is said to have harps; for in public worship all should join; the little strings go to make up a concert, as well as the great; though we have but little grace, yet would not God's worship be complete without us: The Papists hence argue from these odours, that the saints in heaven offer up the prayers of the saints on earth; but this company here are the church of men on earth; and besides, they offer not the prayers of others, but their own; for themselves make the new song, and the benefit they praise God for therein, is their own, "Thou hast redeemed us to God by thy blood:" therefore "the prayers of the saints," are only John's interpretation, that these were saints, and that their odours were prayers.

VERSE IX.—"*And they sing a new song.*" 1st, When David had a new occasion in a further degree to praise God, he saith, "I will sing a new song," Ps. cxliv. 9; so here there was a new occasion given. 2dly, It is called *a new song*, in opposition to that of the Old Testament; as Christ's "new commandment," (John xiii. 3, 4,) of the gospel, is opposed to that of the law. In c. iv. 11, these elders had sung the creation-song, but here they sing the redemption-song. 3dly, The "new song" is here sung; for their eye was on the "new Jerusalem," where is Christ's and the church's kingdom, ("for we shall reign on earth," v. 10;) "all things are made new," (c. xxi. 5;) and for the instalment of the new king, there should be "a new song," Ps. xcvi. 1, 10, 13: even as we should frame new matter of praise, and have fresh affections, upon every new occasion; and should bless God both for our creation and for our redemption; taking in the mention of old blessings when we give thanks for new, like the good scribe, "bringing out of his treasures things new and old," Matt. xiii. 52. The matter of this song is *praise to the Lamb*, for "*Thou art worthy*," (in answer to v. 2, "Who is worthy?") even *thou* only, "by whom and for whom are all things," Col. i. 16; and "Worthy is the Lamb" to be praised, for his *dying* to redeem us and make us *priests*, and for his *rising* as one who was slain, to make us *kings*, v. 10; (see Rom. xiv. 9;) "*For thou wast slain, and hast redeemed us to God by thy blood, out of every kindred and people and nation*:" Whence, *N.B.* 1, That Christ's blood was paid as a price to God for the purposes of our redemption, see 1 Cor. vi. 20; 1 Tim. ii. 6: yet, 2, Christ hath not redeemed all men, but some *out of* every nation, &c. 3, Christ's worthiness to receive the book, because he was slain, should make the Revelation the more prized by us, as a special fruit of his death; before which, we have his own word for it, that he knew not the day of judgment, Mark xiii. 32.

VERSE X.—"*And hast made us unto our God kings and priests, and we shall reign on the earth:*" because Christ is the Lion-lamb we shall reign on earth as king-priests; the consideration of which latter-day glory of the church, comforted the saints of old; and how peremptory are they, "We *shall* reign!" in the faith of which they are confirmed by Christ's undertaking to accomplish all; whereof this is the issue, being the end and scope of the Revelation, and the conclusion of this book, when the seals are off, and the contents fulfilled.

VERSE XI.—Introduces the other company of angels and their song; who, 1, For their number, are "*ten thousand times ten thousand and thousands of thousands*," as in Dan. vii. 10. (*N.B.* God hath another world of rational creatures, which we see not; what a story then will the latter day produce! and what need we fear, where there are so many for us, and all our guardians too? 2 Kings vi. 16, 17, Heb. i. 14.) 2, For their *station*, they are behind the elders, yet "*round about the throne*," having all in a ring, and being as the queen's guard, Ps. xxxiv. 7.

VERSE XII.—Is the song itself, wherein Christ is hymned, 1, As worthy, by *purchase* as well as by inheritance, for "*worthy is the Lamb that was slain*." 2, As he hath seven horns and eyes, so he hath a seven-fold praise. 3, To express their strong desires to give him due praises enough, they heap up many good things, of which they pronounce him worthy. 4, None is worthy to be universal king but Christ the Lion-king; angels were top-heavy of their glory and reeled out of heaven, but Christ hath the God-head to poise him. The seven excellent things attributed to him are: "*Power*," or authority over all, John xvii. 2: "*Riches*," or possession of all the creatures, 2 Cor. viii. 9: "*Strength*," joined to his authority; whereas other beings are personally no stronger than other men, but Christ hath seven horns, and can work anything: "*Wisdom*," as large as his power and dominion; whereby he knows all God means to do, and sees all with his own, and not like earthly kings, with others' eyes: "*Honour*," respects what all creatures bring in to him, Phil. ii. 10: "*Glory*," is his own personal excellencies, as "the brightness of the Father's glory," (Heb. i. 3,) and all that his Father gives him, as sitting at his right hand and governing with him, till he come again in glory to judge the world: "*Blessing*," respects the glory given him by his saints, for his special goodness to them: devils honour him; but they only bless him whom he blesseth first.

VERSE XIII.—"*And every creature*," in its kind, is here introduced so worshipping Christ, (Phil. ii. 10, 11,) because when his kingdom is set up, they shall be renewed and delivered into a glorious liberty. *N.B.* The church of *men* began the song, and the same continue it as containing their mercy, and the instauration of their king; and the more should they be stirred up, seeing all creatures, with so much concord, therein united.

VERSE XIV.—"*And the four beasts said, Amen.* The officers beginning and ending, and with them the elders joining. The *Amen* seems an ordinance for closing the worship, as in 1 Cor. xiv. 16. I now come to

THE SCHEME AND DIVISION OF THE WHOLE PROPHECY.

The stage being set, c. iv. and the prologue acted, c. v. the prophecy itself in several scenes and visions, begins c. vi.: but before I can proceed with the first six seals of the same, (or indeed with any of the visions,) I must needs give the arguments and parts of the whole book; which will afford a more delectable prospect, than that view of the glory of all the kingdoms of this world that was once made in the twinkling of an eye, Luke iv. 5; for what can be more pleasant than to have even a general insight into God's design and project upon the world in which the church is seated, and into the church's condition in the world since Christ's ascension? Here it is as artificially, and in as many scenes, in this book presented, as ever was story in any poem. Now for a general insight into this prophecy, serving both as compass and chart in our sailing over this sea, that we may know still where we are; I premise these general propositions or assertions concerning the whole prophecy.

PROP. I.—*The ensuing prophecy, running to the end of the Revelation, contains two distinct prophecies;* to represent the giving of which to the church, and its execution by the Lamb-lion of Judah, the book in c. v. is introduced. Two things are distinctly to be considered as given with that book, the *seals* on its backside, and its *contents*. Now, 1st, As the *book* contains matter of pophecy, so do the very *seals* also, the visions of which take up c. vi.—ix. both are mysteries, and contain matter of prophecy; its very backside and cover are prophetical; and the seals not only designate its difficulties, (as in Isa. xxix. 11, 12,) but serve to contain a matter of vision to be delivered. Therefore, 2dly, In revealing and delivering this prophecy, two difficulties are distinctly mentioned, in c. v. 2, The *loosing* of the *seals*, and, The *opening* of the *book*. Now if the seals imported only the difficulty of this book, the opening of the book would not have been made a new difficulty in delivering *another* prophecy. Hence, 3dly, In c. vi. when the Lamb opens the first seal, a vision is seen, and therein a prophecy is delivered; so in the second, &c. to the seventh, which produces seven angels with seven trumpets, six recounted c. viii.—x. and the seventh in the end of c. xi. Again, when these seals are taken off one after another, and their prophecies and visions seen and ended, an angel comes with *a little book open,* as containing a new prophecy for John, who was bid eat the seal-prophecy that was past, to be enabled for the new one, to "prophesy again before many peoples and nations and tongues and kings;" whence it is said that "the same voice he had heard before spake from heaven again," (see c. x. 2, 8—11:) Now he had heard it but twice before, and that at the giving of a new prophecy; once at the delivery of the epistles to the seven churches, (c. i. 10,) and then at this general prophecy, c. iv. 1: and now a-again c. x. 8, as beginning another new and third prophecy. *N.B.* In that the seals themselves contain a prophecy, there is nothing in God's book without a meaning; "not a tittle shall pass," Matt. v. 18: the very cover of the book here is prophetical; much more does every word in it contain matter of instruction: let not a jot of the scriptures then escape us, but let us search them narrowly, though we understand not many a tittle of them; there is enough in what we understand to admire, and in the rest to adore: every syllable of the word of the great God hath its weight and value.

Prop II.—*Both the seal and book-prophecy run over the same whole course of times from Christ's ascension to his kingdom;* containing in them several events and occurrences successively to the end of this book: viz. The *seal*-prophecy, c. vi.—xii. acts over one story of all times to the end of time; and then, The *book*-prophecy from c. xii. (beginning at the same time again,) acts over another story of all the same times unto the end: so that the whole race of time is run over in both, but with several and distinct occurrences; even as the books of *Kings* and *Chronicles* contain the stories of the same course of time, from David to the captivity; but the former handles most of the affairs of the kings of Israel, and the latter of Judah. To demonstrate this apart, First: *For the seal-prophecy,* I lay these three things together, (whereof the two first were never denied by any,) 1st, In c. vi. the six seals begin, in the first of which Christ goes forth in preaching the gospel, so to lay the first foundation of his kingdom; which going-forth refers to those primitive times: and in the fifth seal is the first mention of the bloody persecution of the saints professing the gospel, in the same times; for they are told that when the rest of their brethren, by the succeeding persecutions, should be killed, they then should have vengeance on their enemies for their blood spilt; shewing c. vi. to contain those *first persecutions:* besides, the former chapters were but a prologue or preparation to the prophecy, here beginning at least with John's time, c. i. 1. 2dly, These seals and trumpets, in successive order, contain continued prophecy of events following one another in a succession of ages downward; for, "In the days of the voice of the seventh trumpet, when it shall begin to sound," (c. x.) imports, That these several trumpets, as scenes in a comedy, share among them the several successive ages and times; and with the seals, do have their *days* proper peculiary given to them: and the ages precede or succeed, as these are placed, *first*, *second*, &c. for the *first* age, &c. 3dly, The seventh trumpet, (c. xi.) ending all time, becomes a period to one distinct prophecy of all time; which appears from c. x. 6, 7, after the seals were passed over, and seen with their effects, and the six trumpets had sounded in c. viii. and ix. the angel swears "that time shall be no longer; but in the days of the seventh trumpet," all shall be finished: therefore c. xi. 15, 18, (where the seventh trumpet is introduced, sounding in the order of its *day* and turn,) must needs be esteemed the end of that prophecy; for it brings us to the end of all times allotted to this world and God's enemies therein to rule and reign: when this world's hour-glass is run out, that of the other world is turned up to run: so that from the first seal to the seventh trumpet, is run over all the time that the monarchies and kingdoms of this world, as in the enemies' hands, should continue and last; being the "time" which towards the end, under thesixth trumpet, "should be no longer," according to the oath; "He sware by him that liveth for ever and ever, who created heaven, earth, and seas, and all in them, *that there should be time no longer, but in the days of the seventh angel,* when he shall begin to sound, the mystery of God should be *finished,* as he hath declared to his servants the prophets:" which words import, That much of the whole time having thus been past and run out already in the former visions of the seals and trumpets, now the time allotted by God was brought well nigh its very last sands: And that the church might have some warning, and be able to make some guess, and computation, when the world's monarchy should end, and the Gentiles' time be fulfilled, and no longer be; this angel gives us in c. xi. towards the expiration of the whole time, the true computation of the continuance of the last of the four monarchies, as serving to compute the period of the whole unto the beginning of Christ's visible kingdom, even the days of the beast, or Pope, who is the last part with his ten kingdoms of Europe, treading down the church, or the holy city: which beast, and his kingdoms supporting him as their head, (whose time from his first beginning, even to the near approach of that seventh trumpet, commencing to sound about his very end, is forty-two months, or twelve hundred and sixty *days,* i. e. *years,*) shall end, and with him all rule and dominion on earth; and Christ shall take the kingdom when he shall have destroyed Antichrist through the "brightness of his coming," (2 Thes. ii. 8,) which will grow brighter as his coming is nearer. This angel gives also to the church a signal of occurences immediately fore-running the period of this time of the beast's ruin, by representing (c. xi.) what shall be her face before the downfall of that kingdom, and her last persecution by the beast, fore-going her ruin; that so she might both have warning, (not thinking it strange for the fiery trial at last to come upon them,) and also be comforted in its being the last trial, introducing the end of time and the world's kingdom. Secondly, *For the book-prophecy* there is a new prophecy, running over the whole race of time unto Christ's kingdom, from the beginning to the end of the world's monarchies from c. xii. to the end of the book; with other occurrences than the seal-prophecy of the same period, ending c. xi.: *First,* c. xii. begins a new prophecy, for the other made an end of all time;

and the vision of the woman and the dragon in c. xii. must needs be of things fore-going the rise of the Antichrist-beast, (c. xiii.) and therefore concerns the primitive times. The dragon in c. xii. endeavouring to devour the woman, is cast down from heaven; after which his striving to drown her in a flood is prevented: and then John standing on the sand of the sea, spies this new beast arising, to whom the dragon gives his throne and power, (c. xiii.) all therefore in c. xii. must needs contain a story of events of primitive times before the rise of Antichrist. *Secondly*, From the first rise of this beast (c. xiii.) there is allowed him to continue twelve hundred and sixty years, at the expiration of which the seventh trumpet begins, which had ended all time before c. xi. 15; and then c. xiv. contains the state of the church during the time of the beast, in her separation from him and opposition to him; and then c. xv. and xvi. contain seven vials to ruin this beast, whereof the last ends all time again, as the seventh trumpet had done; for 1st, The angel swears "That time shall be no more;" and the voice says, "It is done," c. x. 6; xvi. 17. 2dly, It is said, (c. xv. 1,) that these vials contain the last plagues, in which the wrath of God is fulfilled; and therefore they must necessarily make an end of all Christ's enemies, and of their rule and time. 3dly, The same things are said to be done in the pouring out of the seventh plague-vial, that are presented to be done at the sounding of the seventh, or last woe-trumpet: for in c. xi. 19, were "lightnings, voices, thunderings, earthquakes, and a great hail;" and in c. xvi. 18, were "voices, and thunderings, and lightnings, and an earthquake," such as never were before on earth; and so great a hail that every stone weighed a talent. *But* if Christ's kingdom, in c. xx.—xxii. ends all, what is the time of c. xvii.—xix.? These in general contain a larger explication or vision of some eminent things under some of the vials; and therefere c. xvii. begins thus, "One of the seven angels which had the seven vials, talked with me, and shewed me," &c. as implying that what follows belonged to their times: more particularly, c. xvii. contains an interpretation of what was spoken of the beast, c. xiii. shewing who it is: and as the Holy Ghost interprets the visions in Daniel, so here: Thus the whore carried by the beast, "is that great city that reigneth over the kings of the earth," (c. xvii. 18,) which is Rome: and the Spirit must needs interpret some things in this book, (leaving the church to search into the rest,) and this especially as giving light to all the rest; which therefore fitly comes in after all. Again, c. xviii. contains a more poetical description of the ruining of that city, the seat of this last monarchy, and therefore is but a copious explication of the fifth vial poured out on the seat of the beast, (c. xvi. 10,) together with the church's triumphing song for the times sung at the whore's funeral, and for the approaching marriage of the

Lamb, c. xix. 1—10, whence to c. xx. is a more full description of that last war of the beast and all the kings of the earth, and their overthrow by Christ; being all one with the last vial and the preparation thereunto, as is evident from c. xvi. 13—21, compared with c. xix. 11—21; the Spirit towards the end of this prophecy giving a more full explanation of the two more eminent vials, and the times of them; after first briefly setting them together with the rest, in their order: as after compendiously setting together in c. xx. the reign of Christ during a thousand years, and the universal judgment that follows, he yet spends c. xxi. in a more copious and magnificent description of the state of the New Jerusalem, and that millenial period. *But again,* Whereunto is c. xi. 1—14, to be referred, which is placed, as it were, between both prophecies? All that discourse delivered by word of Christ's mouth, between the seal and book-prophecy, belongs to both, as containing an exact chronology of that last period of the time of the world's monarchies; whereby we may easily compute the whole time of both prophecies; and there is withal a signal given of such eminent occurrences befalling the church, as should be most proper and suitable signs of the dawning of Christ's kingdom and ending of these prophecies; that as Jerusalem had signs of its impending destruction, so hath New Jerusalem of the approach of its rearing. Now that these passages in c. xi. belong to both prophecies, appears; In that, The Holy Ghost speaks of matters contained and afterwards mentioned in the book-prophecy, c. xiii. and xvi. as likewise of matters mentioned in the seal-prophecy; viz. of the ending of the sound of the sixth trumpet; which is declared in c. xi. 14, "The passing away of the second woe:" And also, The angel therein mentions how and when the expirations of the times of both prophecies meet in the sixth trumpet of the seal-prophecy, ending about the time of date of the beast in the book-prophecy: and thus to insert, as it were, a chronological table between both prophecies, serving them both, and knitting together the times of both in one period, in c. xi. is agreeable to the way of historians affixing a table of times to their history, when they run over much time and several matters.

PROP. III.—*What is the matter or argument prophesied of in this whole book? and more particularly what are the differing subjects of the seal and of the book-prophecy.* I shall unfold and clear this by several steps and degrees in these heads following: *First,* The subject of both prophecies are the fates and destinies of the kingdoms of the world, after the ascension until Christ takes the kingdom to himself: therefore at the end of the seal or trumpet-prophecy, there is an acclamation that the kingdoms of the world were become Christ's, (c. xi. 15.) after being in other monarchs' hands, (as shewn throughout the former part of the prophecy,) till "time shall be no longer" for the wordly kingdoms: therefore the book-prophecy also beginning c. xii. when first given c. x. 11, hath this prologue or preface, "Thou must prophesy again *before* (EPI, *about*) kings;" having prophesied about them previously in the seal-prophecy; and now again to do so, together with new occurrences relating to the church. *Secondly,* The whole prophecy concerns only such kingdoms or monarchies of the Gentiles, as had to do with the church; for, 1st, At the beginning of both prophecies the church is made the stage or scene upon which all is acted, and so the prophecies extend to no other kingdoms than where the church hath been: as in the fifth seal, (c. vi. 10,) we have blessed martyrs there calling for vengeance of their blood; and under the trumpets, (which are miseries upon kingdoms,) there are the sealed servants of God, scattered and mingled among those nations upon whom these trumpets blow: so in c. vii. Thus, The Indies, Tartary, China, &c. are not here mentioned; as in the Old Testament also, only those kingdoms are named with which the interests of the Jewish church were interwoven. 2dly, This book being written for the comfort of the church; and all the judgments therein proceeding from the throne of that temple, upon the prayers of the church; it contains therefore the fates of such kingdoms as the church should have to do with. *Thirdly,* The Roman monarchy or empire, with the territories under its jurisdiction both in the east and west sea, then in its height and flourish, (with which the church had most to do, and in the almost alone jurisdiction of which it had always been seated,) must needs be, in its several revolutions and changes, the main subject of this book, together with the state of the church under it. Now the circuit of this empire and its dominions, was extended nearly as far as the dominions under the Turk in the east, and the ten European kingdoms in the west; all in John's time under the emperor of Rome: and here God placed his church and gospel, and here is the seat of Christendom to this day; and it is therefore called the *world,* and the *whole world,* or *all the world,* (Matt. xxiv. 14; Luke ii. 1; Acts xi. 28,) for its greatness, and as set up for God to act his great works upon: and beyond this *line* the apostles' preaching never stretched to any considerable purpose, see 2 Cor. x. 16; Rom. x. 18; Ps. xix. 4. The reasons why this empire, with the church in it, should be the main subject of this book, are; 1st, It is the seat and circuit of the church, and by the several successions of its power the church hath been mainly oppressed in all ages: and if judgments, set out under seals, trumpets, and vials, come on her enemies for her sake, they must eminently light upon this grand enemy: and so this prophecy must note out the judgment and wars that ruined the Roman empire for persecuting the saints who cry for vengeance; and the trumpets are the answers to their prayers, c. viii. 3. 2dly, The Roman empire, and its eastern and western successions, was the fourth and only great monarchy left to oppress the earth, when Christ ascended; as the prophets of old spake each of the reigning monarchy and its successions; so Daniel spake of Greece, and of Rome as most terrible of all. 3dly, The scope of this book is the instalment of Christ into his kingdom, and his putting down all opposing powers in his way to it: Christ's empire is to succeed the Roman, under which he therefore upholds his church till his kingdom comes and forms a fifth monarchy: the same is the scope of Dan. vii. 7—11, only here more largely and particularly set forth. 4thly, That such should be the subject of this prophecy suits also with the chief prophecies of the other apostles; which were reduced to three heads, and were ordinarily preached by them and more expressly written by John: As 1, The foretelling the ruin of the Roman empire, called "a taking out of the way him that lets," 2 Thes. ii. 2—9, with c. vi.—ix. 2, The discovery of the Pope, the man of sin, and the last head of the fourth monarchy; and his ruin, c. xiii.—xix. 3, Christ's coming and kingdom, c. xx. and xxi.

PROP. IV.—*What is the difference of the subject of the seal and book-prophecy?* for in the story of the several successions and revolutions in the Roman empire, we are to consider the state of the political body itself, and also of the church under it; whence some write the ecclesiastical history apart by itself, and others the story of the several revolutions of the Roman empire; as the Book of martyrs relates chiefly the church's conflict with Anti-Christ, but Speed's Chronicle gives several invasions, wars, conquests, and intestine broils of the kingdom. The difference of the subjects of these two prophecies appears in the several characters, and also in the very place and situation of the visions themselves. 1st, For the differing shews or faces of these representations: In the first prophecy are seven seals and four horses, (c. vi.;) and then the seven trumpets, (c. viii. and ix,) noting sealed judgments and devastations on the empire, by plagues, famines, and wars, (trumpets being the signal and symbols of war in all nations, and put for it in scripture:) But the chief actors in the book-prophecy are women, fit emblems of the churches; viz. a travailing woman, c. xii. a virgin, c. xvi. a whore, c. xvii. xviii. and a bride, c. xix. Thus artificial is the Holy Ghost in handling things of differing nature apart. 2ndly, The difference of the subjects of these two prophecies is shewn also from their differing situation and place. The seals were on the *back-side*, as containing state-matters *without* the church, (c. xxii. 15,) but the book itself contains things *within*, (1 Cor. v. 12;) and so the prophecy thereof is cast to be, as it were, *without* the book, even upon the *seals* thereof, touching the outward temporal state of the church; whereas the book-prophecy treats of spiritual things *within* the church: and this appears in the interpretation of all particulars throughout the books, as well as in the general division;

for John, like the best historians, puts things of a sort together: yet not so as that nothing at all of church-affairs is found in the seal-prophecy, or of the affairs of the empire in the book-prophecy: as the matters of Judah are intermingled in the book of Kings, and those of Israel in that of Chronicles. I have now therefore to present

A SYNOPSIS OF THE WHOLE PROPHECY.

This book is a tragi-comic vision of the occurrences of the world, and of the church in the world, through all times and ages; and we may entitle it, "*The story of Christ's kingdom, and the removal of the several difficulties of his coming to it.*" 1st, The stage is set up in c. iv. where is represented the universal church in all ages, set forth according to the exact pattern of a church visible and instituted, into which all saints on earth should be cast: then enters, 2dly, The prologue (c. v.) in which is set forth, in Christ's taking the sealed book, his taking on him the kingdom and government, as God's commissioner, to execute the decrees contained in this book, and to give the vision of all to John: at which instalment there is a doxology to the Lamb by the chorus of elders and beasts, with a triumphing assurance of our reign on earth in the issue. 3dly, The scene or place where the effect of these visions was to be acted, is the Roman Empire and its several eastern and western dominions, called OICOUMENEE, *the whole world.* 4thly, The story itself, begun at c. vi. the general argument of which is, That whereas Christ's government was to be executed and seen, not only in putting down all opposing rule and power, (as in 1 Cor. xv. 24, 25,) but also in a visible taking the kingdom to himself and his saints, under the fifth monarchy; so here the story of this book first shews how Christ puts down the Roman power by successive revolutions, till all are worn out who were ordained to stand up in it, (and these oppositions and persecutions render the story of Christ's kingdom more glorious:) and then it ends in a glorious visible kingdom set up on earth, and peaceably possessed by Christ and his saints, as the catastrophe of all. More particularly the story is this, according to the several contents of each chapter: 1, When Christ ascended to heaven, he found the Roman monarchy, (whose room he was to possess,) stretched east and west over all those parts of the world where he was to seat his church and kingdom; the subjects of the Roman emperor being heathenish and idolatrous, and wholly under the power of Satan the god of this world; whereupon; 2, Christ first sets upon the conquest of Satan's dominion and worship therein, and by the preaching of the gospel overturns its Heathenism, dethrones Satan from the height of his glory, and subjects it to himself, turning its emperors to Christianity within three hundred years: This is the sum and mind of the seal and book-prophecies in c. vi. and xii. But, 3, This empire, (though now professedly Christian, yet whilst idolatrous having persecuted Christ's church, and after also when Arian,) advances to its ruin by the trumpets in c. viii. and ix. at the prayers of the martyrs, and in vengeance of their blood, c. vi. 10, 11, and viii. 4. 4, The empire thus becoming divided into two parts, the imperial Western state in Europe is first ruined by the four first trumpets, (the wars of the Goths by four several steps,) in c. viii. and the imperial Eastern state afterwards, first by the Saracens, and then by the Turks, under the fifth and sixth trumpets, and these possess the eastern parts: These are the contents of c. ix.: only before the trumpets bring those evils on the empire, a hundred and forty-four thousand Christians in the east are sealed up, (c. vii. 2, 3,) to be preserved and continued in the true profession of Christ's name under these two severest and longest *woe woe* trumpets to fall on the earth, where were these sealed servants, see c. ix. 4; and this sealing is the sum of c. vii. 5, The old Roman empire being in both parts removed; as the east is possessed by Turks, (c. ix.) so the west is broken into ten kingdoms by the Goths, all whose kings consented to give their power to the beast, (the Pope,) who thus becomes a successor to the western emperors, and possesses their seat and power, (though under another title,) and so heals that wound given to the Roman monarchy, thus restored in and by him: c. xiii. describes this beast, and gives the vision of his rise, power, and time of reigning, which c. xvii. expounds and interprets. 6, Under this Antichristian tyranny, (as great as that of the Turks themselves,) Christ yet preserves another like company of one hundred and forty-four thousand virgins, or sealed Christians in the west, (c. xiv. 1—4,) &c. and so he keeps possession still by preserving his church, under both these parts of the empire, as being his inheritance. But now, 7, These two enemies to Christ, (Pope and Turk,) thus succeeding in the empire, and sharing the two parts of it between them, Christ is still kept out of his allotted dominion in these territories; for Mahometanism tyranniseth in the one, and Popish idolatry overspreads the other, as Heathenism had at first done over the whole empire: and so Christ hath a new business of it yet, and as difficult as ever, to come unto his kingdom: Therefore, 8, He hath seven vials containing the last plagues, (for he means to make this the last act of this long tragi-comedy,) to despatch the Pope and the Turk, and wholly root them out; even as the seals had done to the Heathenism, and the trumpets to the civil power of the empire: the plagues of these vials are in c. xv. and xvi. the first five of which dissolve and gradually ruin the Pope's power in the west: then the sixth breaks the power of the Turk in the east; so making way for the Jews, (whom he means to bring into the fellowship of his kingdom, in their own land,) therefore called "The kings of the east," c. xvi. 12. But, 9, Their power and kingdom being not wholly ruined by these six vials, both the Turkish and Popish party join their utmost forces, (and together with them all opposite kings of the whole world,) against the Christians both of the east and west, (who, when the Jews are come in and converted, make up a mighty party in the world;) unto the help of whom against these and all opposite power whatsoever, Christ himself comes and makes but one work of it, with his own hand from heaven destroying them: and so, (c. xvi. 17,) "It is done." 10, In c. xvii. is an interpretation concerning the beast, who he is, and where is his seat. 11, In c. xviii. is a funeral-song of triumph for the whore's ruin, (which is the fifth vial,) before the preparations for the new Jerusalem kingdom consisting both of *eastern* Christians, (who enduring the bondage of the two woe trumpets, under the Saracens and Turks, yet continued to profess Christ's name; and therefore to those hundred and forty-four thousand in c. vii. is said to succeed an innumerable company with palms in their hands, having the same promises of the new Jerusalem mentioned in c. xxi. which shews their interest therein;) and also of *western* Christians, (whose hundred and forty-four thousand in c. xiv. arise also to an innumerable company, and after the rejection of the whole world, are brought in c. xix. 1—9, singing in like triumphant manner, decking themselves for the marriage in fine linen;) besides *Jews* especially all over the world, (from whom this kingdom hath the name of the *new Jerusalem,)* with whom come in also other *Gentiles*, as attendants of their joy, who never had received Christ before. Thus, 12, Both east and west, and the fulness both of Jews and Gentiles, become one fold under one shepherd for a thousand years, and one kingdom under this root of David their conqueror-king; even as it first was one under one Heathen idolatrous emperor, when Christ had first set to conquer it: And so that in Isa. lix. 18, 19, is fulfilled; where after the final destruction of all Christ's enemies, "They shall fear his name from the east to the west; and the Redeemer shall come to Zion," at the final call of the Jews, and at the restoration of the world with them, Rom. xi. 26.

THE SIXTH CHAPTER.

Having given a scheme and division of the whole prophecy, and a general argument of the story of it, briefly set together in one view; I will now run over each chapter apart, insisting largely on this only, and glancing more slightly on the rest; for I aim especially at the second part of my Exposition: and though this Commentary rise not to a full and copious interpretation, yet it will serve to shew the true portrait of the Holy Ghost's mind in this story, to be what I have made it in the preceding general argument. The seal-prophecy concerns the state of the empire from John's time downward; considered, *Either*, As Heathenish, (when Jupiter, Mars, &c. were worshipped, and Christians were persecuted and massacred; the empire standing whole and undivided under the entire government of one emperor of the east and west, for three hundred years after Christ;) *Or,* As Christian under Constantine; when it was subjected to Christianity, though afterwards broken into two parts; which rent was established by Theodosius; the east being allotted to one emperor, (now possessed by the Turks, whereof Constantine made Byzantium his seat, from him called *Constantinople,*) and the west to another, (having Rome for its seat,) which the Pope for many hundred years hath had entirely under him. Now, according to the division of the eastern and western empire, the seal-prophecy divides itself into "The first six seals" in this chapter, and "The first six trumpets," which the seventh seal brings forth in c. viii. and ix. from the woe of which trumpets the servants of God are sealed, in c. vii. In this chapter the first prophecy begins with the primitive times; for in the first seal is the "going forth" in the preaching of the gospel, "conquering and to conquer;" (which is the foundation of all God's after-proceedings, the corner-stone of Christ's obtaining and setting up his kingdom;) and the fifth seal mentioning the first martyrdom of saints crying out for vengeance, must refer to those great persecutions under Heathenish Rome, which were soon followed by the Arian, as in v. 11.

THE FIRST SIX SEALS

Are several steps or degrees, setting forth the moving causes and means of God's plaguing and ruining the empire of Rome Pagan. Christ being to put down all adverse power, finds not only this empire to stand in the way, but the worship of idols and devils: first, therefore, he encounters Heathenism, backed by all the power of the empire; and then, in the trumpets, he encounters the empire itself, "*going forth conquering and to conquer,*" (v. 2,) by degrees. The first judgment on that empire left it standing; therefore the martyrs, after the punishment of the second, third, and fourth seal, cry yet in the fifth seal, for vengeance on the empire itself. The seals are so called, First, In a general relation to this whole prophecy; as, 1st, A book of decrees to be executed by Christ having these seals: 2ndly, This book is not to be opened "till the time of the *end,*" (Dan. xii. 4, 9,) being *sealed* till then, when the same angel of Daniel comes in c. x. with an *open* book in his hand, both to give a new prophecy, and also to shew that when all the seals were off, (all the judgments now being executed in the world,) then the book of Revelation should be understood. Secondly, The seals are, 1st, Judgments decreed by God *certainly* to befall that empire; (so the salvation of the elect is *sealed,* 2 Tim. ii. 19; so judgments, Deut. xxxii. 34; and sins, Job xiv. 17:) 2ndly, They are judgments *hidden,* (and so seals do hide,) stealing in upon the world unawares, and not understood: accordingly we find by the apologies of Tertullian, Cyprian, Arnobius, &c. That the Pagan Romans observing such strange, unheard-of famines, civil wars, and pestilences, (typified here by horses, red, black, and pale,) exceedingly wondered at the reason of them, imputing it to the anger of their Gods against the new sect of Christians: but Christ here opens the cause of these sealed judgments, viz. contempt of the gospel: 3rdly, They are *sealed* for pledges and assurances of all that follows; (as the seal of the Spirit is to assure,) which should certainly come to pass in their time, God first sending them judgments as seals; so that from the history of what has already been fulfilled, we may assure ourselves of the accomplishment of all the rest. *N. B.* Here is a ground of confirming our faith about all those things prophesied of by God, in that the fulfilling of one is a seal assuring that the other shall be fulfilled. That Heathenism is ruined, which was more firmly rooted for four thousand years than ever Popery was, is a seal to us that Popery shall be destroyed. The beast of Rome, though not risen in John's day, is now up in our days; which may confirm our faith that he shall as certainly be ruined, the same prophecy foretelling his fall, (c. xviii.) as his rise, c. xiii. and that after this there is a glorious kingdom to come, of which all these are *seals*. We find in c. xi. the temple measured anew, and the outward court of carnal worshippers and worship cast out; and we see it now in our days fulfilled; yea, ourselves fulfil it: we may therefore as certainly expect and prepare for what follows in the same chapter: Thus Zechariah begins his prophesy, so to assure the people of the truth of it, as if saying, "Did you ever know prophecy fail? 'My words did they not take hold of your fathers? (whom the threatened judgments arrested;) and like as the Lord thought to do unto us, so hath he dealt with us:' therefore believe the rest."

THE FIRST FOUR SEALS are represented to us under the vision of *four horses*. The allusion is to Zech. i. 8, 10; vi. 5; where Christ is represented riding on a *red* horse, and behind him stood other horses, *red*, *speckled*, and *white*, who are angels "that walk to and fro through the earth," and are "four spirits (or winds) that go forth from standing before the Lord of the earth;" (see Heb. i. 14, with Ps. civ. 3, 4;) so evil angels are sent forth to do mischief, as in 1 King xxii. 21; Job. i. 7: the angels are the executioners of all God's great designs; and therefore whatever is done in this book by men, is still said to be done by angels. Here the vision of *horses* thus commissioned from God, and the allusion, shews either, That those executions under these seals were conducted by Christ on the first horse, accompanied by other horses, his angel-followers; or, That as the angels on horses in Zechariah went their circuit over the earth, so here were commissions sealed to these executioners, to traverse and compass the earth, as angels are used to do. God begins here to war with the world, and sends out four horsemen to give the first onset. That this vision is presented under that of *horses* is but for variety's sake. The Revelation makes use of all the eminent visions of the Old Testament; and the elegancies of all the types in the Prophets, serve but to set forth and adorn the visions of this book, like a picture composed of all beauties. The vision of the *throne* is from Isaiah and Ezekiel; from Daniel is the *sealed book;* the *horses*, and also the *olive trees*, and the *candlesticks*, are from Zechariah; and so on. *N. B.* 1, How perfect is this book! what a posy of all flowers! what a vision from all visions! (as Solomon's was a song of songs;) all the types and stories of Moses and the prophets, are borrowed to adorn it. 2, The occurrences in the New Testament, with its story of the church, have all the perfections appearing under the Old, which is more eminently acted over in all passages of providence. Here is a more glorious *temple*, and a far worse *Egypt*, *Sodom*, and *Babylon;* Here is a *restoration* of the temple, and that also at twice, and by degrees; Here is a new *Jerusalem:* Did the bond-man of old persecute the free? even so it is now, Gal. iv. 24, 29: What befel them, befalls us much more: Had they *persecutors?* we more and worse: Had they *Pharisees* that sinned against the Holy Ghost and crucified Christ? so have we such as shall, after great convictions wrought by the gospel, prove like a generation of Pharisees, scorched with the heat of hell-fire, (as in the fourth vial,) who shall kill the witnesses, c. xi. "Now all these things happened unto them for types, (so also did their visions,) being written for our admonition, upon whom the ends (or perfection) of the world are come," 1 Cor. x. 11. We have the perfection of every thing under the Old Testament, good or bad.

FIRST SEAL, and its "*white horse*," (v. 1, 2,) whose *crowned Archman-rider* is Christ himself, "*going forth*, (in the preaching of the gospel,) *conquering and to conquer;*" alluding to Ps. xlv. 4—6; for Christ must win the crown and sceptre before he wears it. Christ goes forth as the general of these horses; and *his* being a *white* one, betokens a triumph, and also is a sign of meekness and candour; he offering at first conditions of peace in the gospel, to the empire of Rome and to all nations, on their submission to him as their king, who goes forth peaceably to challenge the nations God had given him for his inheritance: all must hold their crown of him, and do him homage: Thus Tamerlane, before denouncing war, suspended a white flag in token of peace offered. The progress of the gospel is here compared to the free course of a horse and his rider, 2 Thes. iii. 1. The weapons here are but *arrows* in the hearts of the yielding; in c. xix. they are a *sword* to finish the conquest: in Ps. xlv. they are both: the threatenings of the gospel are arrows striking secretly, and darting and wounding mortally; "*Hæret*

Lethalis Arundo." This horseman is "*crowned;*" (for God made Christ king when he first ascended, Heb. ii. 8, 9;) and "*he went forth conquering*" whether men obey or not; (Paul speaks like a conqueror, in 2 Cor. ii. 14;) for if men turn, There is a triumph of grace pardoning, and so subduing, traitors; and if not, The gospel is a savour of death, like a box of venemous ointments, poisoning by the smell; it is a step of ruin and a sealed judgment; and though a blessing in itself, it was a curse to Gentilism, (as the first vial, by converting men from Popery is called a vial on the earth,) causing Satan to fall "like lightning down from heaven," (Luke x. 18,) as the sixth and last seal shews; for the devil was struck dumb in his oracles, when Christ only began to publish *his. N. B.* 1, Christ is so meek and merciful that he goes not forth first on a *red* war-horse, but on a *white;* but if men turn not, he hath other horses to do that work of destroying them. Who would stand out against such a Saviour who loves unbloody conquests? 2, Christ's course to get his kingdom by no other means at first than the gospel, is strange: his weapons are the bow of the tongues of men, to dart their words, and "to shoot out bitter arrows" into the hearts of them that resist: Twelve fishermen conquer the whole world of the Roman empire! what should we think of a dozen poor men sent into Turkey to overthrow the grand Turk and Mahometanism? see Zech. iv. 6. 3, When Christ begins, he goes on to conquer. Let us not fear the cause of God in England: there is a battle to be fought; Christ and his angels growing more and more holy and full of light; and Satan and his, growing worse and worse, deceiving and being deceived: Christ coming up with fresh supplies of new light, with his bow and arrows bears up as hard as they, and will not be foiled· Though the light of the primitive churches grew dimmer and dimmer, yet they conquered Heathenism, much more must these now conquer.

SECOND SEAL, and its "*red horse*" of *war*, v. 3, 4. After the going forth of the *white* horse there follow three other light-horsemen, attending this their general; as in Zech. i. 8, where Christ was on the *red* horse, as about to revenge himself on his church's enemies, but here on the *white* gospel-peace horse, followed by war-horses, whose colour is suitable to the plagues successively brought on the empire: This second horse's colour is the redness of blood, (Isa. lxiii. 1, 2,) and is therefore a war-horse "*to take peace from the earth,*" by civil war, (not by persecution, but) in the empire, wherein "*men should kill one another:*" for, if men take peace from the saints, it is a suitable plague, that God should take peace from the earth; and if men embrace not the Gospel of peace, their peace shall be taken away; but if men will kill the saints, is it not a proportioned judgment that their swords should be turned into their own bowels? Now this "*power was given to him;*" it proceeded from a commission to this horseman; and so "*there was given to him a great sword:*" God commissions the sword he puts into the enemy's hand: and as magistrates bear God's sword, so soldiers, whom the prophets often call God's *sword*. History shews what wars and most dreadful broils were in the eastern empire. John wrote his Revelation just before Trajan's time, in Domitian's reign, A.D. 94; and he died ten years after, in the sixth year of Trajan, in whose time these wars began. When the apostles had preached the Gospel to the world, and were all dead; the Jews rise, and with armies rage through all parts of the empire; and so devastate and depopulate Lybia of her inhabitants, that Adrian was forced to send thither new colonies: about Cyrene they destroyed twenty-two hundred; in Egypt also and in Cyrus twenty-four hundred; and a great number in Mesopotamia: but Adrian destroyed fifty-eight hundred of the Jews in turn. After Trajan, in whose time the empire had its largest extent, the Parthians revolted, and it was lessened. Under Antonius, A.D. 140, all the northern nations came down upon the east and upon all Illyricum, yet were dried up, as a land-flood; so that the empire stood entire: and that these wars might be the more eminently noticed as following upon the apostles' deaths, (before which, and for forty-four years after, there were none;) there was universal peace.

THIRD SEAL, and its "*black horse*" of *famine*, v. 5, 6; as in Lam. iv. 7—9, where the Nazarites' visage is blacker than a coal, from famine. The rider "*that sat on him, had a pair of balances in his hand,*" to sell corn by weight and not by measure, as in Lev. xxvi. 26; and then a *chœnix*, or day's allowance only, was sold for a penny, (about our seven-pence half-penny, or eighth of a crown,) which was a day's wages: there was however a commission "*not to hurt the oil and the wine.*" Now historians being silent about any notable universal famine in the empire, after these, Mr. Mede interprets it of the balances of justice, for which Severus and others were eminent, especially for their theft-laws and corn-laws: but it would be heterogeneal to the other steps for ruining or plaguing the heathen empire, for the Holy Ghost to notice and insert a moral virtue in the midst of judgments: but this scarcity of corn only, might be slipt over by historians, while Tertullian and other Christians mention such a famine of bread, as a judgment for the empire's contempt of Christ and persecution of the saints. I have searched diligently for such footsteps in dearths of that age, two hundred years after Christ, and upwards, as might confirm the truth of this; And first, I find in Commodus' time, A.D. 190, there was a commotion made for bread within the city of Rome by the poorer sort; *(Fames Romanos Afflixit,* says Herodian,) when the store-keeper Cleander, his great favorite, detained the corn from the people; whereupon they mutiny and demand his death, in their rage throwing down houses, opposing the soldiers, stoning the captains; so that Commodus was forced to cut off his favorite's head and set it on a pole, and to kill his children also, to pacify the people: even Mr. Mede's quotation about Severus' justice, and his care about oil, &c. intimates an exhausture of corn from the stores; as also his care, A.D. 118, through Heliogobalus' having overthrown the public stock of corn: And then, secondly, For the Christian writers of these times; Tertullian, A.D. 203, in his apology for the Christians, speaks of the calumny of the heathen laying the cause of all their misery upon the Christians; "If it rained not, if the Nile overflowed not, (Egypt being the granary of the the empire,) if there was pestilence; at once they exclaimed, "*Christianos Ad Leones*, Away with these Christians to the lions;" who were then punished most as a cause of famines, and therefore used to fast in times of such judgment, especially when their *Annona*, or annual stock of corn, was in danger of being spent; whilst other Romans poured out themselves to all licentiousness: Also in his apology to Scapula, the African president, shewing that no persecuting city went unpunished, he instanceth how lately, under Hillarian his predecessor's presidentship, the Christians begging a floor of corn, a voice was heard underground, "*Areæ Non Sunt;*" and they had no corn to thresh in their floors the next year, a great wet having spoiled the harvest: This *vexation*, following a condemnation of the Christians to the beasts, Baronious there understands to be the lack of corn. Origen about A.D. 226, writing on Matt. xxiv. and taking occasion to answer the same general calumny against the Christians, as causes of their wars, famines, and pestilences, instanceth in famines especially, as the eminent punishment of that age.

FOURTH SEAL, and its "*pale horse*," v. 7, 8, with "*Death his name that sat on him*," whose horse brings death "*on the fourth part of the earth*" or empire; and his work was "*to kill with sword, and with hunger, and with death, and with the beasts of the earth*," even all God's plagues let loose at once, for their impenitence; (not as before, civil wars alone, or famine coming alone, but now) all four judgments mentioned in Ezek. xiv. 21, all the treasures of his wrath. Pestilence is here called *death*, as it is by the Chaldean paraphrase, and the Greek; by the Fathers it is called *the mortality*, and by us *the sickness*. It is wonderful to read what a stage of misery and blood the empire became, from A.D. 240, through all these plagues raging at once. In the space of thirty-three years, ten emperors were killed in the civil wars. Under Gallus and Volusianus, A.D. 250, the barbarous nations came down upon the empire, and harrowed it; and the Scythians amongst them, whose rage exempted no part of the Roman jurisdiction, depopulating almost every town; which was followed by extreme famine: "When we had a breathing from these, (says Dionysius Alexandrinus,) there came the greatest and worst plague of pestilence, that ever was read of in any age"—"of fifteen years continuance, says Lypsius: and to add the last hand for completing the misery of these times, God let loose these tyrants at once, as so many wild beasts, to prey upon and make havoc of the empire.

OBSERVATIONS ON THE ABOVE SEALS.—1st, During the first four seals, bringing us to A.D. 260, the officers of churches remained according to institution in the purer churches; but afterwards we hear not of them, (corruptions coming in upon the churches, and preventing their right end,) till the vials begin, (c. xv.) in the first separation from Popery; and then we read only of one of the beasts giving these vials: but after a second measuring the temple, (c. xi.) before Rome's ruin, we read of four beasts, (c. xix.) in their right order again, praising God. 2dly, After the white horse of the gospel, go forth the other three of terrible judgments on the world, for contempt of it: "Judgment must begin at the house of God," (1 Pet. iv. 17,) but not rest there: Soon after the first preaching of the gospel, wrath fell most heavily also upon the empire and its idolaters: as we look for storms in autumn, and frost in winter, so we expect judgments where the gospel has been preached: "the quarrel of the covenant," (Lev. xxvi. 25,) must be avenged and vindicated: if men despise it, God cannot hold his hands. The churches in Germany, Bohemia, &c. had the gospel first, and so the cup of tribulation first; but God will visit them in their order; and those perhaps last, that have had the gospel but a little while. 3dly, God is wont to rise higher and higher in his judgments: He began in the empire with civil wars; and they not working, he sent famine which is worse; and then war, as in Lam. iv. 9; and then he came upon them with pestilence and all the other three at once; which agrees with Lev. xxvi. 21: so the three last are the woe-trumpets; and so in the vials, God will also rise higher and higher. 4thly, All plagues have their commission from God, and go forth only when Christ opens a vial: Of the second, it is said, "Power was given him and a sword:" A commission of restraint was given to the third, "not to hurt the oil and wine;" and to the fourth, "only to kill the fourth part:" as horses guided by their riders. Providence chalks out the way for them; as a path was made for God's anger, into what houses of the Egyptians it should enter, Ps. lxxviii. 50: so in Jer. xv. 2, "Those that are for the sword, to the sword," &c. Now in all these circuits in the way of God's judgment, let us wait for him to turn towards us in mercy, Isa. xxvi. 8. 5thly, Though plagues were ever common in the world, yet these were more eminently to be set down; for being as eminent in the Roman empire in those first ages, as in any other afterwards, yet these were all the plagues it had whilst Heathenish, and so were properly punishments of Gentilism, and of contempt of the message of the white horse, without at all ruining the empire, as the after-plagues did. But the Holy Ghost more especially names these plagues here as visitations consequent upon the gospel; whence the Heathen observed and objected, "That since Christianity began, wars, &c. raged more than ever, through the indignation of their affronted gods:" This calumny stirred up Cyprian to write his apology; which he did in the very language of the fourth seal, under which he lived. But though the eyes of the Heathen were sealed from seeing the up-lifted hand of God against them in these *sealed* plagues, yet the four beasts instructed John, (who personates the church,) concerning the true cause of them; and therefore every seal hath a voice of one or other of the beasts, saying "Come and see:" for the officers or ministers of the churches instructed the people, how that all these plagues were for despising the gospel, and for persecuting its professors.

THE FIFTH SEAL, v. 9—11, Is that bloody persecution which followed after all these plagues in the time of Dioclesian, about A.D. 300, which being the greatest of the ten persecutions, (for under it suffered a hundred and forty four thousand in one province only of the empire,) is put for all the rest; for those other plagues, for the contempt of the gospel, did but enrage the Heathen the more, who imputed these to the anger of their gods, for suffering the Christians to live: and this being the last and greatest, calls for vengeance in the name of all the foregoing martyrs. This vision is, First, Of souls severed from their bodies, even of men slain, or of martyrs; who, Secondly, Are presented as newly sacrificed, and with their throats cut, lying bleeding at the foot of the altar of burnt-offering, (see in 2 Tim. iv. 6; and Phil. ii. 17,) as in c. viii. these "prayers of all saints" are offered up upon the altar of incense. Some understand this altar to be heaven; but that comes in after, when "*White robes were given to every one of them.*" Thirdly, "*The souls of these that were slain for the word of God. were under the altar crying aloud, How long, O Lord, dost thou not avenge our blood?*" It is not simply the *blood* that cries, (as Abel's did,) but the *souls* do cry for vengeance and ruin upon the empire; and this their cry is doubly satisfied; *For,* A reason is given why vengeance is delayed; because the empire having to stand yet in power for a season, they were "*to rest a little while, until their fellow-servants also, and their brethren that should be killed as they were, should be fulfilled:*" so that here it refers not to the persecutions of the Popish Antichrist, (which were a thousand years after,) but the Arian; when under these emperors, about thirty years after this, there were raised as cruel persecutions for the time, as ever were before; and then the trumpets sound, and the empire itself is ruined through their prayers, as c. viii. *And also,* They are meanwhile received to glory, expressed by their *white robes,* 1st, As a sign or badge of heavenly glory; c. iii. 4, and Matt.

xvii. 2; 2dly, To denote joy; such robes being worn in triumphs, Eccl. ix. 8: 3dly, Robes were worn only by noble personages. Now this giving them white robes, is an allusion to the first bringing of the priests into the temple, when their thirty years were expired.

OBSERVATIONS ON THE FIFTH SEAL. 1st, It is God's manner to bring severest trials just before deliverance; as the above was the last and greatest of all persecutions: so it was with David at Ziklag a few hours before he was proclaimed king: so in c. xi. is a persecution and war of Antichrist yet to come, for the space of three years and a half; after which, the witnesses shall cast off their sackcloth for ever: I fear it, for it is the last. 2dly, Though great punishments had befallen the empire by the three preceding horses; yet for martyrs' blood, this is not vengeance enough, which nothing will satisfy but the ruin of that bloody state; as nothing pacified Manasseh's blood-shed but the captivity of Judah. 3dly, In matters wherein many ages have an interest, the saints in each preceding age put up their prayers in the strength of all prayers and cries of blood preceding: so the souls here in the name of all preceding martyrs, cry, "*How long*" &c.! As in a generation of wicked men, the last of them inherit the sins and punishments of all their forefathers; so do a generation of godly men go forth in the strength of all their fore-fathers' prayers and blood-shed. How comfortably, therefore, may we pray against Rome, and all the bishops, her abettors, who have even wallowed in the blood of saints, and against whom we have the prayers of all ages, to join their forces to ours for their more sure prevailing; while we pull together in our cry, "*How long*," &c.! like the linking of many cords with such artifice, that by a pully even a child might draw up a mighty weight, for he pulls in the strength of all the cords. It is but a little resting, till our brethren, (it may be ourselves,) the witnesses, are killed; and then down goes Rome, and the hierarchy with it: in which respect it is good living in these last ages of the world, for we drive a trade with all our fore-fathers' stock. 4thly, The power of persecutors stands no longer than till they have finished the great work of persecuting the saints; which is the reason here given for the empire's standing so long: "Thou hast ordained them for judgment, (on themselves,) and established them for correction," (of thine,) Hab. i. 12. 5thly, The *soul* is here said to cry for vengeance, and not (as when the wicked are murdered,) the *blood* only; God will, therefore, speedily avenge his own elect, whose cry enters his ears with so much clamour. And again, If Abel's blood hath such force in its cry, and his living soul a still greater force; how much more Christ's blood, and still more Christ himself, who lives to intercede for us! 6thly, The souls in heaven, following their interests on earth, prosecute the revenging of their blood; and why not also the interests of their friends, children, businesses and the like; for which they prayed on earth? 7thly, The spirits made perfect know, and are satisfied with the reason of God's dispensations and councils: (as here God opens his utmost reason why the empire was as yet to stand, viz. for the slaughter of a few more martyrs:) for being prophets, as well as priests, they are guided by a spirit of prophecy, as Christ is. 8thly, If we knew the reason of all dispensations, we should rest, as these souls do in this standing yet of the empire. Let our faith apprehend that God hath a reason for all our persecutions. 9thly, Saints yet unborn are here called "their brethren," as in God's election; (for this persecution came not till forty years after;) as Christ calls all his people, whom God gave him before the world was; and Jesus knows the names and the number of his own in all ages, and chose not *qualifications* but *persons;* as he saith, "I have sheep which are not of this fold:" Let us then love the Jews, as those who are to be called; and the saints departed, as those who are our brethren. 10thly, Martyrdom is a perfection, as Christ calls his sufferings, Luke xiii. 32; so here, "till they are *fulfilled*," PLEEROOSONTAI: if we have all holiness, without this *coronis*, we are not so perfect as martyrs. 11thly, Saints departed presently enter into bliss; they sleep not, but have "*white robes given them*," as the priests had at their introduction into the temple; and their robes of glory are new, as given them afresh; their souls are clothed with glory, till they meet their bodies again, as rich robes reaching from head to foot; they are all over happy and glorious. 12thly, Those in bliss reckon us fellow-servants and brethren, though we be sinful; and they hold a communion with us: let us do the like towards our weakest brethren, between whom and ourselves, there is far less distance for holiness, &c. 13thly, The saints are reckoned martyrs, "*for the word of God, and for the testimony which they hold;*" and therefore for the least truth of that word. 14thly, God may defer his answer to prayer; for he puts even those in heaven upon staying a while; yet he will recompense this demur some other way, satisfying us by other blessings; as he gave those saints white robes of glory.

THE SIXTH SEAL, v. 12—17, Expresseth the final accomplishment of "*the wrath of the Lamb*," in throwing down the Heathenism of the empire, and in confounding its idol-worship, (as the former seals contained several punishments on the empire itself,) "*for the great day of his wrath is come;*" which some interpret of the day of judgment, certain phrases also being used concerning it, as in Matt. xxiv. 19: but John was now come only to the tenth and last persecution, about A.D. 300; and also after this, the seventh seal is to be opened, producing seven trumpets of new punishments in succession upon the empire: and as for the phrases here used, they frequently express great mutations and overturnings in kingdoms, and calamities therein;

as in Joel ii. 10, 11; Isa. xxxiv. 4; ii. 19; Hosea x. 8: These passages speaking of the overthrow of kingdoms by wars, therefore Mr. Forbes would have this seal to be the utter overturning of the western empire itself by the Goths and Vandals, about A.D. 400, and not of its Paganism: But, 1st, The first seal, v. 2, 3, beginning only with the conquest of Paganism, (for the gospel at first attacked nothing else,) this sixth seal accomplishes the victory; and so Christ's first step or degree of conquest in order to the kingdom, is fully presented in this chapter, with his first full victory over the first enemy he encountered in the world, even Satan and his false worship; and so this book still goes on to shew, That when he begins, he makes an end of despatching such enemies first, as he first encounters: thus Heathenism was first met by the gospel; then by plagues; and finally as one growing angry, Christ completes the victory by power and might, and by a violent concussion and shaking of the state. Thus having despatched this enemy, and made clear work of it, (as conquerors do,) he falls on the empire itself in the trumpets: therefore the last act of this tragedy is represented under metaphors suited to the judgment-day, when he shall triumph for ever over all enemies. 2dly, The trumpets that come after, are reserved for the ruin of the empire itself; and the vials, for the overthrow of Popery and Mahometanism: thus, 3dly, The parts of this prophecy run on similarly, and things alike are put together in distinct visions; for here are three sorts of enemies, and three sorts of plagues to ruin them: The six seals are the beginning of sorrows to the world, and they fall on Satan's false worship, which stood in Christ's way: The six trumpets fall on the empire itself, for its persecutions of the church: The six vials, (called the last plagues, chap. xvi.) fall on the Popish and Mahometan factions. 4thly, Chap. xii. which hath the story of the primitive church, as this hath of Rome Pagan, doth wonderfully agree with this chapter, describing the same space of time, and the same conquests over Satan in the imperial heaven; only here, (as belonging to the seal-prophecy,) are set forth the calamities and confusion of the kings or emperors, and chieftains of Heathen worshippers, who sought to uphold idolatry still; and then, (as belonging to the book-prophecy,) is described only the dragon's confusion, in being thrown down; that being the story of the church, and this of the empire, more eminently. Under these phrases and metaphors, two things are distinctly set out: *First*, By the *sun, moon*, and *stars*, being darkened, (according to the analogy of the prophets,) is expressed the deposing of those Heathenish emperors and governors in the Roman state, as striving to keep up Heathenism; and with these fell also Satan and his worshippers: for though the state stood still, yet its Paganism, and those governors, were removed, and destroyed, and thrown down from their *heaven*, (the superior government of that state,) by

Christ's inflicting madness and diseases on its emperors, Dioclesian and Maximinian, who resigned their government in the meridian of their glory, (to the wonderment of the world,) from a sense of "*the wrath of the Lamb*:" and afterwards the emperors Maxentius and Maximinus were overcome by Licinus, who favoured the Christians, and was colleague with Constantine; but on Licinus' revolt again to the idolatries of Rome, Constantine subdued him and his chieftains, (for Heathenism went not down without blows,) and after deposing all the persecutors, he turned the whole state to Christian: Such a subversion of state-governors and their armies, (as well as of the state itself,) the prophets express by "darkening the sun, moon, and stars:" so Isa. xiii. 10; xiv. 12, 13, signifies the king, queen, and nobles of Babylon, all deposed from their high stations; the monarch himself being the sun and the lucifer-star; whose heaven was cast down, and it "*fell to the earth*." Now v. 15, may express the same thing, expounding it literally of "*the kings of the earth*," or Roman emperors; those *suns* of this firmament, who were stepped off from their glory; the *stars* of their nobility, those "*great men and rich men*," being also deposed; and *their mountains*, (Isa. ii. 14,) or "*chief captains and mighty men*," removed. Now the rest of the trumpet and vial-prophecy proceeds also with plagues on the sun, moon, and stars; the earth and trees; and therefore one literal explanation to serve for all, is here first mentioned, that we may learn to interpret by the Holy Ghost's own analogy: Every state or kingdom being a *world*, the superior part of the same is its *heavens*, with the *sun* above all, then its *moon*, *stars*, &c. the inferior parts being the *earth*, with its *sea*, *rivers*, *trees*, &c. Judgments on this "*world*" are therefore pronounced like as in Hag. ii. 21, 22, which there expresses the change of the state itself and all places of rank therein; but sometimes, only the deposing of their proprietors is meant thereby, the places and dignities standing still. Thus under the trumpets, the casting down of the sun, stars, &c. means abstractly, an altering the very state, power, and dignity of the empire, together with a deposing of the persons; but here concretely, the *persons* only in power are meant, their *places* remaining for others to fill. *Secondly*, These expressions hold forth, not simply an overthrow of stations or station-holders by political mutations, but changes of religion in a state: for as bodies politic, so religious bodies are compared to a world; thus Christ in Ps. viii. 3, hath his world, whose heavens have their moon and stars, &c. (where the sun is not mentioned, because it is Christ himself,) as interpreted in Heb. ii. 5, 6: so Rom. x. 18, interprets Ps. xix. I, 4: and in chap. xii. 1, the apostles' ministry is compared to twelve stars with which the primitive church was crowned: and so in Heb. xii. 27, "the heavens" partly mean gospel ordinances, that frame of worship which Christ hath erected; (as the legal worship is there "the earth;") though in Dan. viii. 10, 11, the temple-worship, with its priests and elders, is so called; which Antiochus caused to cease, so as to magnify himself even against the Sun of righteousness, who is "the prince of the heavenly host:" So Antichrist hath his Popish world too: so Satan hath his Pagan world, where devil worship and idolatry are practised; whence the Heathen gods are called "the host of heaven," in Deut. xvii. 3; not only because the sun, moon, and stars, were immediately worshipped, but because Greece and Rome called the stars by the names of their gods and goddesses; of their heroes, heroines, and demi-gods: hence Apollo and the sun, Phœbe and the moon, (or "the great goddess Diana,") being worshipped together, and under them Satan himself and his devil-angels, as in 1 Cor. x. 20; from this his heaven Christ saw Satan fall like lightning, (Luke x. 18;) which overthrow began by the apostles' casting out devils, and was fulfilled in c. xii. by the subversion of idolatry in the empire, that "shaking of the heavens and earth," here set forth by "*the great earthquake*," (the only proper word we have to express such a convulsion of nature;) as Hag. ii. 7, expresses the change from Jewish to gospel-worship; and as there will be another shaking, "not of the earth only but of the heaven also," even of the present variegated outward gospel-worship to be yet succeeded by that apostolic simplicity, which shall again be revived and continue for a thousand years; after all false religions shall be trodden down, (in which Satan is the prince of this host of heaven,) by the sun of this firmament, whose stars, (or devils of demi-gods,) fall therefore, as he is put out. Again, as the moon is Christ's church and the queen of heaven; so the college of Pagan priests then in Rome, (as the Pope and cardinals are now,) were the moon in his heaven, as instruments of devil-worship; and so his consecrated places, his "*islands and mountains*," were displaced, and diverted from the use they were once put to under Paganism. Thus this change of the Heathen religion, (the extirpation of which took about a century from Constanine's time,) is here set forth by two things distinctly and apart laid down: 1st, The subversion of the religion of Rome Pagan, signified, 1, By an eclipse of "*the sun*, which *became black as sackcloth of hair;*" and of "*the moon*, which *became as blood:*" the glory of their gods, and the priests of the same being darkened. 2, By "*the stars of heaven* which *fell unto the earth, even as a fig-tree casteth her untimely figs when she is shaken of a mighty wind:*" shewing that Pagan men's hearts were not loosened of themselves at first, but forcibly shaken to a dislike of that religion. 3, By the vanishing of the whole "*heaven*" of his worship, "*as a scroll when it is rolled together:*" (for the Jews wrote on rolls of parchment, or *vellum*, which being folded up they call *Volumen*, or *volume:*) importing that as thus *every letter* is hid, so the names of these gods and their worship have disappeared for more than a thousand years, being as a book unopened and not in use. 2dly, This change is represented, by the confusion of such upholders of that ethnic worship as were the Atlases that supported these heavens, opposing Constantine and other emperors in their introduction of the Christian religion: for the devil leaves not the hearts possessed by him, without the blows of one stronger than he: so he left not his station in the empire without resistance, egging on imperial kings and generals, and the populace, to unite in support of the old religion: but the Lamb encounters these and confounds them in his wrath. The very names given to the Romans in their several ranks, are here used of "*The kings of the earth*," (for the Greek has no other word than BASILEIS, which is the word for Roman emperors in 1 Pet. ii. 13, and 1 Tim. ii. 2,) who were the *monarchy;* "*The great men*" (called "their great ones," and connected with *kings* and *rulers*, in Mark x. 42, Luke xxii. 25,) were the *aristocracy;* "*The chief captains*" over legions of seven *thousand* men each, (called CHILIARCHOI; as *centurions*, or HECATONTARCHOI, were captains of *hundreds*,) were the *military;* "*The rich men and the mighty men*" may be the gentry; while "*Every bondman and every freeman*" may designate the *commonalty*, or plebeian community, the populace in general and lower rank. Now, the confusion of these is expressed, 1, By their overthrow; they fled for shame and disappointment, and "*hid themselves in dens, and in the rocks of the mountains*," as in Isa. ii. 10. 2, By their despair of help, intimated in their saying "to the mountains and rocks, *Fall on us and hide us:*" The language is taken from the Jews, (whose country abounds with rocks,) as in Luke xxiii. 30, Hos. x. 8; the Jews, when Rome destroyed Judah and Jerusalem, wishing to be crushed to death by the falling in of the rocks, into whose caves they fled for hiding, rather than to live and see the miseries that were come upon them; which other people express by wishing the earth to swallow them up. 3, The phrases import, that all this is done with a sense and conviction in these enemies' hearts, of Christ's power whom they had derided and anathematized, though now their conqueror and the world's king; and therefore they cry for a hiding-place "*from the face of him that sitteth upon the throne, and from the wrath of the Lamb, for* (add they) the great day of his wrath *is come, and who shall be able to stand?*" or abide it, as Joel ii. 11. Now the story of the times of the empire's conversion from Ethnicism to Christianity, presented such a face of things as doth this seal; for Dioclesian and Maximinian, (the greatest persecutors the church ever had,) in the height and ruff of their imperial glory and rage, abdicated so unreasonably, that Historians could impute only to insanity, what they did "to hide themselves from the face of the Lamb." Gallerius, Miximinus, and Constantius, (father of Constantine,) succeeded. Maximinus, persecuting the Christians, was smitten with a strange disease; and under conviction of Christ's being king, recalled his edicts of persecution, afterwards putting them forth again, like Pharaoh, till at least he died miserably, acknowledging "the wrath of the Lamb." Maxentius was then set up to defend the Heathen cause; but being overcome by Licinius, he threw away his imperial robes, and fled, and lay hid for the safeguard of his life, and acknowledged Christ by a decree: his flesh was eaten of worms. Then Licinius opposing his co-regnant, Constantine, was overcome by him; and being condemned with his accomplices, at the place of execution, he acknowledged Christ to be God. Afterwards the apostate Julian attempting to re-establish Heathenism, being shot in his wars against Persia, flung his own blood and bowels into the air, saying, Thou has conquered, O Galilean!

OBSERVATIONS ON THE SIXTH SEAL.—1st, When we see any notable overthrow of Christ's enemies, let our hearts be raised up to think of the day of judgment, which is described by similar language, as in Ps. xviii. and elsewhere: particular judgments strengthen our faith in that of the great day; and the general judgment to come assures us that Christ will now avenge his own elect, and be here avenged on his own enemies. Christ hath many great days before that great day; and wicked men and wicked causes have days of judgment here. 2ndly, How easy it is for the Lamb of God to alter the religion of a kingdom, and to make his new one prevail! In a few years the whole Roman empire was turned Christian, even when Gentilism was rooted in all men's minds, and Satan's throne apparently fixed for continuance; but Christ got possession of the emperor's heart, and "turned the kingdom about," (1 Kings ii. 15,) and that, when men of themselves were not turned, but were as figs not fully ripe, yet shaken off by the wind; and he folded up the heavens as a scroll, not a constellation of all these false deities having shined in the world these many hundred years: so will he do to Popery, which being the image of the heathen empire and religion, shall bear the like punishment. As there was a mighty change wrought in the hearts of kings and princes, upon the first reformation; so before Rome is destroyed, God will put it into their hearts a second time to ruin her utterly. 3rdly, Christ will not only confound his proud enemies, but make them acknowledge his truth, as he did Nebuchadnezzar, Antiochus, &c. and as the false church and synagogue of Satan come and acknowledge, that God hath loved the Philadelphian church, Rev. iii. 9: "They shall know that I am the Lord," is the fruit of men's punishments; for not only "every knee shall bow," but "every tongue shall confess to his name." It is ill standing out with Christ in any thing, or against convictions of any kind; for men shall render his victory in their punishments more complete by their own confessions; in dispensing which punishments, 4thly, He meets persecutors in their kind; they caused the primitive Christians to flee into caves and dens and to worship the Lamb in corners; and he with open face drives them into corners to hide their heads. 5thly, What a long and glorious time the god of this world had, when devils were specially esteemed and worshipped as true gods, for three hundred years, and more generally for some thousands of years; and, though reserved in chains for hell, as the immortal possessors of heaven, having their seat above the stars, and all the world for their devotees! What is it then to have a great name; or even the best of names, the name of *saint;* if only for awhile here? 6thly, No wonder the wicked prosper so long, seeing the devil encountered no stop in his way for so many thousand years, wherein he had all nations for his inheritance; and God was worshipped but in one poor corner of the earth, while Satan possessed the heavens, as the sun in the firmament; and his priests, as the perpetual ordinances of the moon and stars. Let us not think much of the continuance of Popery for twelve hundred years; Heathenism stood for longer; and Christ will make quicker work in the last days than in the past days. 7thly, Men have all such sweet thoughts of Christ, as if he had no anger in him: but the meek lamb is also a furious lion; and "when his wrath is kindled but a little, blessed are all they that put their trust in him," Ps. ii. 12. 8thly, God punisheth idolaters and idols together, as he removed Rome's emperor and her religion and gods together, (see Isa. ii. 17—19; Num. xxxiii. 4; Jer. xliii. 11—13; l. 2;) so God punished monks, pulling down their monasteries and idols together; and so superstitious ceremonies and will-worshippers will down together. 9thly, How fearful and terrible will be the day of judgment, when Christ shall come as the Lion of Judah; if now reigning in the meekness and patience of the Lamb, he brings forth such confounding judgments! all terrors men suffer here are but "the wrath of the lamb," compared to the roaring of the lion at that great day. "Now consider this, O ye that forget God, lest I tear you in pieces and there be none to deliver." Ps. l. 22.

THE SEVENTH CHAPTER.

God, to shew his care of his people, in this chapter seals twelve thousand out of each of the twelve tribes, before the trumpets blow, in the several ages, and on the several parts of the world, (named in the two following chapters, to which I refer the reader,) whence the sealed were chosen; who are called in v. 3, "*the servants of God,*" being true believers, and who in the language and types of the Old Testament are called *Jews,* as all Christians are "the *Israel* of God," Gal. vi. 16; even as false idolatrous Christians are called *Gentiles* in c. xi. 2, "who say they are Jews, (profess themselves Christians,) and are not, but do lie,"

c. iii. 9. These who are numbered by thousands, (in allusion to the "thousands of Israel," and to the sealing of the mourners in Ezek. ix.) are preserved by a miracle, in the midst of all the Mahometan tyranny under Turks and Saracens in the eastern part of the world; (so seven thousand were preserved under Ahab's tyranny, who bended not before Baal;) as the hundred and forty-four thousand were preserved under the like Antichristian tyranny in the west, as will appear in the book-prophecy in c. xiv. only here they are numbered by twelve times twelve thousand, to shew their more scattered and divided condition, happily alluding either to James i. 1, or to the twelve tribes as living apart in several quarters of the land of Judah, and not assembled at Jerusalem in the temple: so likewise these, dwelling scattered in the several nations to be overcome by the trumpets, and not assembled in public worship or churches, but remaining single, are mentioned by a set number, to shew that they who shall thus be acceptable to God shall be few, in comparison of that innumerable company to grow out of them in v. 9; and their number being multiplied by twelve, (as their root,) and by a *thousand*, (as a *long* number extending much further than in breadth,) shews that John speaks not of Christians amounting to such a number in one age, but through many ages continuing: and their being multiplied by *twelve* shews their breed and kind to be from the apostles, and of the apostolic faith, (which in c. xxi. 14, is made the mystery of this number, "And the wall of the city had twelve foundations, and in them the names of the twelve apostles of the Lamb;") and they are presented in one uniform state during all that time, even unto the new Jerusalem, of which because these and their successors are to be made partakers, those promises of the new Jerusalem, and the representation of it, comes in from v. 9, to the end. But those in c. xiv. do not remain till the new Jerusalem, in that dark and loose condition, upon mount Zion; but do break forth long before into a separation from Antichrist, and set up glorious temples, filled visibly with the presence of God, as with smoke, out of which come the vials; whereas these continue in one uniform state until the very approach of the new Jerusalem, when they come out afresh from under a sore and long bondage of "*great tribulation*," having been more scattered and divided, and spread here and there, as in several tribes: but those in c. xiv. are summed up together, (yet both alike in number and fewness, and in ages of darkness and desolation,) and grow up long before to a glorious light, and then outgrow that number. Now John enquires, Who are these hundred and forty-four thousand predecessors of the "innumerable company," that shall together with the Jews, possess the new Jerusalem? and one of the twenty-four elders would have him specially note it, as one of the wonders of this book, strange beyond all thought, that the names of such scattered myriads should be found among the denizens of the new Jerusalem:

"*What are these and whence came they?* even a company of poor elect believers, called the Grecian churches, dispersed over the now Turkish dominion of the once eastern empire: And that the Holy Ghost designates these, appears in that, *First*, Their *sealing* here is for their preservation from hurt, (as in v. 3, "*Hurt not the earth, neither the sea, nor the trees, till we have sealed the servants of our God in their foreheads*,") by the four winds let loose, (as in v. 1, "*After these things I saw four angels standing on the four corners of the earth, holding the four winds of the earth, that the wind should not blow on the earth, nor on the sea, nor on any tree*,") meaning the desolations of wars, (as in Jer. xlix. 36;) which winds are the blasts of the trumpets, (c. viii. ix.) to prevent the hurt of which the servants of God are sealed aforehand; which sealing has chief respect to the times of the chief plagues, and therefore to the fifth and sixth woe-trumpets mentioned c. viii. 13, in respect of which the four first were gentle: but these two being the over-runnings of the Saracen and Mahometan nations, were the greatest plague of war and bondage that ever befel the Christian world, being more than five times the two hundred years' duration of the other four. The wars of the Goths indeed rather relieved the church against the flood of Arian persecutors, (as in c. xii. 16,) however it brake and harrowed the empire; and after ruining all the cities of Thrace, Macedon, Thessaly, and Greece, (except Athens and Thebes,) for five years, they fell on the west; even as some of the winds of the four first trumpets devastated also some of the eastern parts: wherefore the sealing hath a respect ten-fold to the eastern Christians. *Secondly*, Besides the above reason for this, the Holy Ghost hath declared that the preservation from the hurt of these Mahometan invasions, was the aim of this previous sealing; and therefore the souls of the sealed ones of the east were alone in danger of apostacy, through the tyranny of the trumpets. In c. ix. 4, when these Saracen-locusts, under their ring-leader Mahomet, were first set loose, and had their commission, then comes in this clause of exception, "That they should hurt only those men that were not sealed," which privilege of *sealing*, then and there only mentioned, argues the chief intent and accomplishment of their sealing to have taken place under the blasts of these locusts, though in the vision it comes in here beforehand; yet the Holy Ghost, as by a marginal hand, points at the real execution of it in c. ix. under the fifth and sixth woe-trumpets. Now though the western church was preserved from all pest by these incursions, the Mahometans being restrained from breaking in on the ten kingdoms, yet they are not here meant; For, *Not only* doth the mystery of sealing note the singling out and marking of some here and there from the crowd; as the door-posts of the Israelites were marked; and as a man marks his sheep, put among other droves; and as the mourners in Ezek. ix. 4, were thus distinguished from other captives: else all the kingdoms of the west should have been said to be sealed; whereas the souls here, were preserved faithful to Christ in spite of all Mahometan seducements and bondage: *But also* being partakers of the new Jerusalem, these are said "to come out of *great tribulation*," endured through the Mahometan incursions; from the hurt of which dangerous locusts they were preserved, though not exclusively of the western Antichrist: *Besides*, the character in the text carries it to these eastern Christians; for the sealing-angel, (v. 2,) ascends from the *east;* and also the sealed are represented as but a few to be numbered in many ages, even to the new Jerusalem times, and as the dispersion of the twelve tribes, and as under the darkness of tribulation from the primitive times: but those in c. xiv. have light and victory in the midst, while the eastern churches have remained forlorn, and corrupt, and superstitious, with but few holy among them, and under the Mahometan yoke, one half of them for more than a thousand years, and the other half for more than two hundred years; and they are still under the Turk, with but little ease from misery, or restoration to light and beauty; yet Christ hath had among them his sects of Grecian and Armenian Christians, &c. preserving the knowledge and profession of his name, and of more truth than is found in the dark times of the Romish church: Now this tyranny being to continue till the new Jernsalem, (for the Turk is to be overthrown to make way for the Jews, under the sixth seal,) accords with the paucity and tribulation of the eastern saints, until such their first and fresh coming out of so great tribulations: And the wonder excited at this gracious dealing with a people so forgotten of all Christians, further confirms it: for the western churches, that have borne the heat of Antichristian persecution, and have overcome Antichrist, (and they shall in the end perfect their victory,) and have set up temples increasing in light and glory, may well attain to the new Jerusalem; for which marriage of the Lamb we find them preparing, (c. xix.) after the ruin of the whore: but who would have thought that these Greek Christians should be God's Ephraims, his pleasant children, Jer. xxxi. 20;! "O the depth," &c. Rom. xi. 33. Therefore one of the elders draws John's attention to this above all, "*These are they who come out of great tribulation*," such as was none ever like it: *Again*, God is wont to choose out of such low estate, that he may *therefore* (v. 15) exalt them, and set all the world a wondering at his acts of grace and mercy: and they, as well as ourselves, having borne the heat of the day, are entitled to their penny also: and being seated in where the Turk's seat is, (whose overthrow opens a way to the Jews' restoration to their own land, as "kings of the east," c. xvi. 12, in the midst of those eastern nations,) is it not probable they shall be thus delivered, on the ruin of the Turk? and if Gentiles partake of their privileges, those Christians who have been oppressed by this their common enemy, and who dwell in countries near, and about the land of the Jews, (especially if their land should be made the chief seat of this fifth monarchy,) are likely to partake most of its benefit to walk in the light of it, as the prophets have foretold. *Thirdly*, Where are the Grecian churches named if not here? The book-prophecy is taken up with the state of the western churches, opposing Antichrist, c. xiv.—xix. they being to ruin him, and retaining the knowledge of Christ, and the shew of themselves in the greatest power and purity; and therefore the Revelation speaks most of them: and are not the Armenian and Grecian churches, amounting to as many as do the professors of Europe, notwithstanding the Mahometan incursion, most fitly here represented under the seal-prophecy? hence we read in all stories of these eastern parts, and hear also to this day, of the continuance of true believers among them; whose confession of faith, printed in English A.D. 1629, is set forth by Cyril, (then patriarch of Constantinople,) and contains all the fundamentals of our own confession: Let us read also Field "Of the Church," book iii, chap. 1, 2, 3, and 5.

THE EIGHTH CHAPTER.

THE FIRST SIX TRUMPETS,

Out of the seven given to "*the seven angels which stood before God*," (v. 2,) contain the several steps and degrees of ruining the imperial government of the Roman empire, when turned Christian, by several wars and incursions of barbarous nations, whereof trumpets are suitably made the denouncers; the Christian blood spilt by the empire, when Pagan, being thus avenged; as the Babylonish captivity did break the Jewish state for the blood shed by Manasseh in its idolatry; though he and all Judah did turn to the true worship of God again. Now according to the division of the empire, east and west; the Goths and Vandals utterly shattered the government of the occidental emperors, breaking it into ten kingdoms; over which the Pope succeeded: and next the oriental parts were overturned, first by the Saracens, (Mahomet their head wresting out of the emperor's hands one great part of the eastern empire, in Arabia, Egypt, and Assyria, and subjecting it to Mahometanism;) then by the Turks, propagating Mahometanism also, who subdued not only what the Saracens before them had done, but also that other part of the eastern empire, (remaining still Christian,) in Natolia, and in Greece; over which the Greek emperors, successors of the Roman,) continued; till now wholly subjected, (together with Constantinople the seat of their empire,) unto the Turks, the sole possessors of the eastern empire: These trumpets are thus, answerably, divided by the Holy Ghost: the first four, (containing lesser evils and miseries,) are the wars of the Goths and Vandals in four several incursions, in this chapter: but the fifth and sixth are among the three last *woe-trumpets*, (v. 13; c. ix. 12; xi. 14;) and contain all those infinite calamities and embondagements, brought on the east by the Saracen wars and conquest under the fifth trumpet, and by the Turks under the sixth; both longer and greater than the four first. The promise therefore to the martyrs under the fifth seal, (c. vi. 11,) is fulfilled in answer to their prayers here (v. 3—5,) offered up by Christ; the trumpet sounding for the time of avenging their blood.

THE FIRST FOUR TRUMPETS, are chiefly on the western empire, extended all over Europe; which was performed by four steps or degrees, falling severally on the earth, the sea, the rivers; the sun, moon, and stars, v. 7, 8, 10, 12: 1st, The *earth*, with the *grass* and *trees* therein, signifying the people in common, both richer and poorer, as in Zech. xi. 2. 2dly, The *sea*, is the extent of the jurisdiction of such an *imperial world*, (as in Jer. iv. 23,) over several dominions; whence Rome is said to "sit on many waters;" and "to arise out of the sea," or collection of many waters or nations: so speak Jer. li. 36, 44, and Exek. xxxi. 4, concerning the Babylonish and Assyrian monarchies. 3dly, The *rivers*, are the several cities and provinces, with the lesser jurisdictions of their magistrates. 4thly, The *sun*, *moon*, and *stars*, shew the glory of supreme magistrates, as in Isa. xiii. 10, Jer. xv. 9. Now of these four trumpets, bringing their four degrees of calamities on Rome and its empire, by the incursions from the north, from A.D. 400, to A.D. 540,

THE FIRST TRUMPET, harrowed the *earth;* wars first lighting most heavily on the people; but it proceeded to no further havoc than "the burning of the *trees* and *grass*," v. 7; "*The first angel sounded, and there followed hail and fire mingled with blood, and they were cast upon the earth: and the third part of trees were burnt up.*"

THE SECOND TRUMPET, fell on the *sea;* the Goths by breaking the imperial yoke from off the nations subject to it, affording them opportunity to set up the European ten kingdoms, which remain to this day; beginning in France, A.D. 413; and by A.D. 450, they were all up. This rending of the kingdoms from the empire, with the sacking of Rome itself by Allaricus, king of the Goths, A.D. 410, is called, (v. 8,) "The burning of a great mountain," (as Babylon is called "a destroying and burning mountain," as overshadowing all cities, till sacked itself by Cyrus, Jer. li. 25;) "*And the second angel sounded, and as it were a great mountain burning with fire, was cast into the sea; and the third part of the sea became blood.*"

THE THIRD TRUMPET, produces the fall of a bright blazing comet, or "great burning star;" or the extinction of emperors, A.D. 476, in Augustulus, (like that of the king of Babel, in Isa. xiv. 12, "How art thou fallen from heaven, O Lucifer, son of the morning!")

who, as a prince of bitterness and sorrows, is truly named "*Wormwood;*" together with whom many provincial, cities and magistrates, (called *rivers* and *fountains,*) had their dignity removed: "*And the third angel sounded, and there fell a star from heaven, burning as it were a lamp; and it fell upon the third part of the rivers, and upon the fountains of waters: and the name of the star is called Wormwood; and the third part of the waters became wormwood, and many men died of the waters, because they were made bitter,*" v. 10, 11.

THE FOURTH TRUMPET, totally deprives Rome, (now in the hands of the Goths, and the seat of those kings, who though they won it, still preserved the splendor of its senators, consuls, and supreme magistrates;) of all its ancient form of government, with the glory and majesty of which it had shined for many centuries ere the imperial power was placed over it; which ancient monarchy, (here called *The sun,* &c.) still continuing under the emperors, was quite subverted in the last war, A.D. 542. Thus the glory of the western empire and Rome had been utterly and for ever extinguished, but for the Pope, (c. XIII. under the book-prophecy concerning the church,) who obtains a power, on a different title, over the ten kingdoms; and by building up a new Rome, possesses the seat of the former beast, which is the empire.

All the above four trumpets falling on, and making such alterations in the west, are but lesser evils compared with those other two here which are to fall on the eastern parts, yet standing whole and entire under a profession of the Christian faith; and as standing longest, God reserved the same unto the severest punishments, which are therefore thus prefaced, v. 13, "*Woe, woe, woe, to the inhabiters of the earth, by reason of the voices of the other trumpets which have yet to sound.*"

THE NINTH CHAPTER.

THE FIFTH TRUMPET, produces the falling of a star from heaven, which opens the bottomless pit, and emits smoke as from a furnace, darkening the sun and air, and letting out an innumerable company of locusts, (v. 1—3,) which are thus described; "*And the shapes of the locusts were like unto horses prepared unto battle: and on their heads were as it were crowns like gold; and their faces were as the faces of men; and they had hair as the hair of women; and their teeth were as the teeth of lions; and they had breastplates, as it were breastplates of iron; and the sound of their wings was as the sound of chariots of many horses running to battle: and they had tails like unto scorpions, and there were stings in their tails; and their power was to hurt men five months.*" v. 7—10: These torment men so that they "shall seek death (because of the calamity of those times,) and shall not find it," (v. 4, 5;) figuring out the introduction of *Mahometanism*, that greatest imposture the world ever knew, which darkens the *sun* and *air*, by quenching the light of Christian profession, through the apostacy of that *star*, who opened hell to bring forth that damned religion of his; to whom numberless of his countrymen-Arabians, (who were as locusts, Judg. vii. 12,) did cleave, and set him up as king, for "*They had a king over them, which is the angel of the bottomless pit, whose name in the Hebrew tongue is Abaddon, but in the Greek hath his name Apollyon.*" v. 11. These wrenched off from the eastern empire, Arabia, Egypt, Assyria, Armenia, and much of Asia Minor; and extending their dominions further over Persia, East India, and a great part of Africa and Spain, they almost vied with the former western empire; Mahomet extending his dominions another way, besides possessing half of the eastern empire: But these are bidden by God, "*to hurt only those men which have not the seal of God in their foreheads,*" (v. 4, see c. vii. 3;) for there were some who remained Christians in that part of the eastern empire. This kingdom began to be set up A.D. 630, and continued many hundred years.

THE SIXTH TRUMPET is ordained to bring calamities on the other part of the eastern empire, still standing under the successors of the Roman monarchy, and professing Christianity in Asia Minor, and Greece, (commonly called the empire of Greece;) to ruin which four angels were ready prepared with four several armies of horsemen, amounting to two hundred millions, as in v. 14—16, "*Saying to the sixth angel which had the trumpet, Loose the four angels, which are bound in the great river Euphrates; and the four angels were loosed, which were prepared for an hour, and a day, and a month, and a year, for to slay the third part of men: And the number of the army of the horsemen were two hundred thousand thousand: and I heard the number of them.*" These armies, with the angels their leaders, hovered for a long time under restraint about the borders of Euphrates, whom the angel of this second woe-trumpet let loose by God's command, like so many furies, to fall on the last remaining part of the eastern empire, and also to conquer those other dominions, which the Saracens under the fifth trumpet had before over-run. Now according to all the characters and foot-prints in Turkish history, no prophecy can more exactly describe any nation or event, than this of the Turks' irruption on the eastern empire; at whose first coming out of their native country, about A.D. 1040, they seated themselves by the river Euphrates, and were divided into the four several governments or kingdoms of Iconium, Aleppo, Damascus, and Bagdat or Babylon: after two centuries, about A.D. 1300, they over-run all Nalotia, (or Asia Minor,) and uniting all into one kingdom under Ottoman, (the fore-father of the present great Turk,) ceased not till they had won Constantinople itself, and all Greece; which last relics of the Roman empire they put down A.D. 1453; and thus they possess the whole eastern empire unto this day: for the number of the Turk being one year, one month, one day, and one hour, (prophetically three hundred and ninety six years,) would not thus be fulfilled, according to the latter date, until A.D. 1849. I shall now proceed to a short view of

THE TENTH AND ELEVENTH CHAPTERS.

The seal-prophecy under the visions of these seals and trumpets, having run over the stories all times, concerning the ruin of the Roman empire, down even to us; (for the miseries of the sixth woe-trumpet will last till near the time of the seventh's bringing in the kingdom of Christ, c. xi. 14, 15; whose sounding makes an end of this first seal-prophecy, and of all kingdoms and times;) The mighty angel of the covenant descends from heaven, 1st, To give the world and the church warning by an oath, that now *time* should be no longer than the expiration of the Turk's dominion, under the second woe: see c. x. 1, 6, 7, with xi. 14, 15. 2dly, To give withal a new entire prophecy under a book open in his hand, (the seals on it in c. v. being now removed, and the visions of them past:) this book, containing another distinct prophecy, John is bid to eat, (as in Ezek. ii. 8, 9,) that he might receive and write the new prophecy, (as in c. x. 9, 11,) beginning at c. xii. after Christ had discoursed a while of the state and face of his purest western churches in these last days, to which the seal-prophecy had brought John, not many years before the introduction of his kingdom by the blast of the seventh trumpet; and after he had also forewarned these churches of a great and sore conflict they were to have with Antichrist, towards the end of all; out of which they should rise again: and then comes the end of both the eastern and western Antichrist, the Turk and the Pope, c. xi. 1, 2, 7--14. Then begins the new book-prophecy c. xii. in new visions, containing the fates of the church in all ages from Christ's time, as the seal-prophecy had done those of the empire.

THE TWELFTH CHAPTER.

The state of the church hath two periods, *The primitive times* including the first four centuries, and *The times of Antichrist:* the *former* may be divided thus, The state of the church until Constantine, the first Christian emperor; and thence under the Arian and other emperors: the *latter* thus, The state of the false church, under the Pope its head; and that of the true church, during the time of that Antichrist, under Christ its head. Now as c. xiii. xiv. shew the state of the church *since* the rise of the

Pope, so this chapter shews its state since, (and that under the two said eminent conditions,) 1st, Under Rome Pagan, until the conversion of the empire by Constantine, (v. 1—12,) represented by *a woman bringing forth a male child,* (that is a Christian emperor,) *to rule all nations;* wherein she is opposed by a dragon, (the devil in the power of an Heathen emperor,) endeavouring to devour her child. The vision and appearance of this woman is such as to fit only the pure primitive state of the church; for though so weak a vessel, yet is she gloriously clothed with the Sun of righteousness; and being honored at her first rise with the preaching of the twelve apostles, and holding forth the light of their doctrine, she binds them on her head as *a crown of twelve stars;* and being above the world, and the rage of Heathenish persecutions, and all things sublunary, (for "they loved not their lives unto death," v. 11,) the *moon* is therefore said to be *under her feet.* Amidst the pangs and throes of ten sore persecutions, she labours with God night and day to bring forth a succession of Christian emperors, who setting Christ to rule in their throne, shall throw down Heathenism from the imperial state, so long subject to the rule of Satan's throne, and therefore represented throughout the Revelation as a *seven-headed and ten-horned dragon.* But while the devil is visibly and openly acting the empire, the church at length prevails to obtain, through the help of Michael and his angels, (i. e. Christ and the apostles, and preachers of their gospel,) his precipitating from the throne, his heaven where he was worshipped as God. 2dly, Is the state of the true church, (v. 13—17,) when the Roman world was turned Christian for the first century, after Constantine; which church was persecuted as much also by the heretical, as she had been by the Heathen emperors; besides being nearly ruined by the multitude of carnal professors; and from these *she hastes to flee into the wilderness* of a hidden retired condition; and in her flight she hath a *flood* of Arian persecution sent after her to *drown* her; but the *earth,* (i. e. the Goths and Vandals, under the first trumpet,) came in accidentally, and through God's providence, *helped* her by breaking the Arian faction, and thus *swallowing up the flood.*

THE THIRTEENTH CHAPTER.

The state of the church, and her conflicts with Satan for the first four hundred years, having been described in the preceding chapter; henceforward is set forth its state during the times of Antichrist, wherein both his false church, and the true church under him, run along together. Now the description of this western Antichrist, (the Pope and his Antichristian church,) in his rise, power, greatness, and extensive dominions and adherents, as set forth in the visions of this chapter, is afterwards interpreted and commented on by the Holy Ghost himself in the seventeenth chapter: the opposite company, or adherents of the true church, who have the Lamb for their head, being described in the fourteenth chapter, in all those several states and conditions they should run under, from the rise of the Papacy until those very times wherein we live; wherewith I take it, the visions of that fourteenth chapter do end. Now Antichrist and his church, is here exhibited under the vision of a two-fold beast, pointing at the Pope, according to his double pretensions of power and headship in the church; viz. 1st, *Temporal*, which he claims over all kings and kingdoms, to depose and excommunicate them and their subjects at his pleasure; and whereunto the ten kings and kingdoms of Europe, (to which the western empire was now by the Goths reduced,) with one consent, tacitly submitted and resigned their power, as is interpreted in c. xvii. 12—17. Thus the Pope, together with the body of these ten kingdoms, joining into one under him as their head, is that first *beast with ten horns*, described v. 1—8; which new beast is a true image of the former Roman monarchy in the twelfth chapter, which being *wounded* and slain in the deposition of the emperors, is *healed* and restored to life again in this beast: and thus the Roman monarchy comes still to continue, though under another head, the Pope; who, 2dly, Besides this temporal power received from these ten kings, (thus together with him making up one beast,) claims also a *spiritual* power, (and his clergy with him,) of binding and loosing so as to pardon sins, and also to curse men to hell; which is peculiar to Christ alone: in this respect he and the body of his false clergy with him, do make up another beast, having two horns like a lamb, as exercising that spiritual power of Christ; for which they and he are properly called *Antichrist*, whose description follows in v. 11—18; for being head of two bodies, ecclesiastical and temporal, he is set forth under the figure of two beasts. Now this spiritual beast, (the Pope and his clergy,) is he who, by his lying doctrines, persuaded the ten kings and their subjects to submit themselves in one body under him as their head; and he is said *to make the image of the first beast*, or dragon, (mentioned in the twelfth chapter, viz. the former Heathenish empire and its idolatrous religion,) which is therefore said to *live again;* for, Not only do these kingdoms become one under the Pope, as their head; being in their very form of government, the image of the former empire, under one emperor, (the Roman monarchy continuing, in this way, still;) But besides, this new beast is called "the image of the first beast," having like form of government and tyranny; and also in that the Pope and his clergy do mould the Christian religion, and its worship, into a true likeness and conformity to the Heathenish religion, whereunto the empire was before framed: for all the Popish worship is but the translating of those ceremonies wherewith the false gods were worshipped, (Jupiter, Apollo, &c. who were cast down under the sixth seal,) into those religious ceremonies in their worship, wherewith they so worship Christ and his saints, that could any of the ancient Heathen Romans come now into their assemblies, and behold their priests in white, their processions, their sprinklings with holy water, their altars, tapers, images of saints departed, and their worship of them, their *Pontifex Maximus*, or great bishop and high-priest, &c. &c. they would cry out and say, "This is just our old Roman Paganism; only *Jupiter* is turned into *Christ*, and the *Priests* of the gods of old into *Popish Bishops;* and our ancient deities, Mars, Janus, Æsculapius, &c. who were *men departed*, are changed for *saints departed:* the life of our old religion remains still, though there be a change of the gods worshipped." Thus as Babel of old made an image, and put to death all that would not fall down before it, (for hereunto is the allusion;) so hath this mystical Babylon set up an image of the old Heathenish religion and worship; and upon the like penalty she enjoins the adoration of his image, and a conformity in worship to all the subjects of these ten kingdoms.

. Now the company who cleave to this beast, and who may more or less be esteemed his followers, are distinguished into three ranks of men in several degrees, (as Mr. Brightman hath well observed on v. 16, 17,) more or less acknowledging him, or cleaving to him, and to this his image and worship; some receiving his *mark* or character; others his *name* only; and others again, the *number of his name:* but so, that those who will not receive or submit to one of these, more or less, during the allotted time of his reign, may not *buy nor sell*, that is, cannot subsist or abide in these his allotted dominions. This *receiving of a mark*, &c. is a similitude drawn from the old Roman custom of printing on the forehead of servants, the names of their masters; and on the hands of soldiers, the names of their emperors or generals: so all those, who belong unto this great lord and his faction, do accordingly more or less receive that whereby they may be known to be his: 1st, Some receive his *character;* as all priests and religious persons do, whether Jesuits or others, who are this Grand Seignieur's Janisaries, his sworn soldiers and prætorian band: their doctrine is, That a man entered into holy orders, doth by his ordination receive an *indelible character*, a secret, invisible, stamp or impress, which can never be rased out. 2dly, Others receive his *name;* and though not in orders under him, yet so cleave to him in his worship, as openly to profess themselves his by appropriation of his name: thus as he is called *Papa* and *Pontifex*, they name themselves *Papists* and *Pontificii.* But, 3dly, What is meant by "*The number of his name?*" this Mr. Brightman carries rightly to a company, taking part with him by a more remote kind of subjection; but not knowing well on whom to fasten it, he brings in the poor Grecians, that are strangers to the Pope, and out of the dominion of any of his ten kingdoms; who, though renouncing all acknowledgment of the Pope as their head, for many hundred years, yet were at last, (through sleights, and the baseness of one of their emperors, together with the conquest that the Europeans made at Constantinople for a while,) so far subjected, as to acknowledge him for their head, and to be called *Latins*, (or of the profession of the Latin Church, by which name some Popish Christians among the Greeks are still distinguished;) so receiving the *number of his name*, LATEINOS, *(Latinus,)* the numeral letters whereof make six hundred and sixty-six, the *number* named in v. 18: But though this forced subjection of the Grecians, so remote, might be intended for those more ancient times, yet I think that it is not only or principally meant: first, Because these Grecian Christians are not inhabitants within the jurisdiction of those ten kingdoms of Europe, the subjects whereof are mainly intended by *the inhabitants of the earth*, (v. 8, 14,) that should be the worshippers of, and cleavers to this beast; of and among whom must be found this "number of his name," as well as those that receive "his name:" And, secondly, Because some of the Christians in the west, (who assist the pouring forth the vials,) are as well said to overcome the number of his name, as others of them do his image, or his idolatrous worship, or his character of lying priests, or the beast himself, as in c. xv. 2. I take it therefore that this "number of his name" must be found in Europe, in some of those ten kingdoms where that company are that pour out the vials.

Now take the times of Popery before the Reformation, (when Protestant kingdoms first began to cast off the Pope;) and none were suffered to have any lax or inferior way of owning the beast; but all received his *mark*, or his *name*, as professed Papists, going to mass, acknowledging the Pope, and worshipping the image; or they could not *buy or sell*, and live quietly as others did. These therefore who receive "the number of his name," must be some generation of men risen up since, within some of those kingdoms that have renounced the Pope: for within the Popish dominions, not only hath the Inquisition suffered none to profess less; but the most moderate Papists have professed, at least, "the *name* of the beast," and therefore more than "the *number* of the name." This "number of his name" then seems to be a company, not proceeding so far as to receive either his *character* or his *name*, by professing themselves either *priests* of Rome, or *Papists;* and yet are they of "*the number of his name*," holding and bringing in such doctrines and opinions, and such rites in worship, as shall make all men reckon, account, or *number* them among Papists in heart and affection; and behaving themselves so as they are, and justly deserve to be accounted and esteemed *Papists*, and to aim at Popery in the judgment of all orthodox and reformed *Protestants*: for though their *profession* deny it; yet when their *actions*, and their corrupting of doctrine and worship, shall speak it to all men's consciences, men cannot but judge that the *Pope*, and the fear of him is before their eyes, Ps. xxxvi. 1: and as those in Titus i. 16, "profess that they know God, but in works they deny him;" so these that shall profess the reformed religion, yet in all their practices and under-hand policies depress it, and advance the Popish party, are justly to be accounted Papists and to have received "the *number of the name*" of the beast. Now the "*number*" of a name is not only taken arithmetically for a name consisting of *numeral letters*, but it is in many languages put for the account, reckoning or esteem that is commonly had of men; as in Latin we speak of "a man *Nullius Numeri*," *of no number*, or account; and so EN POLEMOOI ENARITHMIOS is used by Homer for one *of great account in war*, being *numbered* or esteemed a soldier indeed: so "the number of the name" of the beast, is the common repute or esteem to be a *Papist*, procured though under-hand advancing of the Popish cause. This "*number*" being therefore spoken in a distinct and lower degree from that "*name*," (or open profession,) doth yet necessarily import so much inclining and cleaving to the beast, (though secretly,) as shall deserve the account and repute to be *numbered*, truly in heart, (though but tacitly,) of his company, equally with those that receive his *name*. Now if in opening the meaning of the Holy Ghost in that phrase, this description shall seem to the life to picture out a generation of such kind of Popish persons as these, in any even of the most famous reformed churches, there will not want good ground for it: for though with an impudent forehead, they renounce the Pope's *character*, and the *name* of Papists, and will by no means be called "*Baal's* priests," (though *priests* they affect to be called,) but boast themselves to be of the Reformation, and opposites to the Popish faction; yet with as much impudence do they bring in an *image* of Popish worship and ceremonies, adding to some old limbs never cast out, other substantial parts of altars, crucifixes, second service, &c. so to make up in the public worship a full likeness to that of the Popish church; bringing in the carcase first, which may be afterwards inspired with the same opinions: and all this, not as Popery, or with the annexing of Popish idolatrous opinions, but on such grounds only whereupon *Protestants* themselves have continued some other ceremonies. Furthermore, As in worship, so in doctrines these men seek to introduce a *presence* in the sacrament, of the Lord's supper, beyond what is *spiritual* to faith, which yet is not Popish transubstantiation; and power in priests to forgive sins, beyond what is *declarative*, yet not that which mass-priests arrogate; justification by works, as a condition of the gospel as well as faith, but not so grossly as in a way of Popish merit: by many such methods they truly set up an image of old Popery in a Protestant reformed way, even as Popery is an image of Pagan worship in a Christian way. Say these men what they will, that they hold not of the Pope, nor any way intend him, or the introducing of his religion into their churches, yet their actions *number* them as such, and gain them such esteem every where at home and abroad; as the Holy Ghost prophesied of them, fitting them with so characteristic a description of the "*number of the name*" of the beast. Such sort of apostates from the profession and religion wherein they were trained, being in a church so full of spiritual light and faithful witnesses, the Holy Ghost hath thought worthy of the character given them in this prophecy, to discover to whom they belong, especially seeing they would professedly deny their intention and conspiracy to make way in the end for the beast; this their duplicity going before, as the twilight serves to usher in darkness. And though haply these men will arise but in one of the ten kingdoms, (the Lutherans elsewhere looking also very like this description,) yet growing to so potent a faction as to have power to hinder others *buying* and *selling* and quiet living among them, and being the Pope's last champions before his fall, whom the true saints are to encounter and overcome; (for the greatest number of witnesses in that last age will belong to that one kingdom;) therefore the Holy Ghost thought not fit to leave such a company of new refined Papists out of the beast's number and followers, although they were to continue but a short time; for the doom, as well as description of such a generation to arise "in the *last* days," (of those "*latter times*" of the Papists rising, 1 Tim. iv. 1,) we have in another prophecy, 2 Tim. iii. 1—9: These shall set themselves chiefly against the power and spirit of true worship, setting up "a form" or image instead of it: but they are doomed to "*proceed no further;* they shall have a stop; and their "*folly,*" madness, and hypocrisy, (to attempt to bring in Popery with denying it; and when it is going down to build such a Babel again,) "shall *be manifest unto all men;*" and being discovered will be overthrown: yet must they proceed further than hitherto, even to the "killing of the witnesses" in that kingdom, or tenth part of the city; as will be shewn under c. xi. And because these last champions of the beast, and healers of the wound given him, should come in *the last days of all*, they are therefore last named and overcome by the witnesses and vial-pourers, as in c. xv. 2. Lastly, The Holy Ghost by a wise transition passing from the mention of one thing to another, agreeing in sound but differing in sense, distinguishes the number of the beast *himself* from the number of his *name*, (v. 17, 18,) the former only being six hundred and sixty-six: such a turn is frequent in scripture, and we have it also in c. xx. 17,

"The Spirit and the bride say, *Come,* (as speaking to Christ to come speedily to judgment, as in v. 20,) and let him that is a thirst, *come,* (as spoken of the believing soul coming to Christ,) unto the water of life." As for "the number of the beast," (to calculate which the Holy Ghost encourages and excites us by "*Here is wisdom;*" see also in c. xvii. 9,) while most interpret it of the *numerals* of which LATEINOS, *Latin* or *Roman,* is composed, others refer it to the number of the year, A.D. 1666, according to "the *number* of a man," or as men reckon dates, leaving out the thousands; and so c. xxi. 17, is "according to the *measure* of a man." Thus they date the rise of Antichrist to about A.D. 406—410, (others two centuries later, making his fall about A.D. 1866,) when "the tenth part of the city fell;" France being broken off from the empire, and possessed by the Goths, who restored Rome, (which they had sacked,) on these conditions. In A.D. 412, Honorius granted the same to the Huns, and in A.D. 415, to the Goths in Spain; and by A.D. 456, all the ten kingdoms were up, who "gave their power to the beast," and "received power as kings *one hour* with the beast," c. xvii. 12. Jerome, who lived in the times of that incursion of the barbarous nations, when he saw Rome taken, and the Goths obtaining pieces of the western empire, said in his epistle to Gerontius, "He that held is taken away, (alluding to 2 Thes. ii. 6,) and we understand not that Antichrist is near." By adding therefore twelve hundred and sixty years to any of the above supposed periods of the rise of the beast, we get the supposed date of his fall.

THE SECOND PART.

CONTAINING THE STORY OF THE CHURCH, SINCE HER FIRST SEPARATION FROM THE POPISH ANTICHRIST-BEAST, UNTO THE GLORIOUS KINGDOM OF CHRIST; AS IT IS LAID DOWN FROM THE FOURTEENTH TO THE NINETEENTH CHAPTER; AND IN THE SUPPLEMENTARY ELEVENTH CHAPTER.

INTRODUCTION.

My chief aim in this Exposition being to search into such passages of the Revelation as concern the last days, and to find out under which of these constellations the present times of the church do fall, and what is certainly yet to come; I have therefore been less inquisitive in expounding *The First Part,* as containing events long since past, and have now selected all I find in the *seal* and *book*-prophecy, (enlarging on this happy notion of Mede for understanding the Revelation,) which may refer to present or future times concerning ourselves. Now that I might begin at the right joint, without mangling the whole, I have chosen the state and period of the church's reformation, and of the separation from Popery, where the book-prophecy begins; my Exposition of c. vi.—ix. only making way for the understanding of what is now to follow. To ascertain therefore what belongs to these latter times in this prophecy: 1st, The *seal*-prophecy, (c. vi.—xi.) running over all time from John's days to the kingdom of Christ, (and the passages in c. x. and xi. being the last under the first prophecy,) belongs therefore to the last times, (as shewn in the General Scheme, p. 563—9;) and indeed c. xi. belongs chiefly to the times of the vials in c. xvi. as will hereafter be shewn. 2dly, From c. xiv. 6, of the *book*-prophecy, begins the great restauration of the gospel from under Popery, until Christ's visible and universal kingdom commencing at c. xx. Thus all these passages in the chapters mentioned out of both prophecies, connected in their due place and order, do fitly fall in together, to make the story of the church complete: and as I have given the more general Scheme and Division of this whole book, I shall now give, as the chief key of interpretation,

A PARTICULAR *SCHEME AND DIVISION* PRESENTING, IN THEIR DUE ORDER AND SUCCESSION, ALL THE CONTENTS OF THESE CHAPTERS CONCERNING OUR OWN TIMES.

I shall begin with setting together the materials contained in the said chapters, either as they succeed one after the other, or as they synchronize, and fall in at the same time, one with the other; reserving in part the full proof of my method to the after Exposition: and for the better clearing of this, let us take the two following representations of the church, from the time of her *separation* unto that of the *new Jerusalem;* wherein she is presented, Either, In the *various conditions* she should in herself run through, in her several ages until then, both in respect of the progress of her separation further and further off from Rome, (and so of the increase of her light, purity, and reformation,) and of the persecutions and judgments upon her, and her restitution and deliverance again from under them: Or, In her *one uniform, entire, and general condition* suiting with all those times of the church, first and last, as partaking within herself of like privileges during the same; and also in special reference to the execution of plagues and punishments, (poured out of the seven vials,) on the enemy. The Holy Ghost hath been pleased to represent the story of the church both these ways. *First,* The church's *uniform state* is set forth in c. xv. and xvi. thus: 1st, In c. xv. 2—5, as within herself; 2dly, In v. 6—8, of c. xv. in the common and like description of the angels, or out-pourers of the vials proceeding from those churches: which representation of the church, and of these angels all that whole time, becomes the immediate sign or forerunner, (great and wonderful,) of *the new Jerusalem*, (v. 1, 2,) or that more glorious state of the church to succeed those vials, called in v. 5, "*The opening of the temple of the tabernacle*," (in distinction from the present state of the church, which is the temple of the seven angels, v. 6,) wherein "there was seen the ark of the testament" (Christ himself,) which stands vailed like the Holy of holies, till all the vials are poured out, c. xi. 19. In comparison therefore with the *other* church or temple to come "*after that*," (as v. 5, speaks,) this *present* is but what the inward court of the priests was in comparison of The most holy place. The erection therefore of the one is the immediate forerunning sign of the other, as proved by v. 1, 5. 3dly, In c. xvi. is the execution and effusion of the seven vials, by the angels, out of this church or *inner temple*, erected since the first separation from Antichrist, all along those times unto the new Jerusalem, here exhibited in one view in their several orders and successions. *Secondly*, The church's *chequered state*, is scatteredly represented in *three parts;* the Holy Ghost being pleased thus variously, and in several places to set it forth, (as best suiting to a special end and occasion,) with such descriptive and infallible characters of their times, of the vials they belong unto, and also unto what times of each vial they belong, as cannot deceive us. *The first part* of the story of the various conditions of the church, during the four first vials, is set forth in c. xiv. 6—20; the first erection of the *temple* of true churches beginning at v. 6, when Waldus and his company first fell off from Rome. Now this preceded the vision of the vials, to shew how the *temple* was first built and reared, ere the angels, and their vials, proceeding therefrom, should be mentioned: and therefore c. xiv. shews that first part of the church's story, in all her first comings forth from Antichrist and laying the foundation of churches; but then it breaks off at the time of the fourth vial; for that so far precedes the reformation of the true church, as is respected a separation from Antichrist, and so runs along with such vials as should by degrees first prepare for his ruin, as the first three or four vials do. *The second part* of the church's story is her next state, from the time of the fourth to the fifth vial, supplied from c. xi. 1—14, where this story comes in most fitly, rather than in c. xiv. because it was to be an immediate signal of Antichrist's downfal, and is an exact chronology of the time of the beast's reign, and the expiration of his forty-two months; to warn and comfort the church against a fatal prevailing of Antichrist over her, just afore the time of his ending: so c. xi. begins with a new reformation of the reformed churches among themselves, and what should befall them thereupon, viz. the killing of the witnessses, between the fourth and fifth, or at most before the fifth seal. *The third part* of the church's story from after the fifth seal until the new Jeru-

salem, beginning c. xx. of the book-prophecy
the seal-prophecy,) is presented c. xix. in its due place: For c. xvii. being but an explanation who the beast is, and where his seat, that the church may discern this Antichrist; and c xviii. being a funeral-song for the pouring out of the fifth vial, when the seat of the beast, (that whore, the city described c. xvii.) is ruined, and Antichrist's kingdom is probably over; Therefore the church's state from the fifth vial's ruining Rome to the new Jerusalem, fitly and orderly comes in after both these digressions; and therefore c. xix. thus begins, "And after these things, (after the description of the city and whore, c. xvii. and her ruin,) I heard the voice of an innumerable company," &c. thus going on to describe the state of that church then and until the new Jerusalem. *Lastly,* As the story in c. xiv. contains the *first* reformation and separation of the church from Antichrist, in several degrees; and c. 11 a *second,* from profane mixture within itself; so c. xix. a *third,* or personal reformation of the saints themselves in the church, as then with might and main preparing and adorning themselves for the marriage of the Lamb, so evidently near, now that the whore is cast off and burned: and here you may see them getting all they can of "the fine linen" of holiness and growth in grace, which is "the righteousnesses (DICAIOOMATA,) of saints;" that so their Lord and husband might greatly delight in their beauty, as in c. xix. 7, 8. Such is the true general coherence and order of what yet remains to be interpreted: from which my Introduction will proceed to

THE PARTICULAR SYNCHRONISM *OF THE SEVERAL VISIONS AND* CONTENTS *OF THE ELEVENTH* CHAPTER, *AND FROM THE FOURTEENTH TO THE NINETEENTH* CHAPTER.

According to the above *Scheme and Division,* the vial-visions of c. xv. and xvi. running along the whole course of time, through divers ages, as the visions of c. xiv. 6—20, and c. xi. 1—15, and c. xix. (the one uniformly and continuously, the other in a scattered successive representation of the church's condition all along the same tract of time through many ages:) it will therefore be expedient to shew, which of these several parts of those two representations synchronize, and which are successive; by setting together a little more particularly the stories of the seven vials (in c. xv. and xvi.) with those other several pieces and scattered passages of c. xi. xiv. xvii. xviii. and xix. and, FIRST, With c. xiv. 1st, That same "temple filled with smoke," (out of which came "the seven angels,") began to be set up in the times of the first separation from Antichrist, (see v. 6, with c. xv. 6, 8;) when also "the everlasting gospel" was begun distinctly to be preached by *Waldus* and his followers, who erected true churches unto Christ, (as the history of the Waldenses shews;) when these "harpers on the glassy sea," began more distinctly to "sing the song of Moses and the Lamb;" or that loctrine both of the law and the gospel, which the hundred and orty-four thousand in the darker times of Popery had but muttered so confusedly that none could learn it; (see v. 3, 6, 7, with . xv. 2—4;) so that the doctrine of the gospel, and the erection f the vial-temple, and the separation from popery, all begin ogether. 2dly, Preparation being thus made by the *first* angel's recting the temple, *The first vial* therefore began with the voice f the *second* angel, crying "Babylon is fallen, Babylon is fallen," . e. the first foundation of her ruin is laid in the beginning of hose desolating vials; as will be shewn in opening them; . 6. 8, with c. xvi. 1, 2. *The second vial* follows with the voice or cry of the *third* angel's preaching, when the sea of Antichrist's doctrine was both proved and pronounced *damnable* by *Luther's* doctrine; and "the waters whereon the whore sat," (i.e. those kingdoms and commonwealths which had subjected themselves to Rome,) fell from her; see v. 9—11 with c. vi. 3. *The third vial* hath been a pouring out (as will be shewn) since that "harvest" began, with its summer-weather, and that settled peace of the reformed churches, meant by "rivers and fountains," see v. 14, with c. xvi. 4. *The fourth vial* began about the time of "*the vintage*," for it was excited by an angel "who had power over fire:" and also the fourth vial-angel is said to have power given him to scorch men with fire; so that these two fall in the same times; and thus the times of c. xiv. reach only to the fourth vial; see v. 18, with c. xvi. 8. SECONDLY, With c. xi. synchronizes the age between the third and fourth vial. 1st, This chapter, under the seal-prophecy, (now about the times of the fourth vial,) begins the expiration of the world's monarchy, Antichrist's times, and the church's oppression; and before the blast of the seventh trumpet, v. 15. It opens with representing the same *temple* of the Reformation as the Reformers erected in c. xiv. 15, who having erred in laying an outward court to it, are bidden in the name of John, (who bears the persons of the godly of this age,) to measure that temple anew, as not being fully conformed to the pattern, and to cast out the outward court; for its further reformation. And as in the vintage, (c. xiv. 18,) the Popish Gentiles had "trod down" the grapes in Germany; so here v. I, the like "outward court" in other churches elsewhere, is given to the same Gentiles elsewhere to tread down, and therewith to end their date of treading down the holy city for forty-two months, (or one thousand two hundred and sixty years,) with this their last re-entry upon the churches of the Reformation. Thus c. xi, begins where c. xiv. ends. 2dly, In v. 5, 6, we expressly have the first four vials, (and no more,) briefly summed up in the description of the witnesses, who are thus shewn, in the latter times of their prophecy, to be the same with the vial-pouring angels, c. xvi. 2—9. Now the angels there describe them to John only in a parenthesis, merely that he might recognize them again in this new book-prophecy, to shew what should befall them after these four vials, (or from the time of the fourth, and before the fifth,) in the expiring of the twelve hundred and three-score years, allotted them to prophesy in the *sackcloth* of a mourning condition; now to end with the beast's reign also ending with the fifth vial. Thus v. 7, "When they shall be about to finish their testimony," and to end their prophecy, they that had the power to execute four such vials on the beast's company, before they fatally darken and overcome his kingdom by the fifth vial, must be themselves once more overcome by the beast: which being thus mentioned after the summing up of four of the vials in v. 5, 6, and at the end of their prophecy, and on the expiration of their time of mourning, must therefore be from after, or upon the time of, the fourth vial, or before the fifth, or at furthest with the sixth: and then, v. 13, "the witnesses rise," and "the tenth of the city falls;" which some make the fifth vial of Rome's ruin. 3rdly, "The second woe passeth way," v. 14, (removing the Turkish power and tyranny, c. ix. 12, 13,) which is all one with the sixth vial, (c. xvi. 12, &c.) "drying up Euphrates," or preparing for it. 4thly, v. 15—19, The seventh trumpet that follows begins the seventh vial; v. 19, with c. xvi. 18, 21, and c. x. 6, 7, with c. xvi. 17. 5thly, As under the seventh trumpet comes in "the Holy of holies," or "The opening of the tabernacle of the testimony in heaven in which the ark is seen," v. 19; so in c. xv. 5, after the vials, (META TAUTA, *after these things*,) "the temple of the tabernacle of the testimony in heaven" is said to be opened; that temple out of which the vials come, being but as the inward temple begun to be erected from the first separation, (for else they had had no true churches,) but polluted with the adjoining of the outward court by the Reformers; but under the times of the fourth vial it is measured and purged, and "its court cast out," v. 1. THIRDLY, Chap. xix. supplies what should befall the church from the rising of the witnesses, (about the fifth vial,) and also her condition from that space between the fifth vial, and the seventh trumpet, and the Holy of holies; (for c. xi. doth setly describe only what befell the church just before the dethronement of Antichrist, as a warning signal:) Now it begins with an innumerable company in heaven praising God for the downfal of the whore, (at large set forth in c. xvii. and xviii. which are but a larger explication of the fifth vial ruining Rome;) and therefore it must set forth the state of the church after the fifth vial until the seventh: And then for the agreement of that great battle, at the Lamb's marriage-supper, with the seventh vial, see v. 11—21, with c. xvi. 14—21; after which come in "the thousand years," and "new Jerusalem," (which is all one with the Holy of holies,) c. xx.—xxii. Having thus introduced the second part of my Exposition, I shall now proceed with

THE FOURTEENTH CHAPTER.

As c. xiii. described the false Antichrist-church, whose head is the Pope, so here begins the description of the true church contemporary, (made up of "the seed of the woman," c. xii. 17, persecuted by Satan through Antichrist's power, during her hiding in the wilderness,) whose head is the Lamb, and whose condition from Antichrist's time until this day, may be reduced to three heads. 1st, Her state in those darker times of Popery, when she was mingled with Papists, though preserved from much of their idolatrous worship and opinions, for seven centuries from the Pope's first rising, until the gospel-light bursting forth more clearly, made an open separation between this confused company, v. 1—5. 2dly, Her state in three several degrees, rising higher and higher, presented under three several angels; when believers first separated from Rome, and created churches and assemblies by themselves, and preached the gospel, from A.D. 1100, v. 6—13. 3rdly, Her state under the Reformation, since the times of Luther and Calvin, for the last three hundred years, v. 14—20.

First, The state of believers mixed up with Antichrist's company, without any distinct worship, though opposed to his gross idolatries, is set forth characteristically, (v. 1,) as a scattered company of "*a hundred forty and four thousand*," united to the Lamb, having *his Father's name written on their foreheads*, (i.e. professing sincere obedience and worship to the true God,) whilst a world of the rest went "a wondering after the beast," having received his mark, c. xiii. 3, 17. These, and the Christians in the east under the Mahometan darkness and bondage of the fifth and sixth trumpets, are set forth by the same number, both being companies of persons singly to be numbered, and scattered up and down, here and there, in the midst of the growing superstitions and corruptions of their two several eastern and western churches, until A.D. 1100. These "*stand upon mount Zion*," called David's city, as not yet having a temple, or instituted churches distinct from Antichrist: and though, (v. 3,) "*they sung as it were a* new *song*," (the truth of the gospel they believed,) yet so confusedly and indistinctly as that "*no man could learn that song*," or understand that they differed from them; the other Papists still going on in their *old* way, while the voices of these were heard secretly "*before the throne, and before the four beasts, and the elders*," (the representative chorus, as a standing company viewing all the visions of this book,) but themselves were not cast into such order of worship as to have churches and officers to begin the song, (as the four beasts elsewhere do, the four and twenty elders following,) their voices being sometimes "*as the voice of many waters*," confusedly murmuring against superstitions daily arising in those times; and "*as the voice of a great thunder*," thundering aloud against setting up of images, A.D. 707, both in France and Germany, and against transubstantiation; and sometimes as "*harpers harping with their harps*," in sweet melodious strains of true devotion, (which believers, and some writers in those times, were full of:) These kept themselves from the gross idolatries of the whore, being "*not defiled with* (the rest of those) *women*," living in the daughter-cities and kingdoms of Rome, and allured to her and their spiritual fornication; v. 2, 4.

Secondly, Having moulded this and the following chapters, according to the Introduction, the Second Part of my Exposition properly begins here with the story of the church's first separation from Popery, before the Reformation, v. 6—13; the scope of the Holy Ghost to the end of the chapter being only to shew, by what degrees the gospel should break forth, and how churches should at first be erected, and a glorious reformation made; therefore v. 6—20, reaches only to the times of that prevailing again of the beast over those churches after this reformation, (more fully shewn forth, c. xi.) about the times of the fourth vial executed by "the angel that hath power over fire," v. 18. Now when the Holy Ghost had here given the story of this first separation and reformation, as sufficient to shew the foundation and progress of this new temple and true church, erected in opposition to the false one; he breaks off, and presents the general and common condition and station of believers in this newly-erected temple-church, separated from the doctrine and worship of the beast; and also shews the judgments to be executed on the false church all that while, until the kingdom of Christ; and this entirely together in one view in c. xv. and xvi. The church's breaking forth therefore from under Antichrist, and so coming out of Babylon and Egypt, unto Antichrist's second prevailing in c. xi. hath three degrees orderly set forth, as light increased, from the olden times before Luther. The voice and cry of three angels, (all the great things done in the church and world throughout this book, are still said to be effected by the ministry of angels,) rise higher and higher, and louder and louder, against Antichrist and his company. *The* FIRST *angel*, who lays the foundation of all, is said to have "*the everlasting gospel to preach unto them that dwell on the earth, and to every nation and tongue and people*," his voice reaching to all, as he is seen "*flying in the midst of heaven*," and calling on men to worship and "*fear God*, (and him only,) *who made heaven and earth*," v. 6, 7: So that the matter of his preaching is *the gospel*, which brings to light the *free-grace* of God in Christ for a sinner's justification, and also the *true worship* of this God alone, (withdrawing men from idolatry, and false worship of saints and angels, then overwhelming the world;) and because this was then called "The *new* gospel," the Holy Ghost in opposition to the calumny, calls it "The *everlasting* gospel," which was now restored and brought to light: By the preaching of these two things, the foundation of the whole separation from the Pope that followed, was first laid. Now this first angel's ministry is a lively description of the first proceedings of *Waldus* and his followers, who first began to separate from Popish doctrine and worship. He was an alderman of Lyons, in France, and about A.D. 1100, being converted on occasion of the sudden death of a friend, as they were walking together, (which mightily terrifying and amazing him, was a means of humbling him and bringing him to Christ,) he fell a preaching in that city, and converted many others to the saving knowledge of Christ. Being also a learned man he opened the scriptures, and turned them into vulgar French; and thinking it his duty, with his followers, like the apostles to preach the gospel to others also, some of their company went preaching abroad, but were prohibited by the Pope as being lay-men: but they, affirming "That it is better to obey God than men," and that it was also an article of their faith, "That it is lawful for any man to preach the gospel," went on their begun course amidst persecutions. Now as it was an occasion of further spreading the gospel to other nations, when persecution arose on the death of Stephen, and after the dispersion of the church of Jerusalem; thus Waldus, being excommunicated, came into Picardy, and so into the low countries, where he made many disciples, and then went into Germany, and last of all into Bohemia; and his followers were dispersed into Savoy, Lombardy, and the countries on this side of the Alps; and Arnoldus his companion went into Spain. "These Waldenses, (says Poplinerius, the historian,) maugre the power of all Christian princes, about A.D. 1100, did broach a doctrine little differing from what the Protestants now hold; and not only dispersed it through France, but over all the parts of Europe:" Thus they professedly "preached to all nations" the only gospel-doctrine which can draw men from idolatry to worship God aright, as in v. 7: see the English history of the Waldenses, and Bishop Usher's book "*De Successione Ecclesiæ*." In an age or two following, their number increasing in all kingdoms, and their light growing clearer, there follows out of this company, (v. 8,) *The SECOND angel*, with open mouth proclaiming, That *Rome* was *Babylon*, and the *Pope* that *beast* and *Antichrist* described in the Revelation, and ordained to ruin: but Waldus at first merely muttered, *That the Pope was only equal to all other bishops;* his followers in the next ages asserting, *That the church of Rome was the whore of Babylon*, and making this an eminent article of their confession. But Wickliffe and his followers, about A.D. 1371, in England, and John Huss and Jerome of Prague, A.D. 1400, more fully exposed Rome and the Pope: whereupon appears *The THIRD angel*, (v. 9—12,) vehementer still: for *Luther* and his followers avowed, That all who cleave to the doctrine and superstition of Rome, "*shall drink of the wrath of*

God for ever," and be certainly damned and go to hell ; for that her worship being "the image of the beast," was so manifestly a lie, that under the clear light of the gospel in that age held forth, it could never stand with salvation to live therein : and thus he urged a separation from Rome under pain of damnation. In v. 12, 13, an intimation hereupon follows, (and that once for all,) concerning those martyrdoms and bloody persecutions of all the three angels and their followers, as the effect of their preaching, and as a trial of the truth of their doctrine, and of their own sincerity: "*Here is* (matter for the trial of) *the patience of the saints,*" who are comforted by this encouraging acclamation, "*Blessed are those that die in the Lord.*" The book of Martyrs informs us what persecutions were raised upon the preaching of all these angels, (the church in the dark times of Popery, for eight centuries before, back to the times of the Pagan and Arian persecutions, having been unmolested;) whence followed the martyrdoms of the followers of Waldus, Wickliffe, Huss, and Luther, and of those that embraced their doctrine, especially upon and after this third angel's preaching.

Thirdly, The state of the church at the time of the Reformation, since Luther, Calvin, &c. is presented under the double vision of a *harvest,* and of a *vintage* used to come after harvesting. *The harvest* betokens that glorious peace and sunshine of the gospel, following the persecutions in Germany, England, &c. for more than sixty years, v. 14—16. The conversion and gathering in of the elect by preaching, is called a *harvesting* of souls; as in Isa. xxvii. 12. 13, (compare John iv. 35—39,) where God threshes the corn growing by the shores, so clean as to be gatherered singly, not leaving one grain of the election, nor one ear unreaped: and what glorious harvest-summers of grace has Great Britain had since the third angel's gospel-voice, under the authority of kings and magistrates! Here the sickle-bearing reaper is represented "*with a golden crown ;*" Christ "the Son of man" being visibly set in the throne, ruling Christian magistrates who use their influences for him : the like expressions are found when the emperors turned Christians; see c. vi. 2, with xii. 5. *The Vintage,* (v. 17—20,) after the harvest of the Reformation, at the end of summer, shuts up the story of the two visions; wherein after the gathering in of the corn, God falls upon the wild grapes and cuts them down with the sharp sickle of vengeance, casting them into "*the wine-press of God's wrath:*" These are carnal Protestants who have enjoyed the heat of this fair long summer, and hung like grapes in the sun; but retaining their sourness, have been ripened only for wrath and vengeance. This sharp sickle hath gone up and down in Germany for well nigh twenty years, from A.D. 1620, followed by such a wine-press of pure wrath, and such a treading down to such an overflow of blood and misery, as hath scarce been parallelled in any age; for it is "the vengeance of the temple" defiled by a profane mixture, whereunto her executioner is provoked by the cries of "an angel that came from the altar," zealous for the ordinances of God's worship; and as indignant that his temple and altar should be pestered and defiled with such as call themselves *the church*, (saying, "The temple of the Lord," &c. and so causing God's name to be blasphemed,) as that idol-Papists (called *Gentiles*, c. xi. 1,) should tread down his holy city and sanctuary; for all are as bad as Gentiles "who say they are Jews and are not, but do lie," c. iii. 9. Now that the vengeance here should be meant of this execution of it upon the Protestant party, (or enemies within the church,) seems evident from its wine-press being trodden "without the city," or jurisdiction of Rome; and from its being mentioned apart from the vials on the Turkish and Popish party, that follow: and although, so far as there hath befallen, (through the German wars,) a plague on the Popish party, (the emperor and these Popish princes under him,) this wrath is to be reduced to one of the vials containing all the last plagues on the Papacy, specially the *fourth*; yet so far as these wars have brought miseries and desolation on the Protestant party, it is represented by this vintage: and therefore it is the angel "*who had power over fire*," (as the angel of the *waters* hath the *third* vial,) because he hath power "to scorch men with fire," (c. xvi. 5—8,) it is he incites this angel here to cut down these grapes with his sharp sickle, and tread them: So that this vintage though contemporaneous, is a distinct execution from that of the fourth vial: these wars so far as they hurt the Popish party, being *the fourth vial*, and so far as they hurt the Protestant party, they are the famous vintage here meant, (as in Isa. lxiii. 1,) trodden by the famous *German war-horses:* and the "*thousand six hundred furlongs*" may agree with the dimensions of the chief seat of these wars in the Protestant part of Germany: But God may bring this wine-press into other vineyards, as England, Scotland, &c. treading down our grapes, or theirs, by bloody wars, keeping still to the same proportion of furlongs, (as Brightman reckons the length of England,) and fulfilling it over and over in other several Protestant kingdoms and dominions: only this may be more confidently affirmed, That the rest of those carnal Protestants in England, and other places, shall yet, before the expiration of the beast's kingdom and "number," be more or less given up to the Papists, and to the jurisdiction of Rome; being trodden down and made to vail to them, if not all of them by bloody wars and conquests, yet by some base and unworthy yielding to them, as a just punishment of their carnal profession of the gospel: This we see they begin to do in England, as foretold, c. xi. 1; which chapter being a fore-running signal of the beast's ruin, and the now approaching expiration of his twelve hundred and sixty years' reign, presents the state of the church just before; and the setting down what should befall it, c. xi. 7—13, must belong to these times, as to be subjoined to this fourteenth chapter, (though coming in there as a common signal of the ending of both prophecies, and therefore standing between both,) to make the story of the church complete: and this I shall handle after opening the meaning of the first four vials especially, which though for order put by the Holy Ghost with the rest, (as in this book things of a sort use to be,) after this chapter; yet they have been a pouring forth upon the beast and his company, from that first preaching of the gospel until now: and these vials I would open before c. xi. as synchronizing with this chapter, and because four vials are poured out, (c. xi.) before the slaying of the witnesses; which cannot be understood till these be first explained.

THE FIFTEENTH CHAPTER.

The Holy Ghost having thus first of all shewed how the Reformation from Popery was to be brought about, and churches erected, here begins to lay before us the uniform state of believers, in this *temple*, and the several degrees of their ruining the false church by several vials: and this, as set together in one continued view throughout all these times, since the first separation from Popery until Christ's kingdom. Concerning which in general, I shall premise three things: *First*, The difference of their condition here, and of the churches under the dark times of Popery, as is uniformly described c. xiv. 1—5. 1st, Those in c. xiv. were virgins, but not separate; but these stand here alone in a temple by themselves, washing themselves from the defilements of Popery, as separated therefrom. 2dly, Those sung a new song confusedly, but these sing "the song of Moses and the Lamb," (law and gospel,) distinctly. 3dly, Those there stood naked on the hill of Zion ere a temple was reared thereon; but these here are gathered into a temple, and roofed over their heads. 4thly, Those sung their song in Egypt; but these are come out of Egypt, and so sing Moses' song. *Secondly*, These seven angels and their vials, and this company here, are called in the preface to their general description, v. 1, "*Another sign great and marvellous.*" 1st, It is a *sign*, which always fore-runs something to come, as here v. 5, "*After* (these vials) *the temple of the tabernacle of the testimony was opened in heaven;*" these vials then are the sign of that glorious Holy of holies to come after, or of the new Jerusalem and of Christ's coming; as "the sign of the Son of man," spoken of in Matt. xxiv. 30; the prophets also describing his progress with plagues and pestilence preceding; and therefore at the approach of the last vial, c. xvi. 15, warning is given, "Behold, I come as a thief." 2dly, It is *another* sign; *that* in c. xii. 3, being the devil's expulsion from Heathenism, *this* from Popery at Christ's coming to set up his kingdom: so that we of this age stand in the midst of the times of those vials, and so may see how much of Christ's train is gone before, and what is to come after, himself being to come in the rear of all. *Thirdly*, They are all called "*The last plagues*:" Christ had three sorts of enemies to subdue by three several sorts of plagues; 1st, *Satan* and his false worship, together with the Heathenish empire; despatched by the six seals, c. vi. 2dly, The *Roman empire*, ruined by the six trumpets. 3dly, The *Pope* in the west, and the *Turk* in the east, who succeed in the place of the eastern and western empires: for whom he hath prepared seven vials, or *last plagues* on these *last enemies.*

To descend more particularly to the several contents of this chapter, There are two things here eminently presented to our view: *The church*, or company of believers standing in the temple, described v. 2, 3, 4, 8; and *The angels*, who are executioners of the vials out of that temple, described v. 6, 7. *First*, For the company from among whom the angels come: 1st, They have a temple over their heads, continually "*filled with smoke*," as in 1 Kings viii. 10, 11; Ex. xl. 34, 35; to shew that during the vials there should be new editions and erections and reformations of this temple; unto all which God still gives the testimony of his presence: as 1, In the first separation from Popery, when true churches were set up by the Waldenses; and smoke filled their temples. 2, In the Reformation under Luther and Calvin, when there was a further edition of the temple; and smoke filled it afresh. 3, In that after Reformation and casting away the outward court, in c. xi. 1, when smoke will afresh fill these new measured temples also; God still giving new testimonies of his presence, as there come forth new editions of purer churches. 2dly, They are stationed in the temple "*upon a sea of glass*," (v. 2, with c. iv. 6,) in allusion to Solomon's brazen sea for the priests; shewing, That this company of believers whence the vials issue, should more and more purify themselves in their several ages from Antichristian defilements of doctrine and worship: and as they discover many and further defilements in their several successions, they are still presented as coming forth out of the sea of glass from the washing, afresh and anew, purer and purer, until they become a bride fully prepared for their Lord and King. 3dly, They become victors through pouring forth these vials, and in the end shall fully prevail "*over the beast, and his image, and his mark, and over the number of his name*," (v. 2,) these being the more gross or refined degrees of Popery and Antichristianism; all which also they gradually and successively go on to discover and to overcome, until they have got a full and perfect conquest over all by the time these vials are all poured out. Mr. Brightman understands it not of this company getting a complete victory over all those before the vials began, but only successively and conjunctively, as generally descriptive of what they should effect by the expiration of their whole time, being victorious after the effusion of their vials: so in v. 1, "*In them is filled up*, (fulfilled) *the wrath of God*," meaning, that when they are all emptied, God's wrath will be thoroughly exercised and fulfilled through them and by them: so here is not a full victory previously, but in and through the pourings out of these vials obtained ere their expiration; themselves being the means of their conquest; for each degree of which victory they sing a triumphant song: for, 4thly, "*They sing the song of Moses*," (Ex. xv.) after drowning the Egyptians, (Papists,) in the Red Sea, when the fifth vial comes; the former vials being in allusion to the plagues of Egypt: but after that they will sing the marriage-song of the Lamb, (c. xix. 6, 7,) coming in after Rome's funeral-song under the fifth vial, c. xviii. Or, Moses' song, (Deut. xxxii.) being doctrinal, it may refer to the doctrine of the gospel now beginning to be more clearly taught; which is here therefore still called a song; and though in the dark ages of Popery, God's elect "sung as it were a *new song*, differing from Popish doctrine: yet was it so confusedly "that none could learn that song: but now that they have "the everlasting gospel to preach," (see c. xiv. 3, 6,) they sing Moses' song and the Lamb's, distinctly, preaching the law and the gospel clearly and rightly; "*for thy judgments*, (or *justifications*, DICAIOOMATA, as Rom. viii. 4,) *are made manifest*," v. 4; (justification by Christ, and the work of redemption, being eminently revealed and made known in the time of these vials:) These do besides set up Christ both in himself and in relation to his church, as "*The Lord Almighty*," and thus her only ruler; "*The King of Saints*," and thus her only law-giver; "*The only Holy One*," and thus the fountain of all her grace, at once to be believed in and worshipped: They magnify, nor saints, nor temples, nor the Pope, nor any else; but say, (as Jer. x. 7, in opposition also to false gods, "*Who will not fear thee*,"? worshipping after God's own ways in his own word, and not after men's inventions and superstitions; for "*just and true are thy ways*," see v. 3, 4. *Secondly*, For the description of these angels and their preparation to pour out the vials, v. 6, 7, (see c. xvi.) They are "*cloathed in white*," as priests, and "*girt with golden girdles*" of alacrity, strength, sincerity, and truth: and "*one of the four beasts*," (church-officers,) is said to give to the angels these vials, filled up, in their several successions, by theirs and the church's prayers, (c. v. 8;) the plagues executed being in the vials; (as in Ps. lxxv. 8, "there is a cup in the hand of the Lord," as Rome's sin is "a cup of abominations," c. xvii. 4;) and the vials being "*full of the wrath of God* that liveth for ever and ever;" for that these plagues being spiritual as well as corporal, (as I shall shew,) are but the beginnings of an everlasting wrath, as Sodom's is called by Jude, "an everlasting fire." Again, These vials "*come out of the temple*," or Christian churches, which some have mistaken for "the temple of the tabernacle of the testimony," (v. 5,) which is the Holy of holies, and the opening of which relates only to the discovery of *the ark* therein, the vials having been previously poured out, as in c. xi. 5, 6, 19; the fifth being after the rising of the witnesses; and the sixth is the passing away of the second woe; the seventh also being the same as the seventh trumpet; and then, The most holy place is unvailed: So here this tabernacle is opened "after these things" (or vials;) META TAUTA in this book always shewing successive performances and different visions, as in c. iv. 1; vii. 9; and the mention of it comes in here only to shew the event of these vials. This temple of the priests whence the angels issue, being "*filled with smoke from the glory of God and from his power*," betokens God's special, glorious, and powerful presence in and with the church during the times of the vials: and this smoke, (of which that at the dedication of the temple was a sign,) signifies 1st, The divine *presence* in Christian assemblies, (as foreshewn in Isa. iv. 5,) and God's *glory*, as in Isa. vi. 1; making together "*his glorious presence*." 2dly, The divine *defence* and protection "*from the power of the Lord*," as in Isa. iv. 5, 6. 3dly, The divine *offence*, as in Ps. xviii. 8: and so one probable meaning of "*No man was able to enter into the temple*," is, That whereas God poured forth and rained abroad upon the enemies of his church plague-vials of wrath, (against which this temple and the horns of its altar, were the only refuge and covert,) he so hardens his Popish enemies, (as we read in the vials,) that they are kept from joining his temple, and so perish by the plagues, not entering in "*till the seven plagues were fulfilled*," i. e. *never*; for so "*until*" signifies also in Gen. viii. 7; 1 Sam. xv. 35; Ps. cxii. 8; Matt. i. 25; Acts iii. 21.

THE SIXTEENTH CHAPTER.

THE LAST TWO VIALS, following the execution of the five first in v. 1—11, do fall on the beast, (the Pope and his adherents,) whom God plagues by degrees, as he did the Egyptians, until the fifth vial falling eminently on *Rome*, the *seat* of the beast, so darkens his kingdom and despoils it of its glory and power, (although it may remain for Christ himself at his coming, under the seventh vial, to have the last blow at him, and the full glory of the conquest,) as that the period of his power to *do*, [POIEIN c. xiii. 5,] for forty-two months, is there set, and the date of his lease expired: these therefore being further off to come, (the seventh vial and the preparation unto it, from v. 13, belonging to, and immediately making way for the kingdom of Christ,) I shall but briefly touch upon and despatch them first: the others, (especially the fourth and fifth,) concerning these times, and chiefly serving for the opening of the eleventh chapter, I shall treat more largely upon.

THE SIXTH VIAL, v. 12, is "*upon the great river Euphrates*," (i. e. the first seat of the Turk, [c. ix. 14, Is. viii. 7,] which the sixth trumpet left standing in the east,) which is to be "*dried up, that the way of the kings of the east might be prepared*," and so the Jews go to re-possess their own land, as in Isa. xii. 13—16.

THE SEVENTH VIAL, v. 17, is general, upon "*the air*," or whole power of Satan, (Eph. II. 2,) all the world over: The relics both of Turk and Pope, and of all the church's enemies *everywhere*, (as in v. 14,) mustering all their forces against the Christians in the west and the Jews in the east, and being overcome by Christ himself and his armies, (as in c. xix. 11—21,) explain this last vial on the world; the fifth vial, (the most eminent on the beast,) being explained in v. 18. Now for the true understanding of

THE FIRST FIVE VIALS, upon the beast Antichrist and his adherents, I shall premise these seven things: 1st, Their *times* began with the first separation from Rome in c. xiv. 6, and thus contain all those steps and degrees of ruining Antichrist, first and last, from the church's onset to come out and separate from this *Egypt;* to whose plagues the first three vials allude, as in the next premise: *Besides*, All these discoveries of the whore's nakedness, and the falling off of these kingdoms from her, (although they for a time should begin to court her again,) must surely be reckoned among the vials, being almost as great plagues as will yet befall her, except that of her last ruin: *Again*, In the vintage of c. xiv. the angel of the fourth vial is mentioned, the times after which must belong to the three preceding vials; and the Holy Ghost hath not left us without some character to discern the time of their beginning, whether at the harvest, or at the voices of these angels that made the separation; the song of the church, in the story of that chapter, when the vials begin, being (as in c. xv. 4,) "Who shall not fear thee, O Lord, and glorify thy name? for all nations shall come and worship before thee, for thy judgments are made manifest," &c. this being one of the two meanings, That the plagues of these vials now beginning, God's judgment are being made manifest. Now the voice and message of the first angel, (who began the separation from Antichrist, and the preaching everywhere,) unto all nations (c. xiv. 6, 7,) is, "Fear God and give glory to him, for the hour of his judgment is come; and worship him who hath made heaven and earth:" .his was but the beginning to warn Antichrist and his company of the vials' approaching; but by the second angel's voice we find that the first vial began as the effect of these two angels' preaching; for that voice not only calls Rome *Babylon*, and discovers the Pope to be *Antichrist*, but says "Babylon is fallen, is fallen:" i. e. the foundation of her ruin is laid; the superstitious world not before suspecting this "man of sin," 2 Thes. ii. 3--10: so the western empire is reckoned as taken away at the beginning of the wars of the Goths, and when the first of the ten kingdoms was broken off from the empire, A.D. 410, (as in p. 603;) and the Pope may from that time be reckoned to rise with his ten horns, though his ten kingdoms were not fully erected for forty years after, and the power of the western empire not wholly extinct till seventy years after: So Isa. xxi. 9, speaks in the same words of old Babylon, when the Medes first revolted, and began to set up a kingdom of their own, which was afterwards thereby to destroy her: Thus the first open and professed revolts from Rome made by our predecessors, laid the foundation of her fall in this beginning of the first of the vials ordained to ruin her. 2dly, These *vials* are expressed in allusion to *the plagues of Egypt*, which at first not so great, ended in the Egyptians' being drowned in the red sea, as these terminate in the subversion of Antichrist's seat: The *first* is upon the *earth*, effecting a very noisome and grievous sore on those with the beast's mark, in allusion to the *dust* thrown in the air, causing a botch on man and beast in Egypt: The *second* is on the *sea*, and "on the waters thereof;" and as the Egyptian rivers were turned by Moses into *blood*, so The *third* doth also turn to blood "the *rivers and fountains*;" both being bloody vials: The *fourth* is upon the *sun*, and "tormenteth men with *fire*, like Sodom, (as the Antichrist-state is called, c. xi. 5, 6;) or in allusion to Num. xvi. 35. 3dly, As in the trumpets the Holy Ghost compared the empire to *a world*, so the several parts of the beast's kingdom to be plagued are here compared to several parts of the world: and as the first four trumpets, (on the *earth*, *sea*, *rivers*, and *sun*,) were so many degrees of ruining the western empire, so are these vials of ruining the beast's world or empire: and as it was there shewed, that kingdoms or bodies of men are in scripture usually compared to a world, with its heaven and earth and sun and stars, &c. so in the Pagan and Papal empire, and its parts and divisions. 4thly, The Pope and his company in c. xiii. were resembled by a *double beast*, one representing the *political* state of the ten kingdoms, making it one body under that head; the other, the *spiritual* state of his church and clergy, making up a distinct body under one high-priest and spiritual head: so this his *earth* and *rivers* and *sun*, (the parts of these his kingdoms,) according to the analogy of this representation, may be interpreted either *politically* or *spiritually*. 5thly, The beast's kingdom being called "*spiritually, Sodom and Egypt*,"in c. xi. 8, in referrence to those very plagues of the vials there enumerated, v. 5, 6; as it is a state claiming spiritual jurisdiction in spiritual things, and over "the *souls* of men," (c. xviii. 13,) and in things *outward* and political *in order to things spiritual, In Ordine Ad Spiritualia;* these plagues-vials on this Egyptian and Sodomitish city must therefore be spiritual on the *souls* of Antichrist's adherents, as well as outward; "the righteous Lord," (v. 5,) proportioning their plagues to their sins, and so "doubling unto her double according to her works," c. xviii. 6. It is not enough that this monarchy be ruined only outwardly; for this beast hath sinned in assuming spiritual power, pomp, and glory, as well as external dominion, in Christ's name; she traded in spirituals, as well as "in gold and precious stones," &c. and therefore the highest judgment in both shall befall her; as "hardness of heart" was called "a sending all God's plagues on the Egyptians' hearts." I mention the first four vials especially, as enumerated in c. xi. 5, 6, where they are *spiritual*, as here they are *outward* plagues; and so both are included. 6thly, Though the vials are successive, and have a *precise* time for their *eminent* effusion and execution, yet *sprinklings* of the one may continue under the following; as the *sores* under the first vial are mentioned under the fifth, v. 11; so the *blasphemy* of the fourth vial is heightened under the fifth: again, some *droppings* of a succeeding vial may begin in the preceding, as before the strength and fulness of a storm: though the fulness of each vial hath a special time in its due order of succession. 7thly, All the plagues on the Popish party, first and last, are reducible to one of these vials; for they are "the last plagues (c. xv. 1,) in which the wrath of God is fulfilled" upon that party: and so every drop and sprinkling of wrath and vexation poured out, goes to fill up some vial or other, as a part of it.

THE FIRST VIAL, v. 2, is principally on the beast's *earth*, the lowest part of his spiritual and political kingdom, and was the effect of the first two angels' preaching, and specially the second, in c. xiv. for the preaching of the gospel and the discovery of the Pope to be *that Antichrist*, drew away many *inferior* subjects in all the ten kingdoms of his *political earth;* so that his authority and interest throughout Europe was weakened, and the number of his worshippers lessened; all the world not now going after the beast without contradiction, as they were wont: This vial affected also his *spiritual earth*, or clergy; for by the preaching of the Waldenses, the uncleanness, idleness, and hypocrisy, of the priests, monks, and nuns, (the beast's enchanters,) were discovered; and these cast dust in their faces, as Moses did, so that "*there fell a noisome and grievous sore upon the men that had the mark of the beast*," viz. his *clergy*, who being exempted from the civil power, are his special subjects and sworn vassals, receiving from him *an indelible character by ordination*, (see p. 599,) and who "*worshiped his image*," as upholders of his idolatrous doctrine: Now all those first gospellers, before Luther, made it the chief subject and end of all their writings and disputes, to render odious and vile the Pharisaical Popish clergy: Nor was this judgment merely outward, in a discovery of the shame of their hateful and abominable iniquities, thus making way in all men's hearts for their ruin; but the light of these preachers proved a curse in order to their breaking forth in filthiness and botches;

God giving them up, in judgment for shutting their eyes against the gospel, to the curse of all uncleanness, Sodomy &c. so as to commit all sin, and that with more greediness than ever, as did the Gentiles, in Rom. i. 24, &c.

THE SECOND VIAL, v. 3, is upon the *sea*, on the *third* angel's preaching, &c. *Luther* and his followers; who being raised up to a still greater light, became a further plague both upon the political and spiritual *sea* of the beast, or his jurisdiction over many people, (as in p. 593,) those "peoples, and multitudes, and nations, and tongues," in c. xvii. 15. Now after Luther's preaching and his followers, not only particular persons (as before) were divided from the Pope, but whole nations were rent from him, (as England, Germany, Sweden, Scotland, &c.) and his sea lessened by a third part and more; some of the ten horns of the beast being wrung off, as when members are divided from the body, and "*as the blood of a dead man:*" and because the Popish faction could no longer, through the alteration of religion by law, live quietly, soberly, and peaceably in their idolatrous worship, "*every living soul died in the sea,*" thus divided from him; there was no free living or breathing for them in those seceding kingdoms: His *spiritual sea* also had a vial poured upon it, even his abominable doctrine and worship, *purgatory*, *indulgences*, *merit*, *&c.* in which sea his *merchants* (the priests) had brought in gain both to themselves and to the Pope's custom-house, c. xviii. 15. this sea is turned into putrifying blood of a corpse, so that those who, after such a clear light of the gospel, will still continue in that damnable doctrine, die and perish eternally, as again in v. 3, and as in c. xiv. 9—11, where the third angel preacheth, not only with the former angel, That Rome is *Babylon*, but That "if any worshipped the beast or his image, the same should drink of the wine of God's wrath" in hell, where "the smoke of their torment ascendeth up for ever and ever;" for they shall be sure to be all damned who know the truth but embrace it not: and this was a further spiritual judgment on them, beyond what their doctrine was unto them in former times, wherein men remaining through ignorance, many more of them were then saved than now there are.

THE THIRD VIAL, v. 4—7, is upon "the rivers and fountains," serving to enlarge, or anywise recover or sweeten his *sea* again by their influx. 1st. These "*fountains*" are the lesser springs, Either, *spiritual* ones; (for when the Egyptians' waters were turned into blood, they dug fountains and wells, which were turned by Moses into blood: and so when the Papists' sea is become bloody, they dig fountains of their writings to live in; their writers since the Reformation, labouring with their learning and eloquence to sweeten and make good some of their sea-waters again; [but in vain;] our writers again confuting them and turning all into blood, as it was before; so that those among them that shall read both, must be convinced that they will be damned, [2 Thes. ii. 12,] if they persist still in their doctrine:) Or, *temporal* and political also, such as the Jesuits and others, who have attempted in all those seceded kingdoms, to restore his lost power and jurisdiction: and many of the *lesser springs, (individuals* among them,) have been turned into blood, by the enactment of laws, (in England, A.D. 1581 and 1605; in Holland, A.D. 1586; in France, A.D. 1584;) cutting off many of them, and "*giving them* the *blood* of martyrdom *to drink;*" so that they have a martyrology as well as we; and are justly rewarded, as cries, "the angel from the altar" (v. 7,) viz. the true worshippers and priests of the altar, whose prayers having procured these edicts, they now return praise to God's justice in retaliating to them and on them: for "*the altar*" here and c. xiv. 18, may signify *worship*, as it doth *martyrdom* in c. vi. 9. 2dly, These "*rivers*" and greater streams, are those armadoes and navies from out of the sea of these kingdoms that continue still to uphold the beast, endeavouring to lay all kingdoms into this one sea again; as the Spaniards, sent out to regain Rome's jurisdiction against England, A.D. 1588, and against Holland often since, but still defeated; as was also that navy, A.D. 1639, being a *sprinkling* of this vial still going on in those times of

THE FOURTH VIAL, "upon the sun," v. 8, 9; and to the angel-executer "*power was given to scorch men with fire*," effecting their *blasphemy*. Here is, The effusion of this vial on the *sun*, and, The *scorching with fire* the beast's adherents; which I still interpret of plagues, the one *outward*, the other *spiritual*, on the Popish party: 1st, "*He poured out his vial on the sun*," meaning the more illustrious light, or prince, adhering to the Popish party, and shining in his *political* heaven, whereof he is the great god, or Jupiter; being either the emperor, or the king of Spain; or both, as of the same house of Austria; those German wars, (then about A.D. 1639,) issuing in ruin, when the Popish party should once have had blood enough given them to drink; for the German empire was for eight centuries the most eminent principality in Europe, and in general the most staunch supporter of the Pope, whose creation it was, as set up in Charlemain, that sun in his firmament: the ruin of the emperor, his first-born, must therefore be a special plague on the the Papal seat. Mr. Mede thought this vial to have been in execution in that great prevailing of the king of Sweden against the emperor, whose glorious victories may well be a vial, if not to throw down from his heavens, yet to darken this sun, as that he should never recover his glory and splendour, though perhaps unextirpated. Others interpret this vial of the Pope's own power and authority, temporal and spiritual, setting in obscurity, (as in Is. lx. 20, Jer. xv. 9,) for the decretals of princes style the Pope and the emperor, the two great luminaries in heaven: but how hath this glory been waning more and more in the consciences of his own vassals, and in the eyes of princes once subject? France denies the Pope that absolute power he once challenged; and the Pope hath been but the moon to the king of Spain, (borrowing light from him, and flattering other princes who once flattered him, and were excommunicated at his pleasure,) and as his chaplain made of use for his own acquiring universal monarchy. 2dly, "*And power was given him* (the angel, not the sun,) *to scorch men with fire;*" referring to a greater height of *spiritual* plagues inflicted on all who continued to adhere to the Pope in these his declining times, especially on those of the learned among them, who took pains to write for him, or re-introduce his authority with those European kingdoms again, where the light of the gospel shone so as to have convinced them of it long since; "their sea being turned into blood" and discovered to be corrupt; "their springs, (their writings so clearly confuted,) turned into blood" also; so that they who labour to bring in Popery again, living in those kingdoms, must resist their own light and knowledge: and to permit so presumptuous and despiteful a "rebellion against the light," thus age after age increasing, this vial-angel hath power "*to scorch men with fire,*" proceeding out of the mouth of the witnesses by prophesying, so that men are *killed with a witness,* for their *wilfulness;* as in c. xi. 5, will be more fully expounded. In both places the allusion is either unto the fire of Sodom, or unto that in Lev. x. 1, 2, or in Num. xvi. to which Heb x. 26—28 refers, as in the Supplement will be more fully expounded. That such wilful or other presumptuous sinning against knowledge, accompanied with terror, is here meant, appears also by men's "*blaspheming the name of God who hath power over these plagues:*" Now blaspheming the Holy Ghost, or his workings in others, (knowing they are his works, as these here know they are his plagues,) is the very spirit of this sin; and then final impenitency is also added, as here, "*they repented not:*" And this plague goes on in the fifth vial, under which sinning against knowledge grows to a further height; for they are so scorched," that they gnaw their tongues," as men in hell. That under this vial the sin against the Holy Ghost grows very rife and common by reason of the abundance of light and conviction shining in the churches, hath long been the observation of godly men who have had senses exercised to discern spirits growing in rage and madness, beyond the supposal of any other principle that should act them in their warped and eccentric motion, and violent proceedings: and it is easy to conceive how many learned Jesuits should come to commit this sin; for bred up in their younger years in ways of devotion, they have truth and light enough to give them "a taste of the powers of the world to come," (Heb. vi. 5,) yet after studying and discerning the truth of our writings, for worldly ends, they wilfully go against it, and despise it, being justly abandoned to malicious wickednesss, and growing worse and worse under increasing light: and as the feeble light of the first vial being resisted, God gave them up to gross sins; their doctrine under the clearer shining of the second and third vial becoming more damnable, God also rose higher in his plagues, and by striking hell-fire into their consciences, sealed up reprobation unto them: and thus it became him not to leave these murderers and opposers of the saints and holy witnesses of God in all ages, till many of them were given up to this highest sinning and fullest measure of iniquity, before the final ruin of the Popish kingdom and state; like as the Pharisees in their last age, on whom were brought the punishments of all their forefathers' killing his prophets in Jerusalem, for the despite done by them to Christ's ministry. But above all, it is as hard not to think, as it is hard to be thought, that such apostates are guilty of "the great transgression," who having lived and been brought up "in the land of uprightness," (Isa. xxvi. 10,) yet becoming of the Popish party, "will not behold the majesty of the Lord" shining round about them, but relinquish the truth they were educated in, and would bring in the worship and doctrine of the beast and whore, after so clear a light and powerful preaching so long enjoyed, and growing brighter then ever towards the latter end of the harvest and summer; yet, "speaking lies in hypocrisy," (1 Tim. iv. 2,) they deny this to be their aim, though their deeds do manifest it, so that all the world accounts them Popish, and of the Popish faction, (thus meriting the title of "The number of his name,") being spirits such as Rome hath not worse, in malice and enmity against God's witnesses; for their venom, rage, subtility, and under-hand opposing the saints, do cause the godly to suspect them of that "sin unto death;" and indeed what other principle could act men so? for the Pharisees were brought up in darkness and ignorance of the righteousness of God and of the Messiah, when the ministry of John and Christ came upon them, and called upon them to acknowledge and embrace the Son, whom they never acknowledged; yet they sinned against the Holy Ghost by smothering that new light, which set up Christ alone, and put all men out of credit: But these men, (compare p. 599, &c.) in this our age, have been brought up in the contrary truth and light; and they have both professed it, subscribed to it, and preached it; and yet they love this darkness of Popery, and embrace this cursed harlot, and would bring her into their tents "in the face of Moses and of the whole congregation," (as in Num. xxv. 6,) and they loathe the truth of the gospel and of the faith they once received, and that in the face of the clearest sun-shine and light round about them. One would think God should destroy them visibly; but they must do a great exploit for him first; their further destiny is, to kill the witnesses for this their *scorching* them through the powerful testimony of their lives and prophecies, and so be even with them, and overcome them yet before the fifth vial comes: and though as yet they have not got a full victory, yet they are now a making war, and shall prevail, and banish and disperse them among tongues and nations throughout Europe. But under the fifth vial, these witnesses in the end shall again have overcome this last of all the beast's company and champions to be overcome, "the number of his name," and "*the names of men*," (ONOMATA ANTHROOPOON, c. xi. 13, with xv. 2,) who shall be killed instead of the witnesses at their resurrection, as the first degree and preparation to

THE FIFTH VIAL "*upon the* (throne or) *seat of the beast*," v. 10, 11, which is Rome, the old seat of the dragon, the Heathenish idolatrous empire, as openly governed by Satan, and afterwards resigned to the Pope at his first rising, c. xiii. 2. The Sybils prophesied of Rome's again becoming a sheep-cote; and the Holy Ghost, (c. xviii. 2, 21,) of her being "thrown down as a mill-stone, and no more found at all, but become the habitation of devils only, and the dwelling of every foul spirit for ever." Of this vial we may say, "Now it speaketh plainly and not in parables," as before, (John xvi. 29;) only as the other vials are to be taken in the largest sense, (though not spiritually or figuratively,) so I think this is: and as the second beast, (c. xiii.) is not the Pope only, but the body of the clergy under their head; so the *seat of the beast* may be other sees, besides the see of Rome in Italy and elsewhere, cleaving to the number and company of the beast, who are here under the fifth vial tumbled down from their usurped seats, thrones, and dignities, together with this their head, whose whole kingdom is now become "*full of darkness*" and obscurity: and although the Popedom remains to be destroyed by the seventh vial, yet its glory is here reckoned as gone and taken from him; and he is now reserved alive only for a further and more glorious execution: his seven-headed kingdom is no longer accounted of, and his period is at an end with this fall of Rome.

THE SEVENTEENTH, EIGHTEENTH, AND NINETEENTH CHAPTERS.

To present Rome in all her bravery, before her ruin, c. xvii. is added; and c. xviii. sings a solemn, stately, and triumphant song for her destruction. Now that the Holy Ghost should make the ruin of this long-reigning city such a triumph above all things else in this book, imports, That the last fatal period of the fourth monarchy, (with Rome for its seat, and the beast for its last head,) is here reckoned as good as at an end; though he may yet make troublesome resistance after the sixth vial, but not *reign* any more;

else the Holy Ghost would have reserved himself till after the seventh vial, and not have raised the shout of triumph before an assured victory. But another manner of triumph is to come, more high and glorious, for the marriage of the Lamb; when Rome and the beast will be forgotten; and therefore God ordained it to be performed at the funeral of the great whore: and two chapters being spent in setting forth the pageants of the church's triumph over Rome, surely here ends her great kingdom, and here begins the church's preparation for the Lamb's marriage in c. xix. Now c. xvii. 18, shews the whore to be Rome, for Rome is "that great city which reigned over the kings of the earth;" and thus c. xvii. and xviii. are but a more full setting forth of the fifth, that most eminent and fatal of the vials upon the beast: instead therefore of spending time in explicating those chapters, I shall hasten to the exposition of the supplemental c. xi. mainly intended by me as con aining the state of the church in these and the approaching times; and I join it next to the vials, because these vials serve directly to expound it; and mentioning the first four vials, it goes on to shew what shall befal the churches of the Reformation under the fourth vial, and before the fifth, ending its appointed months and years. And as c. xiv. shewed the condition of the church within itself, to the times of the fourth vial; so c. xi. begins where c. xiv. ends: hence the supplement of the story of the church's various and chequered condition is to be fetched, as will appear in the opening of it.

THE SUPPLEMENT

CONTAINING A MORE ENLARGED EXPOSITION OF

THE ELEVENTH CHAPTER.

I.—FIVE INTRODUCTORY PREMISES

I.—For the better understanding of this chapter, I shall shew, *who* is the angel here spoken of; *what* is his purpose; and *when* he comes down here in this vision. The *angel* who delivers the contents of this chapter, (v. 1—14,) immediately by word of mouth to John, is CHRIST HIMSELF, for he *gives power* to *his* two witnesses, (v. 3;) nor does he speak anywhere but on this occasion, and in c. i. and he is the same who came to Daniel at the end of his prophesy, where he useth the same gesture and ceremony, and the same oath, and that about the same thing and to the same purpose; see c. x. 6 with Dan. xii. 7. The prophecy of Daniel contains the very same matter, more obscurely, as doth that of the Revelation, more clearly, viz. the tyranny of the fourth Roman monarchy, and the oppression of the church thereby, first under the Heathenish empire, and then under the Pope its last head, of whom Dan. vii. and xi. 36—45, prophesied; after whose time expired, a fifth monarchy of the saints should come in: and in both prophecies the *time* of Antichrist's reign is defined to be the same; at the end of which, (in this first seal-prophecy, according to the course of time run out,)this angel here descends in vision. Now first of all he renews the oath then taken, and here swears again, (c. x. 6, 7,) "That there should be *time* no longer; but in the days of the seventh angel, when he shall begin to sound, the mystery of God should be finished, as he hath declared to his servants the prophets;" see Acts iii. 21, speaking of the same reign of the church: These words of the angel's oath imply, that the visions of all times past in the former seal-prophecy, from the primitive times, having brought things to the last scene of the world's time, now "*time* (or *delay*) shall be no longer:" it is but a little, and the last sand drops; the blast of the seventh trumpet will end all. Accordingly the angel here explains distinctly what was the Pope's time mentioned in his former oath to Daniel, and what was the "accomplishing to scatter the power of the holy people," there made the immediate fore-runner of the fulfilling of all things; and as "willing to shew the immutability of his promise, he confirms it with an oath, that we might have a strong consolation," (Heb. vi. 17, 18,) speaking thus in effect: "*I come* now, *beloved, after so long a while worn out, to bid you lift up your heads; for* time, *now in the days of the sixth trumpet, is expiring, and my kingdom is at the doors: the times of the beast, (prophesied of by Daniel,) of whom you shall hear more in this little book-prophecy brought with me open in my hand to give you, do now shortly end and determine; the* "time, times, and half a time," *allotted the beast, (the Pope, the last head and king to reign in the fourth* Roman *monarchy,) is shortly to expire; and with him the times of this present oppressing world: and that you, my church, may know and have infallible warning, when it shall be, I will both explain to you,* How long, *in Daniel's prophecy, the beast is allotted 'to scatter the power of the holy people,' my witnesses; and also, What shall be the* manner *of that eminent last* scattering, *the immediate sign and precusor of Antichrist's ruin, and of the fulfilment of all these other things; and I will shew you also, The face of the church in that age immediately preceding: Thus you may have together a true computation of the* time, *and also of such* events *(and face of the sky) as may be an eminent sign to you; that when you see these things, then know, that the time is expiring and determining. And of this I myself do thus immediately inform you, because that last scattering will be so great a one, as all the faith you have will be put to it: and therefore also I have now in these times* sworn *to it, that you may eye my oath, and remember it; for even now 'your redemption draweth nigh,' nigher than you are aware of.*"

II.—The angel here enters on the stage, and acts his part in a fit scene or *place* in this comedy, or vision of all times successively, hitherto acted before John to be by him penned for us. The seals and trumpets, c. vi.—ix. (containing one prophecy,) run over all times from John unto the end; as doth "the little book" in c. x. containing another prophecy of the church. Just now, as in the last age, and towards the expiring of the sixth trumpet's first revolution of all time, this angel steps in with his new or second prophecy in his hand ready to be delivered; and as some sands of time under the first prophecy were not yet run out, he conveniently and admirably fills up the little interim with an additional discourse of his own, to inform the church what special occurrences were to fall out therein before the final consummation of all under the seventh trumpet, and thus to give warning when the end of both prophecies should be. The Turkish empire is still standing, and the sixth trumpet must be still blowing. Now the sixth seal had set forth an utter end of the Roman empire all it could; being however to continue yet some hundreds of years before the blast of the seventh trumpet; which space the angel here fills up with relating what special occurrences, most intimately concerning his people, should fall out in the western church, (over which the Pope had the dominion,) now towards the end of both Turkish and Popish empires; and so, in this last age before the ending of these times: And though such occurrences properly fall under the cognizance of church-matters in the book-prophecy, yet they are fitly introduced here between both prophecies, as the signal of the ending of the full course of both stages of times. The angel's discourse thus filling up that remaining time in this interlude, with what was indeed yet to fall out together with it, before the sixth trumpet ends; he concludes with "The second woe is past," q. d. "The sixth trumpet ends also hereabouts;" and then in order he blows the seventh.

III.—The *manner* of the angel's delivering all this to John, is as the narration of a chorus, or as the speech of an interlocutor in a comedy; explaining by word of mouth what could not have been well understood by vision; so the angel in c. xvii. also doth, interpreting who the whore is, as this angel interprets the *times* of her and the beast, and the tokens immediately fore-running the ending of them. The narration here is indeed first occasioned by a vision of the church's face and state in the last age of these accomplishings, viz. a *temple*, with its surrounding *outward court*, and its *altar* within, and *two witnesses* standing and ministering before the Lord: else John could not have been bid, v. 1, &c. to "*rise and measure the temple;*" for to such supposed vision alone is the angel's discourse adapted: and this is made the first occurrence belonging to the age wherein time is to expire, and the ground of his discourse; which, after explaining how much time the beast was to have, and how and when it should end, closeth again with the relation of another after-occurrence, and last signal of that age, (v. 7,) just as one of the vial-angels being to describe the beast and the whore, in all the times allotted her, yet takes his rise from a vision of her, as then in her last old age, under the vials, "drunk with the blood of the saints," just before her ruin: So here this angel first enters on the stage as an actor, in the very declension of the sixth trumpet, under which he swears; and then, (after presenting the vision of a measured temple, and its courts falling again unmeasured into the hands of the Gentiles, to tread it down, and thus "to scatter the power of the holy people,") he plays the part of an interlocutor, narrating the whole times of Popery, to expire after this their last revival; and introducing also the opposition of the witnesses during the same, (v. 3—6;) till he returns back to the last catastrophe of the age of the commencement of his speech, (towards the end of the sixth trumpet;) with which he determines his speech about the witnesses, (v. 7, &c.) now thus made clear by his previous statements concerning them.

IV.—The *oath* in Daniel fitly accords with all here, v. 1—14; wherein there is both an interpretation of the period of time, and eminent events signalizing its close: for in the angel's oath, 1st, The beast's reign there lasts for three *times* and a half, and here for forty-two *months*, (of thirty *days* i. e. *years* each,) not one of which shall pass over, without his reigning; and of the one thousand two hundred and sixty *days*, i. e. *years*, not one shall pass over without the sack-cloathed and oppressed saints' opposing him. 2dly, The holy people in Daniel, are the two witnesses in Revelations, who yet, 3dly, Towards the end should obtain some "*power of the holy people*" against him: so here, v. 3, &c. they had power to erect a temple, (backed with a mighty party of an outward court;) whence they had already poured out four vials, so as to scorch their injurers with *fire*, &c. v. 5, and at their weakest, to prevent rain, v. 6, &c. 4thly, This their *power*, as well as the people themselves, the beast should in the ending of that time, eminently *scatter;* as the *accomplishment*, or last act of his so doing, before his ruin and their sorrows cease together: so here when ready to cast off their sackcloth, and "*about to finish*" (TELESOOSI) their testimony against this beast, then their "outward courts shall be trodden down," and themselves exposed to the beast's fury and outrage, to be by him *scattered* among the nations and killed, where "their dead bodies shall be seen lying in the streets," &c. which oppression is described, v. 7—10, with their gathering together again, to be scattered no more for ever, v. 11—13.

V.—The *times* and *events* are here *mentioned together*, to shew that the whole series of the one should end with the other;

so that it is not only making a *computation*, but defining the *period* of months or days; the angel hitting hereby the very aim of his former oath to Daniel, viz. the expiration of the three and half *times*, and the accomplishment of the *scattering*, &c. the whole term being fulfilled in the particular exploits this beast shall play, to the very eve of taking away his kingdom. In c. xiii. 5—7, The beast had "power to *do*, (POIEIN,) forty-two months," and therein "to make war with the saints and overcome them; and power was given him over all tongues and nations and kindreds," of the ten European kingdoms. Now the Gentiles here, and that idolatrous company in c. xiii. 3, 4, that set up this power of the beast to be worshipped, are the same, and have the same lease of months; only here is shewn how the whole term should be fulfilled, through all those times, and by all those wars and slaughters of Antichrist: For, *First*, The treading down of the holy city for twelve hundred and sixty years, comes in here upon the court of the temple being given up anew to the Gentiles; as if the angel had said, "Cast out the court of this age, (which though it hath helped against the Papists to keep them off, hath yet defiled the churches,) and leave it out of thy measure, for it is given to the Gentiles in this last age to re-enter thereupon, and to get power over:" which last treading it down and overcoming it, (having before both possessed it, and then lost it from their dominions,) will carry them on to the destined period of the beast's reign in Europe, that holy city, which is the seat of this church: So that, notwithsandinding intermissions and occasional losses of parts of their dominions, yet the last recovery of all will justify their claim to possesesession for the whole forty-two months, first and last; as in the last payment, the whole sum is mentioned as paid. Interpreters therefore do mistake this temple-measuring and its court-delivering, for the Papists' possessing throughout all ages the *face*, (which they call the *outward court*,) of the temple, because "the forty-two months' treading down the holy city," follows thereupon: as if they were to reign many years after its being delivered up: If so, it could not be meant of some special event or act relative to the church and its outward court in this last age of these latter times: For, 1st, Not the *court*, but the *city* is to be trodden down; for the Papists were lords over the greater part of Europe, even when the outward court was separated from them; the one stands indeed in the other, as the temple stood in Jerusalem. 2dly, The scope of here naming when the term of years ceaseth, is to shew, That in this latter age the beast should re-enter into full power and jurisdiction over the holy city, by the court of the temple being again laid common with the rest of the city; as a king is said to reign fifty years, though obliged to leave his throne for an interim of revolt: and so Antichrist hath his whole number of *months* of reigning from time to time; he reigns not by *days*, for the Goths at first much interrupted the exercise of his power. 3dly, "And they shall tread down," &c. comes in as a reason for the court's being in these last times given to those Gentiles, and therefore Antichrist hopes by repossessing it to recover all Europe again: CAI also, ("*and* they shall," &c.) is often a causal particle, noting out the reason of a thing: So then the term of the Papists' commission over all the nations and tongues of Europe, (only those exempted in c. xiii. 1, 8,) being leased out to them; though the outward court of carnal Protestants and unregenerate hath made a separation together with the true worshippers, yet being inwardly Gentiles, and their names not written in the book of life, they are given to these Gentiles again as their allotted inheritance to be re-entered, the lease not being yet expired: as in a law-suit, a man pleads at the end of eighteen years for restoration to a part of an estate withheld from him under a lease of twenty-one years: so the court here being land within the bounds of the city, and belonging to the Pope by gift for so long, and his forty-two months lease not being expired; therefore, he must *accomplish to scatter* the court and to tread down the city, according to the angel's interpretation here of his own words in Dan. xii. 7. *Secondly,* The computation by *days* is introduced to shew how this long description of the witnesses, and this numbering of their days, is but in order to their last accomplishment; as v. 7, calls it the "*when*" of finishing their testimony: and as more than half of this discourse sets forth this their last scattering hereupon, it shews the scope of the former part to have been the same. And though the Antichrist-beast hath already had some famous overcomings and killing of these witnesses, yet this one is here singled out, (about which the whole book-prophecy is silent,) not perhaps for the eminency of the prevailing, but as the last struggle; which also herein is eminent, that after taking away so much ground from the beast, and winning from him a temple and court set up on his own ground, he should prevail again, though for a short time: and such a remarkable prognostic is here therefore mentioned. *Thirdly,* The series of coherence and connexion of one thing with another in these first verses, is briefly this: The period of *months* for the Pope and his company to reign, and of *days* for the witnesses to prophesy in sackcloth, is the same; and both refer unto the two of these last occurrences in the reign of the one and the oppressed state of the other: 1st, The whole time of treading down the holy city shall *end* with a recovery and treading down of the outward court of the temple of the reformed churches; and the date is therefore added to show how it ends: and accordingly the vision of the temple-measuring is but an introduction to this last occurence. 2dly, In the date of *days,* the order is inverted; and the whole time of the witnesses' prophesying, is first mentioned in continuation with the whole time of the adversaries, (the juxtaposition of the *days* serving to elucidate the *months;*) after which their last scattering comes in as the accomplishment of the time: and the dates go together also, because the witnesses are the continual opponents of these Gentiles, and the chief objects of their malice: CAI also, in v. 3, is often used adversatively, "*But*, I will give power," &c. q. d. "*Whereas the Papists have their forty-two months for treading down the* holy city, (Europe *the chief seat of Christian profession,) from whom the Protestants have, meanwhile, won a temple and outward court; yet to make good the period of their reign, they shall regain that court of the new tabernacle separated from them;* But *they shall not carry it thus, unopposed by my two witnesses, whom I will empower to testify, though in sackcloth, all those days; and even in this their last treading down to avenge themseles with fire &c. of these* Gentiles, *who shall yet go on, and in the end of their days prevail even over these my two witnesses also, so as to kill and destroy them when about to finish their testimony.*" Thus though their appointed time comes in a good way off before, it is in order to this their last slaughter; to shew, (as in Daniel,) how it should be accomplished.

II.—THE TEMPLE MEASURED.

AND THERE WAS GIVEN ME A REED LIKE UNTO A ROD: AND THE ANGEL STOOD, SAYING, RISE, AND MEASURE THE TEMPLE OF GOD, AND THE ALTAR, AND THEM THAT WORSHIP THEREIN; BUT THE COURT WHICH IS WITHOUT THE TEMPLE LEAVE OUT, AND MEASURE IT NOT; FOR IT IS GIVEN TO THE GENTILES: AND THE HOLY CITY SHALL THEY TREAD UNDER FOOT FORTY AND TWO MONTHS, v. 1, 2.

I.—*The double computation by days and months explained, and why they are here set together.*

The contents of this chapter, to the fourteenth verse, are reducible to three heads. I. The above double computation of times; II. The occurrences in these times of Antichrist; in the age (wherein we live) just before their fatal period; unto the accomplishment of which those occurrences conduce. III. The description of the two witnesses interwoven in the angel's discourse, in order to the explanation of what should at last befall them. Now for the *times* here mentioned; First, They are both the same as Daniel's "time, times, and half-a-time;" which, Secondly, Are shewn, by the forty-two months, to be three years and six months; meaning twelve hundred and sixty years; (reckoning thirty days to the month, which prophetically are so many years; as a week is seven years, a month thirty, a twelvemonth three hundred and sixty, &c.) Thus the "*three days and a half*," v. 11, must be so many *years*, wherein the witnesses are to lie in the view of all nations, (as perhaps banished among them,) their enemies meanwhile sending gifts to one another. Thirdly, By thus linking the two modes of dating the times, they are shewn to be the same when mentioned also apart in c. xii. and xiii. Fourthly, Though here and in Daniel, only the times of the Pope's reign, (the last head of the Roman monarchy,) are mentioned; (not bearing date from John's days;) yet the whole period of the Revelation may hereby be calculated, and the contemporaneousness of things in both prophecies; the principal aim being to shew the time and end of the beast's reign, as c. xvii. 8, shews who he is, and what he should be at last. Now to demonstrate all these; 1st, This explication of the times is a date whence to compute the whole period of the Revelation, if we know either the beginning or ending of the Pope's reign: but c. xvii. 12, shews his rise to be *one hour with the ten kings;* which being after A.D. 400, he must continue till after A.D. 1660, (see p. 603); and the Turk's ruin is yet to follow under "the second woe" of v. 14; and then comes the new Jerusalem state of the church; whence we may conjecture the space from the incarnation to that fifth monarchy. 2dly, This computation shew the synchronism of the seal and book-prophecy; and here most fitly between them both; for the sixth trumpet of the seal-prophecy, (v. 14, with c. viii. 13,) ends with the Pope's reign, whose story belongs to the book-prophecy; and the passing away of that woe is the sixth vial in the book-prophecy, affecting the Turk's ruin, or a preparation thereto by the calling of the Jews: and then the seventh trumpet begins with the seventh vial; and so the beast's times, and the rising of the witnesses, end with the fifth vial; after which the sixth shall not stay long. 3dly, The division of things into the double series of six seals and six trumpets, is suited to the angel's division of all times; the primitive being those before the beast's rise and reign: so that ascertaining how the two prophecies meet towards their close downward, we conjecture how they run along upwards. For the seal-prophecy being branched into two such equal divisions of six seals, c. vi. and the six trumpets, c. viii. ix. the seals containing the story of the empire through all that tract of the primitive times before the beast, the trumpets do likely contain the story of the empire during the beast's times; and as they end, so they no doubt begin, not far off from each other. 4thly, The Holy Ghost specifies only the times of the beast, as a rule and measure whereby to sum and cast up the account of all the times of this book; For, The beast's was to be the longest monarchy after Christ, and the Pope the most long-lived of all the heads of the Roman monarchy fore-going him; indeed as long as from the rise of Rome itself, to the rise of Antichrist. 2, The matters of this book being not so fully to be opened "till about the time of the end," (as in Dan. xii. 4;) if the beast's times should then come to be known, the whole time from John downward would be known also by them that live in these latter days, for whose benefit and comfort this computation was given. 3, This last head of the Romish monarchy, (which but for him had failed, but was in him healed and restored again,) is inkling enough of the approach of Christ's kingdom. 4, This beast being the most eminent oppressor of the church in the times after Christ; the computation of this time, (beginning and ending,) and the oppression of the witnesses by him, being most acceptable to be known, would be most enquired after by the church.

II.—*The several occurrences of measuring the temple, altar, &c. leaving out the outward court; and of treading down the holy city; towards the expiration of the above times.*

First, *For a general view and division of these occurrences:* As Christ was careful to give us the above computation of *times*, so for our comfort he relates such *events* to fall out towards the end of these times; which is the second head to be explained, and it is also twofold; The re-delivery of the outward court to the Gentiles, with the treading down of which ends their reign of the time of the city's treading down; and, The killing of the witnesses, which terminates in particular the *days* of sackcloth-prophesying, as the former terminated the *months* of the beast's reign in general, each of which occurrences have two others with them as congenial appendices to them, or occasions of them: The giving up again the outward court is accompanied by, The measurement of the temple, and The killing of the witnesses is much occasioned, and specially provoked by, The *hurt* done by the *fire* of these witnesses just before, in revenge of which they are encouraged to kill them: Or thus: John and the angel standing here in the very extremities of the times of the fourth vial, (the present age,) wherein Antichrist's reign is drawing near to the end; John hath represented to him, (as an introduction to all that follows,) the face of the church in this age, and is himself bidden to represent the work of the godly towards her: and, *First*, She is represented to him as the inward temple standing in the holy city Jerusalem, (as in Ezek. xl. 1, &c.) into which the priest only was to come, and wherein stands the altar, with a company of true worshippers; but a vast outward court lies around it, into which all sorts of professors of true worship come, as used the crowds of Jewish professors. This temple-church is also represented as adorned within with golden candlesticks and two stately olive trees, (v. 4,) being two eminent witnesses and prophets that minister before God therein. Now the Gentiles have for a long time possessed the city, and are still to possess it, till the expiration of their months; but the temple, and its court of late erected in this city, they have been kept out of, and so could not come at these witnesses who are within the temple, nor overcome and kill them as formerly; yet are they mad again with vexation and eagerness for vengeance, because of their being tormented by them with fire and other plagues out of this temple: But now, before the termination of their months, The angel, (being angry both with the carnal worshippers in the outward court so profanely mixing themselves with his worshippers, and laying themselves to his building and temple; and also with the carnal gospelling of the two witnesses among them; and with the imperfections of this temple-building, not yet answering the pattern,) intending to erect a purer temple, *Secondly*, Bids John, (the representative of the godly of this age,) to measure the temple anew; and so begins to make a new reformation therein more answerable to the pattern in the mount; for he is not pleased with the old one that hath stood so long, and whose outward court John is to leave out, as to be given up to those Gentiles, (after that his purer churches shall thus, as it were, have excommunicated them;) who having already taken possession of the city, and kept it a long time, shall now again enter on and over-run this outward court, as within their lease and demise; thus accomplishing their reign over the whole city; and then they are to be driven out of all for ever; which makes them so *angry*, v. 18. *Thirdly*, Having thus won the outward court, which fenced and kept safe the witnesses from Popish persecutions, the beast, (vexed and plagued by their shooting wild-fire out of the temple, and in turn shooting back what had hurt him,) can now come to them to overcome them and kill them quite, and scatter their power; ending withal the period of his oppression, and the last war wherein he shall any way prevail; for though he shall again make head, (what of him is left,) before the seventh vial, it shall not come to another victory.

Secondly, *For the holy city, temple, and outward court*. It is wonderful to me to see how exactly this vision, in the whole series of it, represents the present face, the affairs, stirrings, and alterations, now a working in the churches of Europe; the type and antitype so fully answering and suiting each other; For, *first*, This holy city, (wherein these Gentiles have a lease of forty-two months' reign,) are those kingdoms of Europe which for more than a thousand years have been the metropolis and chief seat of Christian profession, as Jerusalem of old was of the worship of the true God; which therefore in the following part of the book-prophecy are made, (from the rise of the beast,) the only stage of all, until the new Jerusalem and holy city from heaven succeeds this: Yet, *secondly*, God permits this city, (for the punishment of the world,) to be trodden down of the Gentiles, (Luke xxi. 24,) for forty two months: But, *thirdly*, towards the end of the times of this idolatrous crew of the beast, who have set up such an image of Gentilism, a great part of this city falls from them; and an inclosure and separation is made, wherein a temple is built of churches separate from Antichrist, (c. xv.) as in the northern parts of Europe, see Ps. xlviii. 2, with Isa. xlix. 12; Dan. xi. 44: Unto this temple, *fourthly*, An outward court of carnal and unregener-

ate persons hath
this building; and who take up so much of the room, that although true churches and temples have been set up by reason of the true worshippers among them, yet they have been defiled with the addition of an outward court, into which all sorts come: so that indeed these Reformed churches have become outward courts more than inward temples; through which mixture great corruptions and defects in the form of the temple, (or church-fellowship,) have been continued among them, and impurities in the worship and about the altar. Now to the temple there went, first, The most holy place inclosed at one end, and separated as our cathedral-choirs; and next, The body of the temple, for the priests only, (where stood the altar of incense,) surrounded by the inner court; and then, The large outer court, (1 Kings vii. 12; 2 Chron. iv. 9; Ezek. xl. 17, 27,) admitting people of all sorts, and encircling the whole building besides, (like our church-yards,) and here said to be "*without*" the compass of the temple: Herod indeed built a *fourth* court for strangers. Thus then the true church with its true worshippers, is the true temple with its priests, (see 1 Cor. iii. 16; Eph. ii. 21; 1 Pet. ii. 5; Heb. x. 22;) and the uncircumcised in heart, not being, by regeneration, Jews and the Israel of God, and having no right to approach this altar, are "the court of the Gentiles:" And whether *temple* or *church* be taken mystically for the elect and sincere worshippers, or for churches instituted and congregations of true public worshippers, (as Eph. ii. 22; Heb. x. 22, 25;) in both cases others are *without* in comparison of them, see 1 Cor. xv. 12, 17; Rom. ii. 28, 29: so that in what sense soever the Papists may be called "The outward court," these also may; as alike arrogating the name of "the church," and in some places, under that name, casting out the true worshippers; for so great is their number, that in view they are only or chiefly the church; the best congregations of the first Reformation, having numberless more bad than good among them; and many being made up of unregenerate persons; whilst the true visible worshippers, comparatively, are a company of hidden ones: Indeed these unregenerate Protestants are much rather to be accounted "the outward court," and so are mainly here intended: For, 1st, "The outward court," is here opposed to all else enumerated for measuring, as *temple, altar,* and *worshippers;* and therefore it means not merely an outward face and place of worship, but carnal outward worshippers also: and as *heaven* and *earth* are put for their inhabitants, so here the Holy Ghost speaks not of the material court, as neither, elsewhere, of churches as material buildings: so that take the *persons* worshipping away, and the *face* of the outward court ceaseth, and its place is lost. Cornelius a Lapide saith, "In that part of the temple where the priests worship, the faithful are symbolically represented; who in Antichrist's time will be the best, most devout,

most close to God, and most stedfast in his worship." By "the court without," are meant, the more unstable and less strict livers, (therefore those further from God,) who are to be cast out without the church; as if the angel had said, "Reject them among the unfaithful and apostate, as unworthy to be numbered with the faithful, because they give way to the Gentiles and those who cleave to Antichrist." 2dly, These outer-court worshippers are distinct from the *Gentiles*, to whom they are *given:* and therefore not being either Papists or true worshippers, must be carnal Protestants filling our churches. 3dly, The Papists, as possessing the outward face of the church, could not so fill this court, as to be the sole contra-distinct and opposite party to the true worshippers; unless all Protestants were of this inner temple, whereas not one of a hundred are so, according to these rules of this reed-measurement: the mere nominal Protestants must therefore be the third party distinct from both, as cast out by the one, and siezed on by the other; and according to apostolic institutions, such ought to be left out of the building, for true churches to be measured anew without them: and therefore if this measuring the temple fall under the sixth trumpet, I cannot but imagine that a new reformation, begun again, is intended; and that the re-entry these Papists are now making upon the outward court of our churches, and our yielding to them, is this giving of the same to the Gentiles. 4thly, The Papists are no court at all to this temple, being by name "Satan's synagogue," and "worshippers of the beast and of his image," and also "Sodom and Egypt," &c. whereas these, being neither such Gentiles, nor such Israel of God, must be "Jews outwardly," who have the same worship as the true Israelites, and therefore are discovered to be "the court without," by the *reed* and light of God's word; and those *treaders* of that court, (Isa. i. 12,) of which the others are *treaders down;* God bringing on such outward Protestant despisers of the gospel and of true worshippers, the worst of the Heathen, to tread them down by violence, either of conquest over their bodies, (as in Germany,) or over their consciences, in making such again submit to their superstitions and idolatries, as they still go on to do in other places. Now all this must be ascribed to the glorious wisdom of God, who means to have a church most holy to himself under the seventh trumpet, in which "the ark shall be seen in the Holy of holies;" and as he perfects her by degrees, therefore about mid-way between the first Reformation long since made, and the seventh trumpet, he sets his builders on work, (here represented by John,) to endeavour to erect a new frame and reformation of that Reformation, and to take the reed, and measure over anew both temple, altar, and worshippers; and to cast out that outward court of worshippers, with these corruptions of theirs which hindered that thorough Reformation; and so to contract his temple into the narrower compass of the inner temple, yet purer and more refined; he delighting more in truth of worship, than in magnitude or multitude of sacrifices and worshippers: thus he makes to himself a church of priests, into which the faithful are called up from that court before common to both. Here then is the inner temple of the first Reformation, more imperfect, unfurnished, and besides, defiled by having a court attached: Here is also a second Reformation more pure, represented by that temple remeasured for finishing and cleansing from similar mixture; for the Holy of holies is opened, (v. 19,) "into which no unclean thing shall enter," (c. xxi. 27,) for though the *reed* of the second Reformation keeps out those whom the godly, (here represented by John,) judge civil and profane, yet many a hypocrite "that loveth and maketh a lie," (c. xxii. 15,) may escape and crowd into this inward temple still: but there shall be "a *golden* reed" (c. xxi. 15,) to measure the new-Jerusalem temple: At present however we must proceed

Thirdly, *For the measurement of the temple, altar, and worshippers therein.* As a reed is put into the hands of a builder, so Christ puts into the hearts of the rulers of his people the light of his word, as the only sufficient rule whereby to square the worship and worshippers of churches; and by no frame of other reeds unwarranted in scripture: This principle was never yet fully taken up and practised by our Reformers, though long contended for as the ground-work of this building. 1st, The *temple* here is not only the church of the elect, (for there is a distinct consideration made of the worshippers therein,) but congregations in church-fellowship, as in Eph. ii. 20—22, where the saints are not only part of the temple of the elect, but as an assembly, are an habitation apart, and a little sanctuary unto God, every particular church bearing the name of the whole; and in such a temple alone the ordinances of church-communion and worship, (the sacraments, excommunications, &c.) are to be administered; as at Jerusalem alone sacrifices were to be offered: Therefore, 2dly, The altar being the main and only ordinance of temple-worship serving for sacrifice here, means the church-ordinances of public worship and sacrifice. 3dly, The *worshippers*, as the priests of old, are those alone to be of this temple and to approach this altar, as in 1 Pet. ii. 5; being persons with qualifications meet for saints, and requisite for the true temple-worship; and thus they become themselves a temple, as gathered up in a church-assembly, according to Christ's institution. 4thly, The *measurement* of temple, altar, and worshippers by a *reed*, is, 1, The *drawing a true platform* according to the rules of the word, by shewing, What a true church or *temple* is, and how to be built; next, What is the way of duly administering all church-worship and ordinances, as excommunications, sacraments, ordaining officers of holy things who partake of and serve at the *altar*, and in short what Rom. xii. 1, called LOGICEE LATREIA, *word-service*, (speaking of a church-body, as the next chapter speaks to the same persons as members of a common-wealth;) and then, What is true saintship, and who are meet *worshippers* in this temple, being admitted or rejected according to the rule and *reed* of God's word, whereby we judge them that are *within*, 1 Cor. v. 12, 13. That *measuring* is "drawing a platform of all these things," appears by Ezekiel's shewing Israel the *pattern, form,* and *fashion* of the house, its *goings out* and *comings in* for administration, &c. all the *ordinances* with their *forms*, and *laws* thereof: and as the prophet saw, distinctly and apart measured, the *temple* and the *altar;* and then heard the laws given concerning the *worshippers*, blaming the admission of *strangers* uncircumcised in flesh and heart, and shewing who should be *priests* and *Levites*, and what their *duties;* so here the outer court of strangers to God, and unclean, who use strange forms of worship, is to be cast out; see Ezek. xli. xlii. xliii. 10—13; xliv. 7—9. 2, It means also that such temple, altar, and worship, should now in this age begin to be *built and erected*, and men set on work to do it; that so the people seeing the true pattern, might be ashamed of their former aberrations, and in future keep to that pattern, and do after it, and square all by it. Nor does the angel speak of the temple hitherto standing, but of a new building, or finishing of a church, as in Zech. ii. 5; iv. 10. 3, It imports also *protection*, as when God is "a wall of fire round about his people, and the glory in the midst of them." So here the worshippers are called up from the unmeasured court, given to the Gentiles; and by getting into this temple, they are preserved from the re-entry of these Gentiles upon them, and from such power over them, as they had over the outer-court worshippers; the saints being thus preserved from the overgrowing corruptions and defilements of these Gentiles; and God being to them "a little sanctuary," (Ezek. xi. 16,) they will be at least preserved for that resurrection to come after, v. 11, 12.

Fourthly, *For the leaving out of the outward court unmeasured.* 1st, This is "to take the precious from the vile," (Jer. xv. 19,) and "to discern between the righteous and the wicked, and him that serveth God, and him that serveth him not," (Mal. iii. 18,) by such marks and signs and spots of God's people, (Deut. xxxii. 5,) as the word of God sets forth. By this exclusive work, way is made for the right constitution of purer churches; and by these excommunicating gifts, (where the ordinance of excommunication is wanting,) men's natural or regenerate states are set forth, whereby carnal men are convinced and discovered to themselves and others: a spirit being set up in the hearts of the godly by this light, to discern between the clean and the unclean, and so to hew and to set apart the material for this temple, as were the stones for Solomon's. 2dly, This implies a rejecting them from church-fellowship and not admitting them into this new-reared temple, as unfit matter for the building; which is a kind of excommunication of them. 3dly, It may further imply a rejecting such forms of administration in worship, and corruptions therein, as are not found agreeable to the word; though left in the first Reformation, (as the filth which the sea leaves behind it at an ebb;) for "the temple, altar, and worshippers," and "the outward court," are in full opposition to each other.

Fifthly, *For the reason of the leaving out the outward court.* Those forms of worship that came from Popery, (the worshippers themselves being inwardly Gentiles,) are ordained, for glorious ends, more or less to be subjected to it again: and therefore God puts it into the hearts of his builders thus strangely and suddenly to reject them, as the time of his decree draws near; only ere these Gentiles seize on them as their prey, the true church-templers leave them out, and they forthwith become as Heathens, cast out and withered, (John xv. 6;) Popish opinions and practices take them again: And how by degrees do these Gentiles win ground upon the outward court in England! and how does their winning ground drive the true worshippers into the inner temple, and cause them to abandon their mixture with the outward court! thus as the new Reformation makes way for ruining the outward court, so the Gentiles' winning more upon the outward court furthers the new Reformation; God carrying on these two works at once. Now this word "*given*" shews an easy kind of conquest obtained by the Popish party, to whom the fort is yielded and given up without much or long holding out: and in such a dispensation towards carnal Protestants, thus to give them up again to the Gentiles, God may have many and glorious ends before he brings in that glorious church to come; as 1st, To have a purer church, according to the primitive institution, these treaders of his courts becoming loathsome to him with their oblations: and though the first Reformation was outwardly in shew more specious and glorious for the multitude of the reformed, and this is to be a much smaller and narrower building; yet this second building of a temple without a court, consisting of purer worship and worshippers, squared by the word, shall in true glory excel the other. 2dly, To let many taste of the fruit of their own ways, who though church-zealots, and defenders of religion against the Papists, yet cast out God's true worshippers and their ministers, saying, "Let God be glorified," (Isa. lxvi. 5,) whilst they beat their fellow-servants, (Matt. xxiv. 49:) yet herein they are retaliated, being cast out in turn; and their protection and defence ceasing, they are given up to the Gentiles. 3dly, God let Popery come into the world, because men "received not the love of the truth," (2 Thes. ii. 10,) and therefore it will overflow again after so clear a shining of the prophecy of the witnesses. 4thly, To throw out the rubbish that would hinder the glory of the temple to be built; for such Protestants, like the Samaritans in Ezra iv. 1, 2, offering to assist the building, yet not called of God unto it, would only be a hinderance. 5thly, That true worshippers only, and faithful witnesses who stood the trial against the invasions of Popery, might have the honour and praise of that glorious restauration and resurrection of the church and witnesses, yet to come, v. 12, 13. This trial upon all the churches burns up and consumes the dross, and discovers the unsoundness of these carnal Protestants, (that have spoken as big words, and talked as hotly as any against Popery, making it the evidence of their sincerity,) by their base yielding to the Popish Gentiles; that when Christ revives his church again, (v. 12, 13,) he may appear to his people's glory and to their shame. 6thly, That the Gentiles might thus accomplish their time and period of forty two months, with an investment of the Pope into his old territories, towards the expiring of his lease, when he will himself expire almost in full possession; that so the confusion of Antichrist, (the greatest work to be done for the church since the apostles' days,) may be the more glorious unto God. Thus Dan. xi. 44, 45, seemed to foretell, That after these "tidings out of the north should trouble him, (the seceding of the northern kingdoms,) as also "out of the east," (through the Turk's prevailing so near his territories;) enraged hereby, he would "go forth in great fury, and plant his tabernacle again, (his power and jurisdiction,) upon the glorious holy mountain, (where the temple stands,) between the seas;" yet after all this recovery of his power over the Reformed churches, "he shall come to his end, and none shall help him." So when the whore of Rome begins to sing her sister Babel's song, just afore he fall, and "saith in her heart, I sit as a queen, and am no widow, (as having her ancient paramours again,) and shall see no sorrow; therefore shall her plagues come in one day, for strong is the LORD that judgeth her," and omnipotently confounds her, c. xviii. 7, 8: and in c. xvii. 13, 17, the ten kings or states of Europe are twice mentioned; first, as giving their power to the beast, and then as *agreeing* to do so through some special hand of God "to fulfil his will," even till the words of God (in Daniel) be fulfilled.

In conclusion, From the above interpretation I exclude not the idea of a measuring the temple, &c. at the first Reformation, when churches were erected by our worthies, in separation from Popery, they casting out that Catholic Romish church as not agreeing with the rule. And so that Reformation and separation falling out when the Turks possessed the eastern empire, (being the sixth trumpet, c. ix. 13, &c.) this chapter beginning with that Reformation, should thereby orderly continue the story of the sixth trumpet, without any chasm between c. ix. and xi. whereas to draw it down to our time leaves an interim or vacuity of near three centuries; yet the one being a true measuring, as the other is the finishing of that building whereof the Reformers' hands laid the foundation, (like Zerubbabel, whose hands were also to finish the temple, Zech. iv. 9,) therefore I verily think that the Holy

Ghost had an aim to both, as two several gradual accomplishments of it, as in other prophecies, (when the last of several in his eye is yet mainly intended :) and this double aspect here, I shall shew when I come to the killing of the witnesses.

III.—THE WITNESSES DESCRIBED.

"AND I WILL GIVE POWER TO MY TWO WITNESSES, AND THEY SHALL PROPHESY A THOUSAND TWO HUNDRED AND THREESCORE DAYS, CLOTHED IN SACKCLOTH: THESE ARE THE TWO OLIVE-TREES, AND THE TWO CANDLESTICKS STANDING BEFORE THE GOD OF THE EARTH: AND IF ANY MAN WILL HURT THEM, FIRE PROCEEDETH OUT OF HIS MOUTH AND DEVOURETH THEIR ENEMIES; AND IF ANY MAN WILL HURT THEM, HE MUST IN THIS MANNER BE KILLED: THESE HAVE POWER TO SHUT HEAVEN, THAT IT RAIN NOT IN THE DAYS OF THEIR PROPHESY: AND HAVE POWER OVER WATERS TO TURN THEM TO BLOOD, AND TO SMITE THE EARTH WITH ALL PLAGUES AS OFTEN AS THEY WILL," v. 3—6.

I.—*The division, order, and times of the particular acts ascribed to the witnesses.*

First, *For their description,* I come now to the angel's discourse concerning the *two witnesses,* who are "the holy people, whose power is at last to be scattered;" to make way for the relation of which scattering, their condition is set forth, v. 3—6: and yet that John might know of whom he spake, as at last to be thus killed, they are described to him as opposing Antichrist in every age, because the angel needs to mention their whole time; but they are specially set forth by what in their latter times, immediately before their killing, they should have power to oppose the beast in, who yet should prevail against them *after* they had set up a temple, and poured out four vials, and that highest fourth-vial plague of *devouring fire.* Now they are described, first, By their *office,* as *witnesses,* (*Testes,*) to prot*est* against Antichrist, especially now at last; and as *prophets,* to *feed* the church in the wilderness for twelve hundred and sixty years, c. xii. 6. Secondly, By their *condition,* as in sackcloth and mourning, whilst the Pope and his clergy are triumphing in their silk. Thirdly, By their *number,* being *two;* 1st, "By the mouth of *two* (or three) witnesses shall every word be established," (2 Cor. xiii. 1.) 2dly, In allusion to these famous pairs or couples who lived in like times, figurative of the various progress of the state of the church through the ages of Antichrist's reign: these were, *Moses* and *Aaron,* prophets to the church in Egypt, in the wilderness; *Elias* and *Elisha,* prophets to Israel in Ahab's idolatrous day, when no face of a church was seen, and there were hid in corners seven thousand of the Lord's secret ones; *Zerubbabel* and *Joshua,* prophets in the days of finishing the temple, after the people were come forth from the captivity of Babylon. That the Holy Ghost here alludes to these appears, From the *plagues* of Egypt executed in v. 6; From the *fire* of Moses twice consuming his gainsayers, v. 5; By Elijah and Elisha's preventing *rain*, v. 6; By Joshua and Zerubbabel being the *two olive-trees* and *candlesticks*, that began and finished the temple. Now all these were eminent *ministers* and *magistrates;* and as such also the witnesses are *two:* and thus we have their *quality*, *office*, *condition*, and *number*.

Secondly, *They are set forth by their several exploits during their prophecy*, as particularly related in each verse following, the recital of which is so ordered as to draw our eyes to two of these facts, as more eminent and nearest the times of this last age of measuring the temple, viz. Their devouring their enemies with *fire*, v. 5, and Their being two *olive-trees*, &c. v. 4: these two things are first mentioned as setting forth these witnesses at first view, according to what they should be in this latter age: For, *First*, The words in v. 5, "*If any man hurt them, fire comes out of their mouths*," &c. refer directly to v. 3; as if the angel had said, "I will give to my two witnesses power—that if any man hurt them, fire shall come out of their mouths," &c. Now the CAI of v. 3, notes out that special opposition these witnesses should have power to make against those Gentiles entering on their outward court; "*But* I will give my witnesses power, that if any hurt them," &c. "*And I will give*" referring to this, as well as to "*And they shall prophesy:*" for whereas he had said three things, in v. 1, 2: That the *temple* was to be measured and finished in this latter age by the godly, (represented by John:) That the *outward court*, fencing the temple and witnesses, was to be regained by the Papists, and trodden down: That the *Gentiles'* whole time of reigning, (on this occasion mentioned,) was to expire. Answerably, and oppositely, with a "*but*," (as CAI is taken,) three things are said of these witnesses: 1st, That the same space of time wherein those Gentiles reign, the same the witnesses have to prophesy in, and to oppose them; the twelve hundred and sixty days of the one being the forty-two months of the other. 2dly, Whereas this temple was in this latter age to be begun to be measured, but interrupted in the progress by the assualt of these Gentiles on the court and temple; yet these witnesses shall be as those "*two olive-trees*, (v. 4,) that minister before the Lord of the whole earth," (whose power is engaged in that work;) Joshua and Zerubbabel being so called in Zech. iv. in respect of their performing the like work of finishing the temple against all opposition. 3dly, Although those Gentiles, in their subduing the outward court, do much hurt to the witnesses, who oppose them in this their assault on it, and on the temple; yet they again shall be able to avenge all the hurt done to themselves, by *fire* returned upon their enemies, and spit out of their mouths against them, in their attempt to regain the outward court. *Secondly,* This power of hurting their enemies is spoken of as a matter of fact, done at the present time, and in the age wherein John, in the vision, stands in the name of the godly meters: and to encourage them, "If any man will hurt them, *fire* comes out of their mouth." *Thirdly,* Whatever is said of their power, in v. 6, (besides the two things, in v. 4, 5,) is added only to illustrate the power besides what they have in their days formerly exercised. "These have power in the days of their prophesy," &c. v. 6. But the main thing, first mentioned, is their "devouring their enemies with *fire,*" which is plainly the fourth vial, following as an adjunct to the measuring of the temple. *Fourthly,* This their exploit hath also an emphasis on it, v. 5, "*In this manner he must be killed,*" (who hurts them;) as noting the greatest plague these witnesses could execute, which so vexeth and tormenteth their enemies, (v. 10,) and so *scorcheth* them, (c. xvi. 8, 9,) that they are irritated to kill them for it, and so to rejoice over them chiefly in this very respect. *Fifthly,* These four plagues being plainly the four first vials, they are here mentioned in an *inverted order* from c. xvi. for the *fire*-vial there is last, and here first in execution; so that on the *earth,* there first, is here last; to shew that the fire-vial belonged to the present times of this chapter and its visions, (when the temple was measured,) and as mainly intended; and the other to come in only for illustration's sake, to prove the witnesses to be these vial-pourers.

II.—*The witnesses' acts in the darkest ages, and also in the separation from Popery.*

The serviceable acts of the witnesses for the name of God all this long time of their prophecy, respect their enemies and the temple-church of God; What in this last age they were to do before their killing, and now when the temple is measured and the outward court to be trodden down, (v. 4, 5;) and, What in the former ages of their prophecy they had also done, (v. 6;) according to the division of the vials, and in c. xiv. 1st, What they did against their enemies in the days fore-going this latter age, wherein John is supposed to stand, as in v. 6; Either, in the first darkest times of Popery, when the hundred and forty-four thousand stood on mount Zion without a temple, and when idolatry overspread the world, (c. xiv. 1—5,) "*They shut heaven, that it rained not;*" as Elijah did in Ahab's time, when he thought himself left alone; and Ahab and his priests of Baal, (as the Pope and his mass-priests,) ruled the world: This signifies their privilege of exclusive grace, and of the dews and influence of heaven, so as to have a truth of doctrine among them to save them; which fell not into the knowledge and hearts of these priests of Baal; see c. xiv. 3. These gracious dews of saving doctrine, restrained from those apostates, were a just curse on their apostacy. Or, 2dly, From and after the times of their separation from Popery, and on their coming out of that Egypt, they execute the like plagues to those of Moses and Aaron in Egypt, even the three first vials, which are therefore in v. 6, (see c. xvi.) and these are the days of separation from Antichrist, and first Reformation in c. xiv.

III.—*The witnesses' acts in this their last age of prophecy.*

First, *The devouring of men with fire.* Towards the time of the new Reformation of the temple, and afore this their killing, they pour out the fourth vial in scorching and devouring their enemies with *fire*, (v. 5,) whether Papists or other injurious persons. And as Moses had brought the people out of Egypt, and long since set up the tabernacle and other ordinances of worship, when Nadab and Abihu were devoured with fire, and the princes in the rebellion of Korah, (Lev. x. 1, 2: Num. xvi. 35:) so after the church comes out of that spiritual Egypt, where these former plagues were executed; and after the public worship is erected and set up by the Reformation, according to God's appointment in many things; this rebellion breaks out against the witnesses' endeavouring to keep to the word of God in his temple's frame and fabric, and against their calling for this at the builders' hands. The quarrels of both those companies then, and of these now are parallelled thus: The first quarrel then was about introducing human inventions in God's worship; and the second was not only a renewing and continuing that quarrel, but a taking away all distinction of persons in worshipping; for Nadab and Abihu "offered *strange* (or culinary) *fire* before the Lord," instead of the altar-fire from heaven; therefore fire consumed them for justifying such unwarrantable inventions: and as for Korah and his company they offered incense, though no priests, and also quarrelled with Moses and Aaron, for excluding some of the Levites from the priesthood. Now in England and other churches since the Reformation, (of the latter days of which time this is especially here understood, for it is the fourth vial,) the quarrel has been about the strange fire of human inventions, continued and justified against the few witnesses for the commands of God to be the only rule of worship: And as for the putting such a difference between man and man, between the holy and profane, this hath been a still greater grievance of hot and violent opposition against these witnesses, who insist that those who have such or such a work of grace on their hearts, and endeavour to walk thus and thus holy, are alone saints: the stream of their ministry in England, hath still run in this channel of distinguishing men from men, "the precious from the vile;" their work and bent hath been to mark out from that promiscuous mixture, who it is God hath chosen, and who only are true priests and worshippers of God in spirit and truth; and for this, their opponents, quarrel with them, and silence them, saying as Korah's company, "Are not all the people holy? (have they not all been baptized?) ye take too much upon you, (out of the pride of your spirits, ye precise ones,) to lift up yourselves above the congregation of the Lord." Or again, The quarrel hath been about God's own election of a few to be priests unto him, (as Levi was chosen from Israel, and Aaron from the house of Levi,) "Who are his, and whom he hath chosen:" so these now plead the cause of all mankind in universal grace and redemption. Accordingly, all the quarrels between the Popish party and the witnesses are reducible to two heads: True purity of worship, and, True holiness and peculiar election of worshippers. The light in both these things hath in our days grown up so high and so clear, that many opponents of these sin out of rebellion and presumption, against their own convictions of the truth; and so their punishment like that of those conspirators against Moses and Aaron, is the *fire* of the fourth vial, a spiritual judgment on their souls, effected by the powerful conviction of the word out of the mouth of the witnsses, who spit fire into their consciences, and begin hell-fire aforehand: and this very allusion is thus interpreted, Heb. x. 26, 27: For, 1st, The sin of both is rebellion. After Moses' conviction of Korah's company, he was despitefully scorned and reproached by them for bringing them out of Egypt; and so these "sin *wilfully* after receiving the knowledge of the truth;" as here "if any man *will* hurt them," which is repeated v. 5. 2dly, As they were struck dead by God "for despising Moses' law," under conviction of it "by two or three witnesses," (as Moses and Aaron:) so here the angel adjudgeth them to this notorious death for despising the testimony of these two witnesses, and the light of the gospel. 3dly, Their punishment was of all then the sorest, even "a dying without mercy;" but "of *how much sorer* punishment shall he be thought worthy," &c.? for "*in this manner* he must be killed," not with elementary fire, nor so much by killing their bodies as their souls: as the Hebrew doctors say of Korah, &c. (who were rather blasted than burnt,) that their *souls* were *scorched;* and thus they were most lively types for sinners under the gospel, to whom God becomes a *consuming fire.* 4thly, That which is here called *fire* is called by Paul *fiery indignation:* and "a fearful expectation of judgment;" God sealing up by flashes of his wrath the eternal damnation of such sinners: aud this "fiery indignation" sparkles forth upon all occasions from the writings and lives, and from the preaching and testimonies of those witnesses' mouths. 5thly, Here is the phrase of "*devouring* their enemies," as the apostle speaks of devouring the *under-hand adversaries,* (HUPENANTIOUS, *Subcontrarios;*) shewing that such sinners, (like the Pharisees,) renounce not always all profession of God; for so they should not have place and opportunity of hurting the witnesses by their under-hand pretensions and opposition. 6thly, Such was the effect of the powerful, burning, and shining light of the ministry of John and of Christ, (whose crucifying is also alluded to v. 7—13;) the Pharisees being *tormented* with it; (as in v. 10, with c. xvi. 9;) and in Mal. iv. 1, the gospel-day became to the Pharisees "a terrible day, burning *their consciences* as an oven," so that in the heat of their wrath they crucified Christ, knowing him to be the Son of God, even as the witnesses were known to be his prophets.

Secondly, *The temple-work of the witnesses,* for Christ and the church, also sets forth their power in these latter days, especially that in v. 1, represented most lively by the olive-trees and candlesticks, in Zech. iv. where Joshua and Zerubbabel having begun to sacrifice after the people's first coming out of Babylon, and to set up public worship, within two years laid the foundation of the temple, and set up the altar, (Ezra iii.) but left the work imperfect, without the roof covered, or the temple beautified with all those holy utensils and ornaments, appointed as ordinances to the complement and perfection of God's worship; and all this, through the opposition of a Samaritan faction, of a mongrel religion, (2 Kings xvii. 41,) pretending "to seek their God as they did," (Ezra iv. 2—5, 23, 24;) but not being taken into this work of building, nor owned by the true Jews, they forced the same to cease, instigating the Persian monarch to frustrate their purpose; until Haggai and Zechariah were sent to stir up Joshua and Zerubbabel to finish the work, which was yet a true temple, and place of worship, all the years it remained imperfect. Among other visions exciting them, was that of *two-olive trees,* (called "*sons of oil,*" as laying out their grace, gifts, and estates, and spending their fatness, in hearty endeavours for repairing and finishing the temple;) and a *candlestick,* whereinto they emptied their oil; for this being the most necessary utensil to complete and shew the glory of the temple, (into which it was brought last of all,) is put for all the rest: Hence Zerubbabel is represented with a *plummet* in his hand, and a *measuring-line,* (as John used the *reed,*) for measuring the temple to be now fully finished; for the hands that laid the foundation, were to finish it, in spite of the Samaritan "*great mountain*" of opposition: Now the meaning of this hieroglyphic is given in the angel's answer to his own question, "Knowest thou what these be? this is the word of the Lord," &c. Thus the church having long since come out of mystical Babylon, hath set up public worship, and by the authority of princes hath begun the foundation of the temple, but hath been hindered from going on to full perfection of discipline intended and endeavoured through the mixture of a *Samaritan party,* interrupting the attainment of the perfection contended for: But in the end God stirs up many of the English spirits, (like unto Joshua and Zerubbabel,) to finish what was before left incomplete, and to begin to make a further and purer edition of churches according to the pattern: and so they stand in this age with a *line* or *reed*, and do empty oil out of themselves unto this work; endeavouring to add to this temple ordinances instituted of God, and tending to the perfection, beauty, complement, and glory of the temple, though not absolutely necessary to the being of a church: And though the allusion includes the foundation of this temple-church laid in the first Reformation, yet it principally falls upon the finishing of it; which is the proper and peculiar aim of the vision. From c. i. 20, it is evident that *churches* eminent for purity, as well as *persons*, are witnesses *against* the false church; though these witnesses may be oil-bearers *for* the candlesticks, which being here two, shew that these are sister-churches now, and not only one mother-church as then; and the proportion is doubled in other respects also, to shew the increase of gospel-blessings, as observed in c. iv. Now this new Reformation of the church in attempts to finish the temple, through now as "a day of small things despised," shall go on and spread till it be perfected, for it is "not by power, nor by might, but by my Spirit, saith *the God of the whole earth*," (v. 4,) whose power backs it, and causes the hearts of the godly to fall to it; and the Romish "great mountain," so standing in its way, "shall yet become a plain before it." And as the vials are to come out of this temple, it shews that the true church is to be the plague and ruin of the false: But however small are the beginnings of such a work, so interesting the divine glory, it will progress, and its progress is in this book noticed, as observed in c. xiv. yet I fear these olive-trees and candlesticks will, (like the rest of the churches in Europe,) have their *power* scattered, ere the building be finished, and they revive again, and "grow up into an holy temple in the Lord," Eph. ii. 21, with c. xix.. Finally, As the witnesses are here in sackcloth, so Joshua (Zech. iii. 4,) was in *filthy apparel;* and as there he had change of raiment given him, so after a few years will these witnesses also have "the garment of praise for the spirit of heaviness," (Isa. lxi. 3;) and their testimony being ended, they shall put off their sackcloth, and put on "fine linen," the wedding-dress of the Lamb's wife, as in c. xix. 8; and so in the end, the glory of this temple, set up after Antichrist's demolishment, will yet be more glorious, (as Zerubbabel's also was, Hag. ii. 9,) by Christ's coming into it; when a Holy of holies shall be added to it, (or rather swallow it up,) in which "the ark shall be seen;" but not till after

IV.—THE KILLING OF THE WITNESSES.

"AND WHEN THEY SHALL HAVE FINISHED THEIR TESTIMONY, THE BEAST THAT ASCENDETH OUT OF THE BOTTOMLESS PIT, SHALL MAKE WAR AGAINST THEM, AND SHALL OVERCOME THEM, AND KILL THEM: AND THEIR DEAD BODIES SHALL LIE IN THE STREET

OF THE GREAT CITY, WHICH SPIRITUALLY IS CALLED SODOM AND EGYPT, WHERE ALSO OUR LORD WAS CRUCIFIED. AND THEY OF THE PEOPLE, AND KINDRDES, AND TONGUES, AND NATIONS, SHALL SEE THEIR DEAD BODIES THREE DAYS AND AN HALF, AND SHALL NOT SUFFER THEIR DEAD BODIES TO BE PUT IN GRAVES. AND THEY THAT DWELL UPON THE EARTH SHALL REJOICE OVER THEM, AND MAKE MERRY, AND SHALL SEND GIFTS ONE TO ANOTHER; BECAUSE THESE TWO PROPHETS TORMENTED THEM THAT DWELT ON THE EARTH." v. 7—10.

I.—*The* time *of the witnesses' killing not yet come.*

The angel's scope here being to shew, according to his oath in Daniel, how Antichrist should "accomplish to scatter the power of the holy people," towards the end of his three and a half times' reign; what is here said of the beast's war and victory, refers not to the conquests and slaughters which Antichrist, during his reign, should make of the holy people or witnesses, (spoken of in c. xiii.) but specifies an eminent prevailing over them, on the eve of finishing their sackcloth-prophesying. We have seen their power to erect a temple to themselves, whence to pour forth four vials upon their enemies: and the better to fence themselves against the beast, thus possessed of the greatest part of Europe, (or the holy city,) they environed the temple with a court, or mighty party of carnal Protestant fellow-separatists from the beast. The treading down this court by the Gentiles, who are again to subdue it to themselves, is a part of this final scattering of the saints' power, or rather a preparation thereunto; for before the beast can get at the witnesses to kill them, the court must be more fully won, (which is now a doing,) and then both themselves and their inner temple will be exposed to the irruptions of these Gentiles, and easily subdued by them, these out-works being taken and recovered. The great question here, is about the time of this killing, whether it be past or to come. Mr. Brightman makes the whole fulfilled in the overthrow of the Protestants in Germany by Charles the Fifth, (A.D. 1547,) and that condemning of the scriptures, (these two witnesses, or the Old and New Testaments,) by the council of Trent, about three centuries ago: but Graserus, Hoe, Mede, Wood, &c. think it yet to come; and if the series of interpretation I have given hold good, it must needs be so; and both what precedes and what follows this great event, confirms the same; nothing of what must follow being yet fulfilled, though several centuries have past since Mr. Brightman's date. 1st, This is to fall out at the close of their mournful state of prophesying, after which they shall cast off their sackcloth, as after Joshua's captivity-garments were taken from him; he had a mitre set on his head; so these on their rising again are to be cloathed in fine linen: but the church is still bewailing her condition under Antichrist, and those other enemies even in the Reformed churches who are triumphing in silk and liberty. 2dly, This "killing" is towards the close of Antichrist's reign in respect of his "*power to do*," for this is that last *scattering* of Daniel, wherewith he is to accomplish his *times:* but his kingdom yet stands, and it is three hundred years since that German havoc, and we are still under the fifth vial; for when Rome itself, the seat and throne of the beast, shall come to be ruined, then his kingdom shall be full of darkness, and his glory so put out, that his reign will be accounted at an end. 3dly, Antichrist is still but in his first march towards this war, to win and recover the court of the temple, that he may come at the witnesses to kill them: and though he hath trodden down Germany, yet he is but setting up and advancing his engines of assault and battery on other such places where God hath most of his powerful witnesses in these last times, in whose siege he is set down by his agents and the receivers of "the number of his name," who are to be his last champions. 4thly, Four of the seven vials are to be poured out by the witnesses before their killing, for in the days of their prophecy, they smite the earth with plagues, (which is the *first* vial,) and turn the *sea* and *rivers* into blood, (which is the *second* and *third* vials,) and then devour *men* with *fire*, (which is the *fourth* vial:) after all which exploits comes their *killing*. But that slaughter three hundred years ago was but in the beginning of the second vial, and we see not yet the full effect of the fourth, which is still pouring out its contents. 5thly, After the witnesses' rising, the second woe of the *sixth* trumpet is to pass away, (v. 14,) its times being expired, or the foundation of its ruin laid; and this is the great power and tyranny of the Turk, whose kingdom yet stands in its vigour and flourish, no fundamental blow of weakening being given it; much less, 6thly, Is the *seventh* trumpet begun to be blown, which yet is to come quickly after the sixth; for although Jesus Christ, in the northern kingdoms, hath been assisted in that his harvest of his elect since the Reformation, by supreme and princely authority, (and therefore that peaceable harvest was reaped by a *crowned* angel,) yet 1, The kingdoms of the world becoming Christ's for him to reign for ever, (and that, at the beginning of the seventh trumpet,) will be different from what he hath yet had, being the fifth monarchy, to begin when the beast's days end, (Dan. vii. 14,) and to be carried on, not so much by deputies and delagated power, as under the immediate rule and government of Christ himself, v. 17; And, 2, When the seventh trumpet shall begin to sound, "then shall the mystery be fulfilled spoken of by the prophets," (c. x. 7, with Acts iii. 21,) even the new Jerusalem and kingdom of the saints, and first resurrection, (v. 15—17, with c. xx. 1, &c.) but since what Mr. Brightman calls the "resurrection of the witnesses," none of these things are begun, or as yet to begin. 3, The seventh trumpet and last vial fall out together, or rather the last vial begins the seventh trumpet, (as v. 19, with c. xvi. 18, shews;) there being the same thunderings, hail, &c. in both: now we are yet but under the fourth vial, and so very far off from the last.

I will however add this, which may reconcile also Mr. Brightman's opinion, and haply serve, in the closure of all, to hint further about the *expiring of times* at the last vial's fulfilling. In the measurement of the temple, the angel might aim both at that first laying the foundation of true churches, and also at this second Reformation now in hand, as degrees of the same work, though the latter is specially intended, (the other yet being a far greater work;) so might he take in *two killings* of these witnesses, following and accompanying both these measurings, the one near the foundation, and the other near the finishing; and so ordered, that the first should be a foregoing resemblance of the succeeding. Many prophecies have had several gradual accomplishments; the former becoming types of the latter mainly intended: and there are many passages spoken of as fulfilled in the New Testament, which yet had a gradual accomplishment in the times after the Babylonish captivity: thus Isa. i. 9, is applied in Rom. ix. 27, to gospel-times, the Holy Ghost aiming at both. And even in the Old Testament the same prophecy is sometimes fulfilled over and over: Thus as there were two eminent leadings into captivity, the one of Jeconiah, the other of Zedekiah; so there is a double reckoning of the seventy years, and of the building again of the temple; (and this instance I pitch on as a type of this *measuring of the temple;*) for Ezek. i. 2, 3, begins the captivity from the carrying away of Jeconiah, in the fifth year of Nebuchadnezzar; and Jer. xxix. 10, comforts the captives with the promise of being visited after seventy years, when Cyrus gave leave to lay the foundation of the temple: and yet after this, when the temple was to be again measured and completed, another seventy years is said to be ended, (commencing from the nineteenth year of Nebuchadnezzar;) as in Zech, i. 12, 16. And why may not the Holy Ghost have an eye here also to a double work, and a double accomplishment of the beast's reign, and of the church's coming out of Babylon, and of the killing of the witnesses, and of the measuring of the temple; though this last be mainly intended? Again, In Dan. xii. 4, 11, (referring to the New Testament, "when knowledge should be increased," &c.) the angel shews, that from the time of removing the Jews' daily sacrifices, and of setting up the desolating abomination, were to be twelve hundred and ninety *days*, i. e. *years*. Now there hath been a double removal of that sacrifice, and also a double setting up of "the abomination of desolation," or Heathenish idolatry: for from the sacking of Jerusalem by Vespasian and his son Titus, to about A.D. 1360, was just so many years; and then began that first great increase of knowledge and discovery of Antichrist, under Wickliffe, Thaulerus, &c. But there was another, "ceasing of the daily sacrifice (of the Christian religion,) and setting up of the abomination" of Heathenism by Julian, the apostate emperor, about A.D. 363: indeed he set up the Jewish sacrifice again, that had ceased, but has never since been restored; God's special hand binding all the Jews from setting up their daily sacifices at Jerusalem again; for the Turk suffers them not to live there, and tolerates all exercises of all religions except that of the sacrifices: and Christians themselves possess the sepulchre of the Lord. Now Mr. Brightman reckons the beginning of Antichrist's reign, and of the witnesses' prophesying in sackcloth, from the time of the Roman emperor's removing to Constantinople, leaving Rome to the Pope for the seat of his power, in fulfilment of 2 Thes. ii. 7; when "the man of sin" was at least *conceived:* the end of those years would thus be A.D. 1550, when the revival of the Protestant cause in Germany began : so the term of Antichrist's power to *do*, might have had one period in the falling off of England, Scotland, &c. before A.D. 1560, (which he interprets of the seventh trumpet, when the kingdoms of this world became Christ's, c. xi. 15,) and so, before that settled peace of the gospel, and Antichrist's ejection; the witnesses having first had their several times of being overcome and killed, in each of their kingdoms, for three years and a half; as in that victory over the Protestants in Germany, about A.D. 1547, just three years and a half before that revival and enjoyment of the peace they have since had: Also in England the martyrdoms under Mary lasted but three years and a half; for the former two years and a half of her reign were spent in making preparations for that war against the witnesses, by statutes made for their *burning*, &c. Again, in France, A.D. 1572, (about twelve hundred and sixty years after Constantine) the massacre of the Protestants began; but the deceased religion had a resurrection in A.D. 1576. There is also another computation from the *birth* of Antichrist, about a hundred years after Constantine, (the two centuries later still, in p. 603, may be his *naming*, or his being *of age*,) when the western empire itself began first to break into ten kingdoms: accordingly since A.D. 1660, there was begun a second measuring of the temple; and before the finishing of it there will follow another great and eminent slaughter of the witnesses by the beast's again prevailing over them.

II.—*The allusion to Christ's passion in this killing of the witnesses.*

In all other passages of this book, the allusions are still to stories of the Old Testament; but this, as standing alone, is in exact conformity to the circumstances of that great centre-story of Christ's death and resurrection, which being typed of old, are now made transcendent patterns beyond all sufferings, (as in Phil. iii. 20, Col. i. 24,) in any former age; whereby we are both provoked to prepare for it, as Christ did; and also comforted against it, as being thereby to be made specially conformable to Christ in his glory also. Thus Christ, after *three years and a half's* ministry, (when he had almost carried it in the people's hearts, the world going after him,) was at length prevailed over by his enemies, and put to death by the sovereign power of Rome, which then had jurisdiction in Jerusalem,) and for *three days and a half* lay in their power: So when these witnesses are about to finish their testimony, their Pharisean enemies, (afraid of losing their own credit and authority, through their prevailing in the people's hearts,) will acknowledge the foreign power of Rome, so far as by and under the authority, and for the sake of the beast, to kill them and have them in their power, for three years and a half; whereupon they feast, and "send gifts for joy," as the Pharisees, ridding themselves of the torment of Christ's ministry, made the passion-passover the most joyful feast they ever kept. But Christ and his witnesses, both *rise again*, and with an *earthquake* too, and also amidst the *consternation* of their enemies; after which, both *ascend* to heaven: and to confirm the allusion, the Holy Ghost puts in a parenthesis, (v. 8,) "*Where* also our Lord was crucified;" meaning either "*Sodom* and *Egypt*," and *Jerusalem* also, "*Where also*," &c. or, referring to "crucified;" q. d. "*where also* the witnesses are in like manner to be *killed*."

III.—*The killing of the witnesses executed by the power of the beast, and not by any previous persecutions in the Reformed churches among themselves.*

To explain somewhat about this great occurrence yet to come in the church: The power authorizing this slaughter is to be that of *the beast*, or Pope of Rome, who having regained more or less influence in the places where these witnesses are, is to kill them, (v. 7,) though they are hated also of all their enemies who are of the Reformed religion among them: and besides, the place where their dead bodies lie, (and consequently where the slaughter is to be executed,) is "*the city* where our Lord was crucified," (c. xvii. 18,) the jurisdiction of the Roman empre being so called in John's time; as Popedom is the church of Rome, and all its kingdoms make up "*that great city*." Now Rome was as the royal palace of the Roman world, whence issued edicts and commands over all; and therefore the sentence of Christ's death was pronounced by Pilate the Roman governor residing in the holy city: thus the beast of Rome shall again recover so much owning and acknowledging, (by secret combination, or by professed avouchment,) in the places of the Reformation where the witnesses are to be killed, as that for his sake, and at his instigation, those *Pharisees*, (either as joining with him, or else using the help of his party,) shall kill them, the beast having so much hand in it as to be said to do it, and that for the further advancement of his power in these places: Now their dead bodies are to lie "in the *street* (or *extent of the jurisdiction)* of the great city," (v. 8,) which is the *outward court* of the temple. Whatever enemies the witnesses have had from among themselves, of the same nation and religion, (as the Pharisees were to Christ,) who have persecuted them from the times of the first Reformation, and made them continue to prophesy in sackcloth, notwithstanding the separation from Antichrist; yet none of all those wars and prevailings are this eminent *killing* by the *beast*, with whom these enemies combine, using the help of the Papists against the witnesses; or perhaps beginning again more openly and avowedly to submit to the beast, (as the Pharisees did to Cæsar,) to advance whose power they shall kill these witnesses, his greatest and heartiest withstanders: Or, if in doing this, they do not so openly avow the beast's power, it may yet be said to be done by him, if done through such agents; and we may be suspicious of this, for there is a generation of men, (as shewed out of c. xiii.) set forth as the beast's last champions, who not at first avowing his name or character, yet receive "the number of his name," and are reckoned truly his, as interdicting commerce to his opponents, in order to advance him: and I fear they shall proceed yet further, if not to confess the Pope as "infallible head of the church," yet as "universal patriarch of the west," so endeavouring to effect union and reconciliation with him; for these men are at first to bring in but an image of Popery, (as Popery was an image of Heathenism,) with intent to introduce more, as was said; whereunto accords this angel's oath in Dan. xii. 7, concerning the beast's *scattering* the saints, &c. And as the Gentiles are to obtain the outward court to tread it down, with the the rest of the holy city, it argues their prevailing so far as to gain a subjection from carnal Protestants, through whom the beast's power may be said to kill the witnesses, as Pilate crucified Christ in the name of Rome; so Rome through her legates will depose and put to death, in those places, these witnesses: that as Jerusalem was to be the slaughter-house of all the prophets, (Luke xiii. 33,) so Rome is to have a hand in the deaths of all the witnesses, (though others may persecute them too,) and to execute this last great martyrdom: for in her downfall she is to be reckoned with, (c. xviii. 24,) as having the blood of the prophets, and saints, and all the slain found in her: until therefore the Romish flag be advanced on the walls of the court of the temple, we must not reckon the time of the witnesses' three years and a half to be come; but when we see that "abomination of desolation" begun to be set up, then let us "flee to the mountain."

IV.—*The time of the beast's enjoying his full victory over the witnesses is but* three years and a half, *though he may be longer a killing them, and obtaining it.*

The Popish Gentiles have already been long a besieging the temple, and making war against it, without prevailing yet, even so far as to overcome fully enough the court, and gain the out-work; but how far so ever this war may be lengthened out, when it once comes to a complete victory, we are comforted that the witnesses shall begin to rise again from their killing within three years and a half: and as the time of the greatest obscuration is specially noted as the time of the eclipse, so in this great and last hour of the church's darkness, the time of its eclipse alone is reckoned. The Pharisees plotted long against Christ, consulting his ruin, but prevailed only for three days and a half, "or the midst (or half) of the week," (Dan. ix. 27,) which *days* of the witnesses must be prophetically *years*, (as are the twelve hundred and sixty,) not only so as to exhibit their dead bodies before nations and tongues, in reports of this beast's victorious putting them down, but for the Papists to rejoice therein and send their gifts and congratulations: Now just such a three years and half had Jerusalem under Antiochus, when the temple was polluted, and "the daily sacrifice taken away, and the abomination (of idolatry) set up;" see Dan. xi. 31, &c. with the history of the Maccabees. And therefore after Daniel had set forth and ended this his tyranny, he begins to set out the tyranny of that "*wilful king*," the Pope, his antitype; as Christ passes from the story of Jerusalem's destruction to its fulfilment in the end of the world: so there is a transition there describing Antichrist, whose ruin and end comes after "ill tidings out of the north," (the northern Reformations,) had enraged him to "go forth in fury," utterly to root out the Protestants; in which expedition he is so far to prevail, as "to plant his tabernacles in the glorious holy mountain," and thus to over-run the church; as Antiochus prevailed over the Jews, and the Pharisees over Christ, in their hour of darkness; so this will be "an hour of temptation coming on the whole Christian world," c. iii. 10: the enemies think to get the *day*, but they shall have only their *hour* in this fearful eclipse; and then will be the revival, as in Hosea vi. 2: For three years and a half also Julian again set up idolatry, after forty years reign of Christianity; and so long shall Popery be again set up on every throne where Protestantism hath reigned, till it be utterly and for ever extirpated.

V.—*The* nature *of the beast's victory over the witnesses.*

Some interpret the *killing* the witnesses only of a *civil death*, as *witnesses*, not as *men;* taking away all power from them, by a general silencing of ministers, and deposing of magistrates, and men of worth, that profess and uphold religion, putting men from their high places, shutting their shops, burning their books, &c.

for that as their resurrection is not from a natural death, so their bodies could not be supposed to lie above-ground for three days and a half, before a spirit of life came into them; who being dead must be the same as were killed. Thus also the not suffering them to be put in graves, would signify only what hindered their enemies from killing them outright, the Protestant party in the nations about them preserving them above ground for a reviving, as we leave unburied any of whose death we are not sure: and "the nations, tongues, and kindreds," seeming a distinct company from the witnesses' enemies, (who "rejoice over them," &c.) favours this notion; the angel thus describing the differing spirits of the two sorts of men towards the witnesses, "they of the nations" kindly keeping their bodies out of the grave, and "those that dwell on earth" rejoicing over them. Again, as it was commonly reported that Christ should rise on the third day, (Matt. xxvii. 63,) so this general notion of the Popish party's prevailing for three years and a half, will influence the witnesses' friends to interfere against their utter extinction and burial underground, hoping, (like the disciples as long as Christ lay buried in the grave,) that they will rise again from their lying unburied above-ground. In answer also to the supposition of this last being the worst and arpest of all struggles, they say, That "*killing*" here is alone ecified thus, as being the signal of the Pope's ruin. But, hough I think it cannot be denied, *First*, That this *lying dead* is, metaphorically, a suppressing by civil death, the now desperate cause of the saints, as *witnesses*, so putting them down that they remain as men laid forth by the walls for dead, of whose testimony there is no likelihood of a revival; whereat their enemies rejoice; (as the Pharisees thought they had Christ sure enough in the grave, after his condemnation and crucifixion:) So the last war of the beast *scatters the power* of all the saints, as *witnesses*, but *kills* them not all, as *men*, however the natural lives of many of them may be sacrificed: Yet, *Secondly*, I fear that so great a victory over and suppressing of the witnesses, will be followed with great effusion of martyrs' blood; and that such a warring, and overcoming, and killing, import further proceedings by which they get this complete victory: I fear all these *metaphors*, lest this same *killing after overcoming* be not really and properly some further cruelty of malicious enemies; for "*overcoming*" would sufficiently express the mere suppression of them: and in c. xiii. (which is a prophecy of the rage and utmost cruelty the beast should exercise against the saints throughout his whole reign,) all those bloody executions and butcherings of the saints are expressed also by "*warring*," and "*overcoming;*" the "*killing*," there omitted, being afterwards expressed so as to shew the cause and manner of the beast's bloody fall and ruin in the end, and what provokes God and man unto it; for "He that *killeth* with the sword must *be killed* with the sword," c. xiii. 7, 10: And though Antichrist's power is there set out generally, in its height and ruff, during his whole reign over all, and here only his last special war against the witnesses is described, immediately fore-going his ruin; yet the expressions here as there, may be of the same nature, and import the same mode of prevailing: for though his last war is to issue in the beast's ruin, yet may he first recover again the like power, and exercise the like cruelty over these witnesses, though for a small space: yea, it may be feared, by that dirge of her own funeral-song which she makes in c. xviii. 6—8, that Babylon shall recover her ancient power again, or fully expect it, through her prevailing over some of her lost kingdoms; for only the day before she is to be burnt for a witch and whore, "she saith in her heart, I sit as a queen, and am no widow, and shall see no sorrow;" and then follows God's omnipotent power in her sudden destruction by plagues at once in the midst of her rejoicing. There is a like intimation of the beast's recovering his power, (Dan. xi. 45;) for "*yet* he shall come to his end," unlikely as it is that he should again be put out of such power as he seems so settledly to have regained; even as it appeared impossible that the cause of Christ should again prevail, after the Gentiles and Pharisees had so glutted themselves with his blood, and so triumphed over him in the grave, "Yet (saith Ps. ii. 6,) I have set my king upon my holy hill of Zion." The cruelties Rome may revive, together with the revival of her influence, may revive also the memory of all her former slaughters, and so provoke God and men, as for this her last blood-shed to bring upon her the blood of all the prophets and martyrs before shed; as the blood of Christ brought upon the Jews the blood of all the righteous down from Abel: and as the ten tribes were enraged against the Benjamites with eagerness to root them out, because of their first great victory over themselves; so may the Protestant party be whetted on by fresh killings of the saints to do execution upon such enemies without all mercy, "rewarding her as she had rewarded them," and "killing with the sword her that killed with the sword." But why should this one particular war alone be mentioned by the angel at last, if it were not different from such as Antichrist was wont to make upon the saints, as in c. xiii? I answer, 1st, This war is thus specified as being the last, because it is a signal of the time of Antichrist's ending, and a manifestation of God's wonderful dealing, both with the church and with his enemies; that after so great a victory obtained by her against the beast, he should yet have *power to do* again for a little space, that he might be overthrown when thinking himself as secure as ever. 2dly, It is the last eminent suffering of the European churches, and probably the worst; for sharpest afflictions fore-run the greatest happiness; and here the witnesses die to rise again, and rise again to die no more, as it was with Christ himself. The king of terrors is the porter to let saints into heaven;

2 X

and, says Paul in 1 Cor. iv. 9, "God hath set forth us the apostles last, as it were appointed unto death;" alluding to the gladiators or fencers in the Roman games, the last of which three sorts, (being usually slaves or malefactors,) wont to come upon the stage, were appointed not to go off, but to fight it out till they were killed. The greatest persecution of the church under Pagan Rome was that of Dioclesian and the fifth seal, and therefore all Rome's former martyrings under the former seals do not raise a general cry of their blood, until the arrival of that most cruel persecution; and yet these saints are bid to wait till another martyrdom: but here the witnesses dying as Christ died, shall also rise likewise to die no more. 3dly, This last conquest is mentioned as an epitome of all the witnesses' sufferings during the whole time of their prophecy, and thus the crisis of their three *days* and a half is interpreted by, and is a compendium of, their whole time of proprophecy for three *years* and a half; even as this period reduced to *days* of twelve hundred and sixty, become again so many prophetical *years*. Now as Christ's sufferings, here alluded to, were all summed up in his death; and he was heard and delivered as soon as they came to this, "Why hast thou forsaken me?" so when the church, in her last brunt, shall utter the like voice, know we that delivery is near. 4thly, The beast having been so chased by these witnesses' prophesying, and having had so many vials emptied upon him and his company, will wreak such vengeance, when once he gets the power again, that "his anger will be fierce, and his wrath cruel," (as in Gen. xlix. 7;) and the northern Reformation causing such opposition to him, will stir him up to this his last invasion of the churches "to go forth with great fury to destroy and utterly to make away many," Dan. xi. 44: Thus having nothing but blood and cruelty in their hearts, where would it end if God "restrain not the spirits of these princes," or cut them short by an almighty work of his power. 5thly, In c. xvii. 6, the whore of Rome, just before her ruin, "adds *drunkeness* (Deut. xxix. 19,) to her *thirst* for the blood of saints, thus increased by her *scorching* with *fire* from the witnesses: and that this refers not to her former bloody martyrings, appears from John's telling us that "one of the seven vial-angels, (probably the *fifth*, who poured on the seat of the beast,) shewed him the judgment of the great whore, with whom the kings of the earth had committed fornication," &c. in so many ages fore-past: for that now in these her old and last days she appears so drunk, it makes me fear her new coming out of her cups of blood, (the draught of some fresh cup making her tipsy again;) but so, that she may be surprised however, *Somno Vinoque Sepulta, buried in sleep and drunkenness,* (like Babylon) to her greater judgment and confusion. Yet, 6thly, God may perhaps "restrain the remainder of that wrath, and make it praise him, cutting short their spirits," (Ps. lxxvi. 10, 12:) yea, maugre all their rage, malice, and spirit of revenge; their own wisdom and policy may move them to forbear the full execution of what they *could* do, so as to moderate the use of their victory, especially in a respect to that Protestant party continuing firm in heart and conscience to the cause of these witnesses, though outwardly overcome. The light of the gospel deeply impressing men's spirits is not to be extinguished, so as men shall suddenly embrace Popery for truth: and as the Pharisees "for fear of the people," forbore many attempts against Christ, so may these for fear of those *tongues*, and *kingdoms*, and *nations* in heart favoring Protestants, forbear the extremity of rage in their power; promising themselves perhaps some future more perfect recovery and settlement of their power, and more mischievous ends, when men's consciences shall be more quieted in Popish ways, and the adverse party more lowered and diminished; till the short date of their full power suddenly expiring, they awake from their dream too late to "destroy and utterly make away many," see Ps. lxxiii. 20, Isa. xxix. 7, 8. We have experience of the wisdom of this generation of men loving easy and gradual conquests, who find, that by butchering the saints the cause of Protestantism is advanced; and their own religion branded with the bloody mark of the false and whorish church: such was the policy of the apostate Julian, who yet sinned against the Holy Ghost: but he knew that martyrdom increased the church here, and brightened the martyrs' crown of glory hereafter; and therefore out of envy and a witty malice, he forbore edicts for killing the Christians, and used subtilty to ensnare and tempt men from the truth to the shipwreck of their consciences; and thus he paddled with profane hands in the blood of *souls*, a sweeter victory to him than that of their bodies: and to mischief and diminish them still more, they were denied schools of learning, and the use of books, and all offices either in war or peace. 6thly, Though these Gentiles are so furious "to root out many," yet the issue being expressed by the beast's "planting his tabernacle, (soon to be pulled down again,) on the glorious holy mountain," may imply no more done in the execution of his destructive design, than taking possession again of the church as his throne; Dan. xi. 44, 45. But, 7thly, Let us fear and prepare for the worst, seeing the sins of the witnesses in yielding so far to the superstitions of Rome as to leave some of them in their churches, like so much filth on the shore from the overflowing of the ocean, (the Romish sea,) and their other sins, as carnal-gospelling, worldly-mindedness, &c. also their base yielding up the outward court and deserting their cause; for many among them "shall do wickedly," Dan. xii. 10. Lastly, The utmost to be hoped is such a time with the church as that under Julian, whose persecution might be a figure of this to come; that the last of Paganism, this of Popery: Julian abstained from *violence* of blood at first, but used *deceit;* he smote with the tongue rather than with the sword; he studied to ensnare consciences by placing his own image among idols in the forum, that in refusing to do homage to these false gods, the saints might be accused of denying reverence to him; which course ended in much bloodshed, though without the public edicts of former emperors; the people persecuting Christians to death in various parts of the empire to gratify his hatred of them. Now though this prevailing to come, may prove worse than death by martyrdom, through manifold temptations and snares and cruelties, yet may it be rather an hour of temptation and trial to believers in general, (accompanied perhaps with the Gentiles' killing of many witnesses,) and *difficult* times, (CHALEPOI, 2 Tim. iii. 1,) of these *last* days of Popery, than the *bloody* times of the *latter* days in 1 Tim. iv. 1; and though the *last* days may be stained with much blood also; yet many shall certainly survive this war, after being "made white and tried," (Dan. xii. 10:) for so sudden a resurrection of so great a multitude as shall possess that glorious state of a church described in c. xix. 1—10, at three and half years' end, would hardly arise from a succession of new converts, but from the same persons surviving and out-riding that great storm.

V.—THE EXTENT OF THE KILLING OF THE WITNESSES.

It is a question how far the generality or universality of this slaughter may reach; and, *First*, Whether to all sorts of professors of religion, or only to eminent persons in the church? as *witnesses*, probably the most excellent saints will be singled out to a duel, or single combat as it were. The Gentiles before this had the outward court of carnal professors more easily yielded; but among these truly godly ones, they find serious and stiff opposers that will never be brought to yield to them: and the Popish party themselves see and find, that the godly of the Protestants are their only real enemies, who put the great bars and impeachments to their plots, and are the great stakes in the hedge of the church, standing in the gap against their irruptions: and these alone *tormenting* the ungodly by their lives and profession, (v. 14,) are triumphed over by the beast: This therefore may not be a massacre of all sorts of professors at large, like that in Paris, A.D. 1572, but a set battle against sincere witnesses alone, whom their enemies have been taught to know and distinguish from others by the *fire* they have shot into their consciences, (v. 5:) so Antiochus' three and half years' persecution fell especially on the teachers and instructors, Dan. xi. 35. But these witnesses being "the golden candlesticks," (v. 4,) a *scattering* of the purer churches will be joined with this *killing*: and if their olive-trees be felled and removed, if their prophets and rulers be scattered, "the sheep will be scattered, the shepherd being smitten;" which

Matt. xxvi. 31, is here alluded to. *Secondly*, Whether this *killing* of the witnesses shall be over all the Reformed churches, and of all Protestant states and kingdoms? 1st, Graserus, a judicious Lutheran divine, thinks it will be universal, and that the angel's scope is thus to difference this last from all former partial eclipses of true churches; that whereas persecutions have never ceased in one place or other, at one time or other, now they will prevail at the same time in all places; and such universality the treading down of the outward court, and the great and general sins of all churches, do at least threaten; and thus "the dead bodies seen in the street, (or jurisdiction,) of the great city" might import, that wherever witnesses are to be found, they shall be killed, and so exposed to view. This I deny not, but think it may be the event more or less; yet I believe that some one kingdom or state, will more eminently be made the seat of this war, the field of this battle, the shambles of this slaughter; for where the witnesses rise from their dead conditions, there an *earthquake* shakes *the tenth part of the city*, or one of those ten European states that have given up their kingdoms to the beast, but shall now in this slaughter begin to fall from, and cease to be a part of the city, no longer belonging to the jurisdiction of Rome, under which it had again been for the space of three years and a half; and there this earthquake is for the special help and furtherance of the witnesses' *rising* in this kingdom, and ascending into heaven, whose slaughter it will avenge by killing *seven thousand names of men*, their enemies, v. 13. Now if this resurrection and ascension be in some one part of the ten kingdoms made more eminently glorious, as the special privilege of the witnesses therein, the death also therein should also be more conspicuous; for the glory to follow is in proportion to our suffering here with Christ: and though the main shock of the storm may fall there, yet the whole heavens may be covered with black, and all churches feel some drops and sprinklings of it. 2dly, The witnesses lie dead in *the street*, not in all the streets or states of Rome's jurisdiction; the Protestant party (the *peoples*, and *kindreds*, &c.) in the other streets (or *nations*) noticing the slaughter, as by-standers aloof, will perhaps prohibit them a sanctuary, or *grave* to hide their heads in, when they flee thither for help. 3dly, If in this last combat the witnesses be singled out as the one party, and if by *witnesses* be meant only such faithful Christians and professors as hold forth an eminent testimony, (not men of learning, but of holiness and zeal, being the real *tormentors* of these their enemies;) surely where such witnesses are chiefly found following the steps of their forefathers slain before them for the same cause, there especially will be the seat of this war. Now, 4thly, In all the Reformed churches how few such witnesses are there! the fire and heat of the first Reformers, (which *scorched* the Popish Gentiles,) have left only a light remaining, and so faint and cold and dull a testimony as the enemy despises: only in the witnesses of great Britain, both the light and heat of religion have been in times past preserved and increased; and more true witnesses will probably be found in it, in the last day, (wherein this slaughter is to fall out,) than in all other of the Reformed churches; and that according to the testimony of those who, in times past of begun scattering, have come hither. 5thly, The place of killing the witnesses will surely be where most witnesses are, in which kingdom also are more eminently found those last sort of champions for the beast, who receive only *the number of his name*, and yet shall be chief executioners of this last slaughter, and are to be overcome last of all the beast's company before the fifth vial on his seat, as in c. xv. Add we hereto, 6thly, This conjecture upon Dan. xi. 44, 45, (which chapter, from v. 36, hath Graserus excellently, [and Mr. Mede on 1 Tim. iv. 1, 2,] applied to the Pope, that *wilful king* typified by Antiochus:) where the angel's scope is, to shew the issue of the beast's last expedition against the Reformed churches before his end, in the last war of Antichrist's "accomplishing to scatter the power of the holy people;" wherein "going forth in such *fury utterly to destroy*, he shall plant the tabernacle of his palace between the seas, in the glorious holy mountain: yet he shall come to his end, and none shall help him." Now this *Holy Mount* is the Zion of Christendom, where stands the temple of the true church, which is "the mountain of the Lord's house," (Isa. ii. 2,) erected in Europe by the *northern Reformation*, against which the beast shall prevail so as to tread it down, and place again the tents of his throne upon it, or at least some part of it, as Alstedius and others confirm, and as accords with the delivering up of the outward court: and this Zion being situated *among the seas*, designates its distinction from every other church. Luther makes it point to Rome, the seat of the beast, between the Adriatic and Tuscan seas: but how could the beast "*go forth to plant*," if some new-gained settlement were not meant, or if the ordinary place of his residence was meant? Graserus hints at Germany, between the Baltic and German oceans; but even so, it could only be its northern parts. I fear for our own isles, our British Zion, which God hath made pre-eminently the seat of the church in these latter-days, and which so stand *between the seas* as to be wholly among seas, ("*Penitus Toto Divisos Orbe Britannos*,") and which "God hath loved above all the habitations of Jacob," Ps. lxxxvii. 2. And as the angel also calls this mountain by this high and transcendent phrase, "the mountain *of delights of holiness*," or as Junius turns it, "*of holy comeliness*;" it seems to note out some "place of uprightness," where God's majesty and glory should shine, so as to render it his *delight*, and *comely* in his eyes, though, for the trial of the witnesses therein, to be again ceded to Antichrist, "to plant there the tabernacle of his palaces," or throne, (or clergy, as Graserus reads it;) even as Nebuchadnezzar planted his throne at Tahapanes, as a sign of his conquest of Egypt: So that he shall be so rooted in his pristine sovereignty, that in hope of recovering all, the whore of Babylon shall sing just before her fall, "*No widow I.*" But this sudden victory is only a pitching tent in a field; and not being a tabernacle of God's planting, it will come to nothing; for "Every plant which the Father plants not, shall be rooted up," Matt. xv. 13: therefore "*He shall come to his end, and none shall help him.*"

VI.—THE NON-INTERMENT OF THE WITNESSES.

Though the witnesses' *lying dead* seems a metaphorial allusion, yet I fear this "*not suffering them to be put in graves,*" rather expressive of inhumanity, whether "these of the nations," &c. be friends or foes; so that the whole is added to shew further the extreme misery and desperate calamity brought on the witnesses in this time of their trial. *First*, If these *nations*, &c. be *enemies*, their *seeing* the dead, and not suffering any *interment* to take place, implies a feasting their eyes as with a spectacle of delight, a gazing-stock to these *seers*, as in Ps. xxii. 7; cix. 25; lii. 6; Isa. lxvi. 24: and in Ps. lxxix. 2, 3, the like miserable desolation of the temple, and slaughter of the saints, whether under Antiochus, or at the Babylonish captivity, is aggravated by this, "that *there was none to bury them;*" the witnesses herein partaking of the humiliation of Christ's lying in the grave, by lying at the mouth of it; though his obtaining a burial and such an honorable burying-place, was an act of humanity in Pilate the Roman governor, which the Roman pontiff makes "the nations" &c. deny the witnesses. *Secondly*, If these "*nations,*" &c. be *friends* in heart, and of the same religion with the witnesses, is their not suffering them to be buried a friendly office? Now "*they* of the nations," &c. seems to be a company (ΕΚ) *out of* these nations, a contradistinct Protestant party, not in *all* nations, nor *all Protestants* in gospel nations; but *some* witnesses in Protestant nations are here mentioned, to shew what part they should play in this tragedy: For this killing the witnesses falling out in an age when so many among the nations continue Protestants in heart, will they endure it, and not put a helping hand in this extremity? says the angel, "They shall see their dead bodies, and not suffer them to be put in graves:" 1st, They shall see their dead bodies lie in the *street*, or *market-place*, for a public scorn, without heart to help them, or however to relieve them; shy of intermeddling in their killing one way or other, they stand aloof as friends and well-willers do from malefactors executed, or as men pass the other side of a corpse: even as when Rome's turn shall come, the kings of the earth, who still cleave to her in heart, shall stand aloof at the sight of her burning, (as when Abraham looked at the smoke of Sodom,) c. xviii. 9, 10, 18. Or, 2dly, In that the witnesses should be driven out among the nations, so that "those of the nations," &c. to which they should fly for refuge, should *see* them; what follows may come in as a further degree of inhumanity, added to the indignities put on them by their enemies, so to complete their affliction: these false friends being prevailed on by the power and dread of the Papists, to refuse harbouring and befriending them: The grave is a resting-place for the vanquished, and a shelter from the shame, contempt, and indignities of insulting foes; but no such resting-place can the witnesses find. *Thirdly,* The allusion here may be, 1st, To the sufferings of Christ; for after a great part of the people had shouted their "*Hosannah* to the Son of David," rejoicing in his ministry, they were prevailed on by the Pharisees to cry out "Crucify him, crucify him," and to run in troops to see him executed, and "to look on him whom they had pierced:" so it is to be feared that the Protestant party will be over-awed by the power and tyranny of Rome, (lest she tread them down also,) and shall comply with her forbidding to protect the witnesses. *Fourthly,* It may allude to putting a corpse into a grave, which is all that we can do for the dead: so when these witnesses are deposed from their station, and perhaps banished from their nation, (a sort of death to them,) and, being cast out to the contempt and malice of their enemies, shall come to those of other nations, &c. for rest and harbouring as in a grave; (they now being laid by the walls speechless, and as dead in respect of their former active life of witnessing by prophecy;) but such shelter not being afforded them, thus "their dead bodies are not suffered to be laid in graves:" Yet the witnesses flying out of England were so far sheltered by the Low-countries; and so were the Protestants flying out of Germany by the English: and in queen Mary's days, the English Protestants found *graves* at last, some in Germany, some in Geneva, and others elsewhere; enjoying liberty of conscience, though not of preaching as in king Edward's days: but the surpassing misery of the three and half last years will stop every hole of refuge, and every grave where they may hide their heads and be buried there. *Fifthly,* This non-interment shall be by edicts, prohibiting the banished witnesses' being harboured, and *not suffering* them to lie in their grave, (Ezek. xxxvii. 12, 13;) and though "being *put* into a grave" is a passive phrase, and notes what is done by others, and seems improper to express men's fleeing for shelter and seeking a grave; yet we must remember that the Holy Ghost speaks also metaphorically of a civil death, wherein those who are dead, as witnesses, may seek a hiding-place, as men: for people are sometimes said, *actively*, to "bury themselves," being *naturally* alive; So these here are *passively*, "put into graves," being *figuratively* dead. Therefore, *Lastly*, This non-interment notes out the fulness and finishing of the afflictions of the church, aggravated thus by the inhumanity and cowardice of her half-hearted friends; seeing all Europe cannot offer them a bed in its graves, and no sanctuary in any of its streets; for they will not now be able, "when persecuted in one city, to flee into another." Now the unfaithful carriage of many Protestant states towards their neighbours and brethren, when this war began its commencement, may give us cause to fear and suspect, that even the Protestant party may turn thus inhuman towards the witnesses. How have the Lutherans in Germany complied to take part with the Papists for the ruin of the Calvinists? and it were happy for other states professing the Calvin religion, if they could wash their hands of the blood of the churches not only not assisted, but even betrayed by them.

VII.—THE RESURRECTION AND ASCENSION OF THE WITNESSES.

"AND AFTER THREE DAYS AND AN HALF, THE SPIRIT OF LIFE FROM GOD ENTERED INTO THEM, AND THEY STOOD UPON THEIR FEET; AND GREAT FEAR FELL UPON THEM WHICH SAW THEM. AND THEY HEARD A GREAT VOICE FROM HEAVEN SAYING UNTO THEM, COME UP HITHER: AND THEY ASCENDED UP TO HEAVEN IN A CLOUD; AND THEIR ENEMIES BEHELD THEM: AND THE SAME HOUR WAS THERE A GREAT EARTHQUAKE, AND THE TENTH PART OF THE CITY FELL, AND IN THE EARTHQUAKE WERE SLAIN OF MEN SEVEN THOUSAND: AND THE REMNANT WERE AFFRIGHTED, AND GAVE GLORY TO THE GOD OF HEAVEN," v. 11—13.

I.—*Four general observations concerning this resurrection.*

First, *The circumstance of it correspond with Christ's resurrection and ascension;* Christ *mystical*, in these last days when his visible kingdom draws near, being more eminently conformable to Christ *personal*, both in his death and resurrection, (those last of his acts done on earth before his kingdom then:) and though there are some evident characters of likeness between his passion and their killing, yet there are still more striking ones between his and their rising again. Secondly, The peculiar circumstances of his resurrection correspond with those of the *killing*, as a well-proportioned reward; for, 1st, A spirit of *life* enters into these *slain*. 2dly, Instead of any longer *lying dead* in the street, they *stand upon their feet*. 3dly, Their enemies, or false hearted friends, who with *pleasure see* them (BLEPSOUSI,) or who help them not, now (THEOOROUNTAS) *with terror behold* them,

4thly, *Great fear* falls on their enemies, who before with *joy* looked on. 5thly, Their dead bodies suffered the contempt of remaining above ground, unburied and exposed; but now they more than live, being called up to heaven thither to ascend. 6thly, Thousands of their enemies are now killed in turn, as sacrificed unto them. By all this, Thirdly, The parallel of Christ's resurrection and ascension is made; the lower was the one, the higher is the other, as in Eph. iv. 9, 10: where he *rose*, who *died:* he went up to *heaven*, who went down to *hell;* he *sitteth* at God's right hand, who *lay* in the chambers of the grave. Fourthly, In this ressurrection there is a fore-running shadow of that last great victory, which brings in the dawn of the kingdom of Christ and the saints for a thousand years, beginning under the seventh trumpet, v. 15. I shall notice these particulars after despatching the following interpretation of

II.—*The steps and degrees of this resurrection and ascension.*

First, "*The spirit of life from God enters into them,*" as Christ's soul coming again into his body was the principle of his future life. This notes a full restoration of their former state of life and power; and it is a reviving, not of their *bodies* but of their *persons*, (as surviving this short storm,) or of successors standing up in their cause: that whereas they were like dead men for three and a half years, in respect of their life of prophesying, (and perhaps through their own discouragements and fears, they lay too still and quiet, suffering their enemies to carry it, by their not opposing them as they ought,) yet now a bold and steeled resolution comes upon them, and they *stand on their feet*, and make head against their enemies, being thus *alive* again from the *dead;* while those who were actually *slain* by the Gentiles may be said to *rise* in their successors; for the saints are a holy nation and community; and what the next succession doth, through the prayers or sufferings of a former, that the former is said to do; as in Isa. v. 8, 12, and as John Baptist rose up in the spirit of Elijah, and as in Christ's ministry John was thought to be risen again from the dead. Now this "spirit of life" enters into the witnesses *from God*, as a special demonstration of the power of his hand, such as he put forth in the resurrection of Christ, Eph. i. 19, 20; Rom. i. 4. Secondly, "*They stand upon their feet,*" 1st, As in their former state or station. 2dly, As men erect, and taking heart; their cause being just, though they were before condemned. 3dly, As ready to defend themselves, and able and resolved to confront their enemies, into whose guilty consciences it strikes a mighty dread; "great fear falling on the spectators," whose hearts begin to sink, (as the hearts of Haman's friends misgave at his beginning to fall before Mordecai,) at the witnesses' first beginning to live; for they see this prophecy fulfilled, beyond all expectation, as Christ foretold his resurrection after three days: and now the church will sing, "Rejoice not against me, O mine enemy," &c. Mic. vii. 8, 10. Or, "*Those that saw them*" may be the *by-standers* of "the nations," &c. who not having relieved these their friends, are taken with fear and reverence of God and his truth, so as now to take part with them, contemplating their wonderful zeal and courage, and awed at the power and majesty of God's finger herein, as in Jer. xxxiii. 9. Thirdly, "*They are called up to heaven in a cloud,*" (as Christ ascended;) where "heaven" means not "the church," (as it often doth in this book,) but a more honourable and glorious condition than they had before, so that they shall die no more (Rom. vi. 9) the death of *witnesses*, whom it became "thus to suffer and to enter into their glory," Luke xxiv. 26: their former state was as a church on earth, this is as a church in heaven. This "*ascending up to heaven*" is used to express new power, freedom, and glory, (as Isa. xiv. 12, 13,) such as is the dawning of the glory of "*the new heaven and earth,*" to the enjoyment of which the church shall henceforward be raised up, as in c. xix.

VIII.—ACCOMPANIMENTS OF THE RISING OF THE WITNESSES.

As there were certain events which accompanied Christ's resurrection, so here there was an *earthquake*, affrighting the watchers: Now, 1st, The *time* of it was "*the same hour*" of the witnesses' rising, as one of the means facilitating it by the removal of impediments, (like the rolling away the stone from Christ's sepulchre;) the power of their enemies being thus scattered and dissolved: and though their resurrection and ascension are mentioned together, and then this earthquake is mentioned, after both, yet it follows not that all three were together; for the two distinct degrees of exaltation need not follow one another immediately, though put together as things of a sort; so this earthquake may refer only to the period of the witnesses' first rising, as falling out *the same hour* when this great turn began. 2dly, The place and effects of this earthquake are expressed thus: "*The tenth part of the city fell, and of the names of men were slain seven thousand*" in the overthrow of the buildings thereof.

I.—*What is the fall of the tenth part of the city?*

First, Mr. Mede thinks it is the ruin of Rome itself, at *the same hour* with the witnesses' rising and ascending, and all one with the fifth vial; for that, (it being an overthrow of the Popish enemy,) it must be reduced to one of the vials, four of which are mentioned before in v. 5, 6, 7, and the sixth seems to be that of v. 14, and then the seventh is all one with the seventh trumpet: for modern Rome is but a tenth part of the ancient imperial city, thus reduced by the trumpets in c. viii. and ix.; and "the names of men slain," are ecclesiastics and other dignitaries, as cardinals, archbishops, bishops, &c. those Italian merchants who have enjoyed so much traffic by reason of this whore's merchandise, are to be deposed and suffer a civil death, (as the witnesses had done,) at this seat of the beast's now falling into Protestant hands. But, *Secondly*, Though this may be ultimately intended, my thoughts have been carried to some other distinct event, by observing the different effect which this earthquake hath on the hearts of the remnant of these slain in the fall of the city, from that which the full and fatal ruin of the seat of the beast, (under the effect of the fifth vial,) hath on the remnant of the beast's company there; see v. 13, with c. xvi. 10, 11: The one having been drawn in through fear, to be of the Popish party, do afterwards repent; while the other cease not to blaspheme: so that it seems some special event connected with and making way for the witnesses' rising and ascending where their chief slaughter was, through a mighty commotion of the state of things, and in men's hearts; that as the Pope's power had again been entertained by that tenth part of the city, through a forced consent and yielding to their slaughter, there is now a great insurrection against that power, and a proceeding to ruin the opposite party, of whom the unslain remnant in their fright "give glory to God," and return to embrace the truth, and the cause of these witnesses. The scope of the Holy Ghost here is, to shew what properly concerns the rising of the witnesses as the means unto it, the earthquake and fall of the tenth part of the city being still reducible to the fifth vial, as a degree unto it, and as the final scope of it; for there are *sprinklings* of the same vial both before and after its acme, yet reducible to the vial of their own kind, to which they are either preparations or appendices. *Thirdly*, "City" being taken in this book, either for *Rome* or its *jurisdiction*, "the *tenth* part" may be either or both; the fall of one being a step towards the fall of the other; and this double interpretation is frequent in scripture. But, *Fourthly*, I rather understand hereby some tenth part of Europe, (probably the same as "*the street of the city*," v. 8,) that one of the beast's ten kingdoms, (by charter allotted to him, c. 17,) where are found most faithful witnesses lying dead for the three years and a half, and where they shall first begin to rise at the convulsion of the earthquake.

II.—*What is the great earthquake and downfal in this tenth part of the city?*

Under the sixth seal, the mighty change wrought in the Roman empire turned Christian, through Constantine's deposing all heathen emperors and rulers and worshippers, is called an earthquake, c. vi. 12; and so is this last shaking of states politically or ecclesiastically, whereby this one of the ten states of Popedom *falls* off from the rest who belong to the beast, and becomes

Protestant again, after having again been so enthralled to the Pope as to be guilty of the last blood of martyrs: and as earthquakes are from inward motions in the bowels of the earth, so this glorious revolution may arise from within that kingdom, either through the supreme magistrate's beginning to "*hate the whore*," (c. xvii. 16,) or through the people's hearts turning against the beast's cruelty, after their consciences are enlightened, while their outward court lies trodden down by the Gentiles, the witnesses also having the spirit of life re-enter, so that with one heart they join together to break their yoke asunder. Mr. Mede conjectures this voice to the witnesses out of heaven, to be that of supreme authority, with which the people also shall join, an earthquake being a commotion in the people and nations.

III.—*What is the seven thousand names of men, and their slaying?*

There is not such another phrase in the Bible as "*names of men*," which are certainly such enemies of the witnesses as had the chief hand in their killing, and in subjecting "the nations," &c. to the beast's power. *First*, Mr. Mede takes it for "*men of name*," (as "riches of glory" for "glorious riches," &c.) meaning men of office, title, and dignity; (as they are also called in Num. xvi. 2;) who here are ecclesiastical dignitaries under the Papacy; as they do themselves speak of all the several ranks and orders of the hierarchical ministry, from the highest to the lowest, (which being so many are here numbered by sevens and by thousands,) thus, "*By what* names *or titles soever dignified or distinguished;*" and these are "names of *men*," being of human invention, and not what the Holy Ghost teacheth: and this phrase is aptly connected with the ruin of the Pope's creatures, brought about by such evil and error of theirs: But it is proper to civil offices and titles to be *of men*, as human ordinances or *creations*, (see p. 5, for ANTHROOPINEEI CTISEI, 1 Pet. ii. 13:) but the foundation of the calling and office of ecclesiastical names is of another building, "not of men," (Gal. i. 1,) though "by man" the persons may be set apart to fill such offices of which Christ is Lord, of whom they hold, as truly as gifts hold of the Spirit, and as *operations* do of the Father; and it is God that hath *set* (ETHETO,) *teachers* as well as *apostles*, 1 Cor. xii. 4—6, 28. Therefore Popish *names*, not being "plants of the Father's planting, must be rooted out" of this kingdom, where they had caused us much mischief even to cruelty against the witnesses; and where the efficacy of working to uphold these names had brought it again under the measure of the tenth part of the city, ere the earthquake causes it again to fall from the jurisdiction thereof.

IV.—*What is the tenth part of the city that fell by the earthquake and resurrection?*

Though it is rash to determine, it is not hard to conjecture, which of the ten European kingdoms or states shall first be privileged with so blessed a handsel of the general revival of the churches: for God makes new choice of nations and churches beyond our thoughts; for "his ways are past finding out," by any designment traced on the face of previous dealings with any of the churches. I will therefore only prognosticate, from the face of the sky in the churches of this present age, where this heaven (into which the witnesses shall ascend;) is likely first to clear up from under these clouds, and from out of this hour of darkness to come upon the world. *First,* The saints and churches belonging to the kingdom of France, God hath made a wonder to me in all his proceedings towards them, first and last; and there would seem some special honour in reserve for them. The light of the gospel by the first and second angel's preaching, (c. xiv.) which laid the foundation of Antichrist's ruin, began from Lyons and other places, which have endured the heat of that morning of persecution, greater perhaps than any since, wherein the French churches have also had perhaps the largest share; and though they have continued a glorious church for so many centuries since their separation from Antichrist, (see p. 611,) yet they have not had that great honor and privilege of a supreme magistrate's professing their religion, (with which other churches have been so blest;) for such have been either their bloody persecutors and oppressors, or else have apostatized from them: we may therefore yet expect their kings to be wrought upon "to hate the whore and to burn her with fire," c. xvii. 16; and the voice which calls these witnesses up to heaven, may yet proceed from the throne of France, where the witnesses have ever prophesied in sackcloth; so that that kingdom may have the first stroke in the ruin of Rome. But, *Secondly,* Viewing the face of the present condition of the saints and churches in Europe, as it presents itself in this last age, (wherein these things are in all likelihood to be fulfilled,) together with a retrospect into the times past also; and putting all together, Great Britain and the islands belonging to it, seem to have stronger claims than any other of the Reformed churches to the glory of being the prominent stage both of this great slaughter, and also of the rising and ascending of these witnesses. For without being swayed through affection only, (which might betray the judgment,) I have seriously and impartially considered and weighed things: for since the fourteenth century, there has been as glorious a succession of godly witnesses and martyrs, (as you may collect among Mr. Fox's martyrology,) as any other nation can produce; and since the Reformation, the *descriptive marks* of these witnesses designed to this slaughter and glory, appear the liveliest upon those of Great Britain. For 1st, Here God hath continued the most *faithful,* and *called,* and *chosen,* (c. xvii. 14,) who are of the Lamb's side, and are to overcome, with him, the kings that shall hate and burn the whore; there being more that hold forth the power of religion here than in all the nine kingdoms besides: and surely where the most eminent witnesses are, there will be the most eminent slaughter, and consequently also, their most glorious resurrection and ascension; magnitude of sufferings, multitude of witnesses, and greatness of glory, being thus commensurate. 2dly, In *this* "*street* of the city," (more than in all other churches,) God hath eminently stirred up men's hearts to breathe after, and contend for, a further and purer Reformation and measuring of the temple; and this more or less ever since the first erection of the English church of Frankfort, in queen Mary's days. Now the bitter persecutions brought on through such contentions against all false worship, have caused our witnesses to prophesy in sackcloth, more apparently than others in other Reformed churches; whence hath followed a greater increase in spiritual light and holiness, and in practical knowledge in the ways and works of sanctification, (by which the worshippers are to be measured,) and also a clearer insight into the institution and true government of a church, (by which the temple and altar are to be measured;) others in the quiet enjoyment of this sort of purity having run out into little better than an outward-court formal profession, with but few priests of the inner temple, those worshippers who worship God in power, in spirit, and in truth. By consulting the Exposition of the first six verses, and by impartially applying the interpretation given to the Protestant professors this day in Europe, how pre-eminently will the state of British saints, and their constant conflict with the beast and his abettors, fit the measure thereof, and approach nearer the life of that face of things presented in the British, rather than in any other European Zion? 3rdly, The description of the eminent opponents of the witnesses in these last days, as authors of their slaughter, also fits those open and professed enemies in these kingdoms, where are found those that receive the *number* of the beast's *name*, who yet have rather denied, and may still for a while deny his *character*, and disclaim his *name*: to whom else shall we liken this generation? or where else shall we find similitudes for them, if the said description in these chapters suits them not? And these *number-names* being the beast's last-named last champions, (as in c. xiii. 17; xv. 2;) are to hold up the last great quarrel of the beast's cause, and to fight the last combat with the witnesses; and so in this last age to be overcome in open field by them, as their predecessors, that had the *mark* and *image* of the beast, have been overcome by the former generation of witnesses in elder times. 4thly, In which of the Reformed churches, except in these kingdoms, are those *names of men* continued, (according to the otherwise unused phrase, "*By what* names *or titles soever distinguished*,") who are to be the killers of the witnesses, and therefore to be slain by this earthquake, in their revenge? which several names and titles and dignities, from the highest to the lowest, may haply amount to just seven thousand, (or a great number,) even besides such ministers of parishes and assemblies, as for the substance of their office have a warrant from God, though their usual names be of man's devising. Yea, is not this very thing made the quarrel now, Whether these same ranks of ministry be names of God or of man, about which the witnesses have contended from the beginning? And is it not the suspicion and general opinion, that to continue and secure these their names, men would again introduce Popery? for this the witnesses have been silenced, fined, deprived, and deposed from their ministerial charge, lest (as the Pharisees said of Christ,) the people's running after their doctrine should endanger their names, credit, and dignity; and so "take away their kingdom." This hath been the secret cause of the continuation of the quarrel, though under other outward pretences; yea, this will be the provocation for the ensnaring slaughter of these witnesses, which now approacheth; they say within their hearts, "Let us kill *these witnesses*, and the vineyard will be ours." 5thly, On all the above grounds, how plainly probable does it seem, that these accompaniments of the witnesses' resurrection, are to fall out in this tenth part of Europe, and in one, or both, of these our kingdoms? and how just were it with God to give up these "*names of men*," (who have been the enemies of his witnesses in all times since the Reformation,) to receive at least "*the number of the beast's name*," and under his name and power, as his trained band and leaders in this his last war, to become in the end the killers of these witnesses? And how wonderful and wise a dispensation of God will it be towards his own in these kingdoms, to have reserved the utter extripation of these long contended for "*names of men*," unto such a time and occasion as this? and that after they shall first have done this feat and exploit for the beast, in killing the witnesses, they should then be sacrificed, (as Baal's priests were by Elias;) when these witnesses, whom they so persecuted, shall rise to die no more? thus the ruin of those their enemies is made their triumph, and the removing them out of the way by this *earthquake* is the foundation of their ascension into heaven: after which the work of measuring the temple, by these Samaritans interrupted, shall go forward in the hands of Joshua and Zerubbabel; and the people, before afraid, shall begin to cry "Grace, grace, unto it:" so the rearing of these purer churches shall be upon the rubbish of this Samaritan mountain of the false church. 6thly, If the fifth vial be also aimed at in this earthquake, and the fall of Rome, the seat of the beast; how comely will it be, and suitable with the long expectation of God's witnesses and holy ones, that the ruin of these sees and seats of those that shall do Antichrist such service, shall fall out with, or be preparative unto the fall of that great bishop's see, (as expounded in the fifth vial;) when both shall go down together, as alike pertaining to the same building of man, not of God! Lastly, If this prove the issue of God's dealings with these kingdoms, how gloriously shall God thereby acquit himself in the conclusion of all his dispensations towards them? For to see two such contrary streams running so strongly one against another in the same channel, hath indeed caused a wonderment in the godly-wise of this last age, what God means to do, and what end he means to make with England: how equally God means to proceed here both towards them that fear him, and towards the opposite party, that are and have been here, is the great expectation of the churches; for it is miraculously strange to see how God upholds in the same state two such contrary factions and parties, one of his own people, rising higher and higher in spiritual light, against superstition, and breathing after further purity of holiness and perfection of public worship; and herewith at the same time another strong party, looking towards Rome, and increasing in superstition, darkness, and an impudent outfacing the light of truth, even when shining clearest and brightest on them. Now for the all-wise God, whose art and skill "*knoweth* how to preserve the righteous, and to reserve the wicked unto punishment," (2 Pet. ii. 9,) to come off at last so gloriously; what more equal and likely dispensation, than the course chalked out in this chapter, towards both parties in our kingdom? which course, according to God's dealing throughout the scriptures, the godly-wise might have hoped he intended to run, even though this prophecy had not been left us in this chapter concerning these very times.

V.—*This resurrection and ascension, is a shadow of "the restitution of all things."*

To make appear yet more glorious all that hath been said about the great privilege and honor to befall one tenth part of Europe, let me add, That this resurrection of the witnesses seems the commencement of the first great turn of things in the church hastening to the new Jerusalem, and the dawn of the fulnes of Christ's kingdom, and the final restitution of the church's liberation from under the yoke of Antichrist. "Wilt thou *at this time* restore the kingdom to Israel?" was the disciples' question after Jesus' resurrection, (Acts i. 6, 7:) Jesus denies not the fact, but denies them only the knowledge of "the times or seasons, which the Father hath put in his own power." But now these times and seasons drawing near, the rising of these witnesses, (which being figured out by his resurrection, and the fulfilment of it, is called in c. xx. 5, 6, "*the first resurrection,*") is here mentioned as the signal of that restitution: and so the ancients generally spake of that day, That this killing and rising again of the two witnesses, (though interpreted by them of Enoch and Elijah,) are the harbinger-signs of that joyful day of Christ's kingdom, which they called *the day of judgment*: And this particular occurrence in but a tenth part of Europe, is here mentioned, rather than others likely to fall out with it or after it, (as the ruin of Rome, in itself a greater one,) that this one passage might more properly become a sign, (to give which is the Holy Ghost's scope in this chapter,) of the approaching of the new Jerusalem, under the seventh trumpet: For it is not only the first step of the restauration of the church after Antichrist's last scattering of it, for ever to go on increasing till the full restitution of all things; being the first turn of the stream after that last low ebb, whose waters still rise to full sea never to ebb again; (these witnesses now rising, as Christ did, never to die again, but to cast off their sackcloth for ever;) But further also, being in many particulars the liveliest picture and model of that great revolution to come, this passage is singled out as the fore-running type and resemblance of what is to begin with the seventh vial, (which is all one with the seventh trumpet,) when "old things are to be done away, and all things made new," (2 Cor. v. 17; c. xxi. 5:) and as here, so there, there is said to be a great earthquake; one "dividing the remainder of Babylon into three parts," and precipitating "the cities of the nations," (c. xvi. 18, 19;) the other precipitating the tenth part of the city, and slaying those "*names* of men:" and as the one is ushered in with *the first resurrection*, so the other with a *revival* of dead witnesses to a better life than they had before: for this wonderful work and change shall be, (like the conversion of the Jews,) as "life from the dead," Rom. xi. 15.

VI.—*Conjectures about the time of the witnesses' killing and rising.*

Two periods have been especially pitched on, by writers of the seventeenth century, for great changes in the churches of Christ; one about A.D. 1650-6, the other A.D. 1666, (see p. 603,) concerning which, and also any other conjectures out of these prophecies, this general caution must be taken in: That in such computations a mistake of a few years may occur, from the years since the incarnation being uncertainly kept; as Arnobius saith, "It is about three centuries, more or less, since we began to be churches;" and therefore Helvicus, (one of the best chronologers,) makes A.D. 1650, to be A.D. 1652; and others allow four years difference: And an unknown English writer, in a little book dedicated to the church of Rome, A.D. 1589, first gave this obscure hint of the year A.D. 1666: "Yet two months, two weeks, two days and a half; and thy number *six hundred three-score and six* shall be fulfilled;" reckoning from Pope Innocent's time, A.D. 406. Simpson, the Scotch abbreviator of the church's story, and Mr. Wood in his manuscript on the Revelation, incline also to A.D. 1666. The other period, A.D. 1650-6, some make the time of the Jews' first calling, and others the expiring of Antichrist, and the fall of the city; so that holy man Hiltenius, (the great forerunner of Luther, in Germany,) who foretold the very year of Luther's rising after him to teach his doctrine; which Melancthon saw written under his own hand; this being one of his last sayings, (recorded among the lives of the German divines, by Melchior Adam;) "That A.D. 1651, shall be the time of the change of this, and the beginning of the new world. Since him Finch, in his book of "The Jews' calling," (and many others also,) makes that the time "when God will leave off to scatter his holy people, for then shall the Turk's first declining come," &c. and the most learned Rabbi in the world communicated this period to Mr. Forbes, as the utmost time of the advent of their Messiah. Mr. Mede also makes Antichrist's commencement, A.D. 395; so that thus there would be as many years from Christ to the beginning of the new world, as from the creation to Noah, to which age Christ compares his coming. In Dan. xii. 11, this same angel says, " That from the time that the daily sacrifice shall be taken away, and the abomination that maketh desolate set up, there shall be a thousand two hundred and ninety *days* " or *years*," added to Julian's time; for from Vespasian and Titus' time, they would have been out near five hundred years ago. Hiltenius, (who was a great studier of Daniel's prophecies,) first made this conjecture; and Wood, Finch, and others followed him, as did most of the Jews. Now these two computations of A.D. 1656, and A.D. 1666, may be reconciled by the two gradual accomplishments of the fifth vial; whereof the one is the preparation to the other, some portions being poured out at the top, and others at the dregs of God's wrath; the first degree of it beginning at the rising of the witnesses, with the fall of the tenth part of the *city*, (or Romish *jurisdiction;)* the other completing the ruin of Rome itself, (c. xvi.) which is but a tenth part of the original Rome. Now this angel here, declared in Dan. xii. 1, 7, That about the same time the children of his people, (the Jews,) should be called by Michael their prince, (Christ,) and be also delivered out of the greatest distress from the Turkish empire, (the second woe to pass away, v. 14,) ever nation was in; after which restoration of the Jews, and resurrection of the witnesses, the church's reign on earth will begin to be established on the ruins of Antichrist, at the blast of the seventh trumpet. But the other period of " the thousand three hundred and five and thirty days," (or years,) being about forty-five years anterior, would have brought it down to A.D. 1690-9; and these two periods are set as two posts, the one at the beginning, and the other at the ending of the whole style of time allotted for the fulfilment of events before Christ's kingdom. Again in Dan. xii. 7, the angel seems to mention Antichrist's " three and a half times," distinct from the " accomplishing to scatter the power of the holy people" by killing the witnesses; and then " all these things, (about the ruin of the Pope and Turk,) shall be finished," or a finishing; for they would scarcely all end together at one time. So that the twelve hundred and ninety years designs not so much Antichrist's time, as the first turn of things at the saints' scattering, preparatory to Christ's kingdom; this expiring of his time being somewhere within these forty-five years: For, 1st, The angel's fixing a latter period for the final end of all, leaving so many years between, augur the former to be the *punctum* beginning the time for the accomplishment of these great things, whereof Antichrist's ruin is one, and that of the Turk is a great one also. 2dly, Having repeated this *scattering*, &c. as a preface to his answer about the time of its being finished; "Many, (says the angel,) shall be made white, and tried, and purified" by this scattering; and then is subjoined, "And from the time that the daily sacrifice is taken away, (under Julian, as some interpret,) shall be twelve hundred and ninety days," to the killing of the witnesses: Now these three years and a half were prefigured by those of Antiochus, and accompanied with the same trial, Dan. xi. 35; "Many shall fall, to try them, to purge them, and to make them white;" the scattering in the apostate Emperor's time being a strong resemblance with that to come under apostate Rome: But the Pope's "three times and a half" would have been reckoned from some more eminent and suitable mark than this heterogeneal passage of Julian's persecution, as homogeneal with this killing of the witnesses. 3dly, As the latter period emphatically blesses him that cometh thereto, it intimates a blessedness also on the dawn of it, forty-five years before, in comparison of the scattering times previous thereto; though thrice blessed are the times of which the angel saith to Daniel, "Thou shalt stand up in thy lot," &c. as he saith in c. xx. 6, "Blessed is he that hath part in the first resurrection." It is in explanation of Daniel, that the angel here insists so largely on this *last* killing of the witnesses, and their first resurrection; the forty-five years *ending also* with another resurrection still more glorious, the Pope and Turk being destroyed utterly in the interim: and in further confirmation of this harmony, the twelve hundred and ninety days are pitched on by some for the conversion of the Jews, and the fall of Turcism; the taking away the Jews' sacrifice being pitched on as the eminent mark and post, whence to reckon the account: for the Jews' last attempt to erect their temple-worship in Julian's time was overthrown by an earthquake; thus fulfilling the prophecy of Christ then again, "not to leave one stone upon another" even underground: The time therefore of their turning to the Messiah is reckoned from temple-matters of which he is the substance; and if the resurrection of the European witnesses, and the conversion of the Jews, should fall out together, how famous would Daniel's *days* be made by two so glorious resurrections, accompanying the foundations of the new Jerusalem; the enemies of Jews and Protestants, hitherto *letting*, being now "taken out of the way," that the Son of man might be revealed; as the Roman empire did let the revelation of "the man of sin" and his kingdom. Thus both these typical resurrections will become pledges of "the resurrection of the just," and that of the witnesses will prepare the effusion of the fifth vial on the ruined Romanist, as that of the Jews will prepare the effusion of the sixth vial on the ruined Turk. And it may be observed, that these forty-five years correspond with the period of the Exodus of Israel, adding the five years of battling for the promised land to the forty years in the wilderness, as in Joshua xiv. 10.

IX.—"THE SECOND WOE IS PAST."

The three last trumpets being called *three woes*, and one woe being past when the fifth trumpet had done sounding, (c. viii. 13; ix. 12;) as soon as the time of the sixth trumpet is being finished, it is said "The second woe is past, and behold the third cometh quickly," v. 14. Now the sixth trumpet being the empire and tyranny of the Turk, and the sixth vial being that great and deadly blow that shall be given to that empire, to make way for the kingdom of "the kings of the east," (the Jews,) mentioned in that vial, Mr. Mede interprets this passing away of the second woe, to be the very sixth vial, and the fifth to be the fall of the tenth of the city. But the last blast of the sixth trumpet seems here to synchronize with the earthquake, and the resurrection and ascension of the witnesses, and the fall of the tenth of the city; all ending in one period: for as soon as the Holy Ghost had narrated all these, he concludes with, "The second woe is past." If then the fifth vial be the period of the Pope's reign, and if the witnesses' putting off their sackloth be at their rising, and at the fall of the tenth part of the city; how can the passing away of the second woe, (if it be the sixth vial,) fall out and synchronize with these; seeing the vials, seals, and trumpets, fall out successively, each after other, if not in equal distances of time? To reconcile this difficulty, 1st, Either the fifth and sixth vials shall fall out about the same time; and so the conversion of the Jews, and the rising of the European witnesses, fall out together as preparations to both: (and so Dan. xi. 45, with xii. 1, seems to connect the fall of Antichrist with the rising again of the Jewish nation from that paroxysm of Turkish trouble, accompanying their first conversion;) Or, 2dly, As the witnesses not only rise with an earthquake, but afterwards ascend also into heaven; there may be a space of years between, (as there was of days from Christ's resurrection to his ascension,) wherein all their enemies and other obstacles are removed: so though their rising be preparatory to the sixth vial, their ascension may not be until the sixth. But 3dly, The angel's scope in introducing this clause, "*The second woe is past*," may not be to denote the exact period of all these occurrences, or to shew the synchronism of the sixth vial and the end of the sixth trumpet, with this earthquake, &c. but rather, (as the Turkish tyranny was one part of the *second woe* on the eastern Christians, [c. ix.] and another part the treading down the outward court of carnal Protestants by the Papists, and killing their witnesses,) having related and put them both together, he comes in with "*The second woe is past*," q. d. "I have now fully declared what a woe God will bring on the eastern and western Christians, perfecting together the *second woe*, and making up the story of the sixth trumpet; and having done with these two parts, I pass therefore to speak of the *third woe*, which now *cometh quickly*," &c. So that this passage seems to shew *materially* what pertains to the sixth trumpet, rather than *chronologically* to shew the expiring of it: and this great punishment from the Popish Gentiles on the Protestant party in the west for their sins, is fitly cast under the trumpets, and joined to that great plague on the eastern Christians by the Turk, as a part of the sixth trumpet; and severed from the vials, as no part of them; they being to fall only on the enemies themselves of both these Christian companions, viz. on the Pope and the Turk. Thus the Holy Ghost homogeneally puts together the punishment of carnal Christians, eastern and western, under the woe of the trumpets; and in like manner involves these other two grand enemies to Christ's profession and religion, wholly under the plagues of the seven vials: and this may be why the "*treading down the outward court*," and the "*killing of the witnesses*," come in here; and why the "treading of the winepress," (c. xiv. 20, which is part of the treading of the outward court,) is reckoned no part of the vials, it being to fall on the Protestant party: yet so as that, what with the trumpets and what with the vials, God will be sure to meet all sorts for their sins, and by a like just and impartial rule proceed both towards friends and enemies, without any respect of persons. 4thly, As the calling of the Jews is but tacitly intimited in this book, which is chiefly written for the Gentiles; may not this passage intimate the foundation of the Turk's ruin by the Jews' conversion happening together with the resurrection of the witnesses? for the height and bitterness of the Turkish tyranny is past, (though the empire may stand for a while,) when the Jews are called; the *woe* of it lying in its hinderance of the Christian religion, now to revive among the Jews in his territories. When the foundation of the ruin of any state is laid, and its dominion is past the meridian, and begins to decline, it is prophetically past; as things are said to be *finished*, when begun to be accomplished: as Babylon is said to be fallen, (c. xiv. 8,) when but the first vial was began to be poured out, and the open discovery of Antichrist made; and again her fall is finally pronounced, when she is unseated for ever, c. xviii. 2. Old Babylon is said to be fallen, (Isa. xxi. 9,) at the first revolt of the Medes: so the second woe, or sixth trumpet, (or Turkish empire,) is said to be past, when the Jews first begin to revolt in their conversion to Christ; therefore the angel proceeds to warn us, that "Behold the third woe cometh quickly," at the blast of the seventh trumpet, introducing the new Jerusalem of Christ's kingdom. Thus this chapter is a complete comment on the twelfth chapter of Daniel, and makes mention of all these things therein mentioned.

X.—CONCLUDING OBSERVATIONS.

On the fulfilment of prophecy relative to this chapter.

I have already observed, that God is wont to fulfil prophecies, and the computations of them, over and over, in several degrees of accomplishment, as in Daniel's twelve hundred and ninety days, and John's twelve hundred and sixty; and also in the witnesses three days and a half, whereof some gradual accomplishments have transpired several times in Europe; yet I have proved a far greater slaughter of them yet to come. Now the observation of the revolution of time in the centuries past, wherein the killings of the witnesses fell out, may indigitate the time when the great and last slaughter, in the centuries running on since, may fall out; that is, as the partial and smaller killings of the witnesses fell out in A.D. 1547—9 in Germany, and in A.D. 1556, in England, (under Mary;) so about the time of the revolution of the same term of a hundred years, in the middle of a following century, the time of this last killing of the witnesses may also be. Thus John Huss who suffered martyrdom at a stake about A.D. 1417, said, "After a hundred years you Papists shall be called to account;" which remarkable speech the Bohemians had stamped upon their coins: accordingly in A.D. 1517, Luther arose, and with him the gospel in Germany; and again after another century, about A.D. 1618, began those notable alterations in Germany, which still go on to this time, the Deformation of the gospel proceeding with as strange a hand against the church as, through God, the Reformation did for it: so that I confess myself suspicious of the revolution of every century, since those former killings of the witnesses, fore-running the final one: and if England, Scotland, &c. as the tenth part of the city, is to be the eminent stage of this slaughter, then will it fall upon some centenary after the former trial of England; and as upon the rising of England and Scotland began that glorious harvest of blessed times, which lasted till the German wars began; so in the revolution of other hundred years, far more blessed times are likely to arise at the beginning of the forty-five years, (before spoken of,) allotted for the accomplishment of all. But I leave these conjectures to further light, lest I presume too far in fixing the times and seasons for God's great works of wonder: for if chronologers even now are not agreed whence to date the seventy years' captivity, how much more difficult must it be to fix the period before the accomplishment of any prophecy? Yet let an indefinite warning that these things are approaching, and ourselves within reach of them, suffice to move us to prepare for them; (which is the only use of knowing them;) as it is said of death, The day is hid, that every day may be watched: And though we may think this dismal and black hour of temptation not likely to come soon, as the clouds rise not fast enough so suddenly to overcast the face of the sky with darkness; yet living in the extremity of times, when motions and alterations, being so near the centre, become quickest and speediest, we are at the verge and within the whirl of that great mystery of Christ's kingdom, which as a gulf will swallow up all time in its haste to make a full end of all. And for the Jews' call, which is conjunct with this killing and rising of the witnesses; as it depends not on ordinary means, there are like to be no preparations at all unto it, until it comes with this extraordinary voice, "Shall the earth be made to bring forth in one day, or shall a nation be born at once?" Isa. lxvi. 8: so that in the year before there will be no more outward appearances or probabilities of it, than there are now, or have been for centuries past: therefore our faith need not be put off from this, by our not seeing any stirring or motion towards it; the truth is, Both the killing of the witnesses and the calling of the Jews, *may fall out sooner than we are aware.*

The Reader will perceive, 1st, That he is left to make his own table of errata, except that in p. 577, is Cyrene for Cyprus; 2dly, That the *Iota subscript* is expressed by ɪ after *Eta* and *Omega*, (or double E and O;) 3dly, That some few passages of Scripture are not quoted verbatim; and 4thly, That he is relieved from the necessity of any reference to the date of the Author's writing, except in p. 603, where the Editor has inserted a short parenthesis, suggesting the year A.D. 606, as that of the rise of the beast, (when Boniface III. by flattering the traitorous murderer Phocas, emperor of Constantinople, procured himself the title of *Universal Bishop;*) to shew how nearly the fall of Turk and Pope would synchronize, according to one of the dates in p. 596. If however our Author looked not beyond his own century, how shall we look beyond the *eventful middle* of ours, as the *centre* of all woes, and "the hour of temptation which shall come upon all the world to try them that dwell upon the earth?" and if the outlines of these our days, which were so strongly depicted by his hand, are being filled up so strikingly by us, "how shall this generation pass away till all these things be fulfilled?" For while our *State* (which by two Acts of the Legislature, tolerates blasphemy against the holy Trinity, and removes the disabilities of idolatry,) holds out her right hand and left to Turk and Pope; our *Church*, by a long-standing apostacy of her members, and by a more recent "falling away" among her ministers, is being robbed of the crown of her *election* of God, and of that brightest jewel on its front, her *justification* by CHRIST ALONE through *faith only*: but if this Jachin and Boaz of our temple be shaken, what can bar our re-union with Rome, between whom and ourselves there will soon appear no more difference in *sense* or *sound*, than between Aholah and Aholibah? Such rapid retrograding into Laudean days must soon precipitate us backwards into the Bonnerian age: and what true Protestant hath not "great heaviness and continual sorrow in heart," anticipating "such a time of trouble as never was, since *England* was a nation, even to that same time?" yet let us "rejoice with trembling," knowing that, although "*all shall worship the beast*, whose names are not written in the Lamb's book of life;" "At that time her people shall be delivered, every one that shall be found written in this book;" see Dan. xii. 1. Rev. xiii. 8.

Preserve us, Lord, by thy dear word;	Both these would thrust out of his throne
From Turk and Pope defend us, Lord:	Our Lord Christ Jesus thy dear Son.

Old Ver.

END OF THIS VOLUME.

ENTERED AT STATIONER'S HALL.

JENKIN THOMAS, PRINTER, PLYMOUTH.

9780332274201

WS - #0011 - 080623 - C0 - 229/152/8 [10] - CB - 9780332274201 - Gloss Lamination